Belong

Belong

GROUP SPIRITUAL DIRECTION *for* CHRISTIAN FRIENDSHIP *and* COMMUNAL DISCERNMENT

Melanie Dobson

Nashville

**Belong: Group Spiritual Direction for Christian
Friendship and Communal Discernment**

*Copyright © 2025 Abingdon Press
All rights reserved.*

No part of this work may be reproduced or transmitted in any form or by any means, electronic or mechanical, including photocopying and recording, or by any information storage or retrieval system, except as may be expressly permitted by the 1976 Copyright Act, the 1998 Digital Millennium Copyright Act, or in writing from the publisher. Requests for permission can be addressed to Rights and Permissions, The United Methodist Publishing House, 810 12th Avenue South, Nashville TN 37203 or e-mailed to permissions@umpublishing.org.

ISBN 978-1-7910-3807-6
Library of Congress Control Number: 2025943448

Scripture quotations unless noted otherwise are taken from the New Revised Standard Version, Updated Edition. Copyright © 2021 National Council of Churches of Christ in the United States of America. Used by permission. All rights reserved worldwide.

Book cover for *Belong* by Melanie Dobson. A field of sunflowers conveys a sense of belonging to emphasize the subtitle, "Group Spiritual Direction for Christian Friendship and Communal Discernment."

MANUFACTURED IN THE UNITED STATES OF AMERICA

For Patience, who taught me the reverence, mutuality, and compassion that comes from group spiritual direction, and for Shalem Institute, which provided the arena to learn group spiritual direction.

For the churches and faith communities who have given me the opportunity to teach and practice group spiritual direction for friendship and discernment with you.

Contents

Introduction: The Power of Group Spiritual Direction 1
How to Use This Book 11

Part 1: Group Spiritual Direction for Christian Friendship

1. A Practice of Friendship with God and Others (The What) 17
2. A Means of Grace (The Why) 35
3. Preparing Participants for Group Spiritual Direction
   for Christian Friendship. 57
4. Equipping Leaders for Group Spiritual Direction for
   Christian Friendship 81
5. Addressing Conflict and Challenges (for Both Kinds
   of Group Spiritual Direction) 105

Part 2: Group Spiritual Direction for Communal Discernment

6. A Practice of Seeking Consensus Together with God (The What). . . 123
7. Holy Conferencing Leads to Harmony (The Why) 143
8. Understanding the Process of Communal Discernment
   for Consensus 161
9. Leading a Congregational Discernment Process. 189

Epilogue: The Miracle of Belonging 215

Appendix

How to Find a Spiritual Director for One-with-one Spiritual Direction 223
Models of Group Spiritual Direction 225
The Steps of Group Spiritual Direction for Friendship 229
Group Spiritual Direction Process for Friendship-Based Groups:
   A Quick Guide 235
Covenant Guidelines for Group Spiritual Direction 239
3-1-3-1 Timing Structure for Group Spiritual Direction 241
4-4-4 Timing Structure for Group Spiritual Direction 244
Two Extended Timing Structures for Group Spiritual Direction. 247
Summary of Timing Structures for Group Spiritual Direction 251
Contemplative Spiritual Practices to Support Listening to God 252
Prompts for Leading Group Spiritual Direction 259
Guidelines for Holy Listening and Life-giving Responses. 265
Belong Leader Training Session: Sample Agenda 269
Opening Worship for Use in Belong Groups and Belong
   Leader Training 271
Guide to the 12-Step Process of Communal Discernment for Consensus . . 273
Group Spiritual Direction in Communal Discernment to Consensus . . . 277
Ignatian Deliberation in Communal Discernment to Consensus 280
Quaker "Sense of the Meeting" Practice in Communal
   Discernment to Consensus 282
Wesleyan Quadrilateral in Communal Discernment to Consensus. 284
Sample Outline of One Church's Communal Discernment Process 286
Abbreviated Communal Discernment Practice for a
   One-Hour Meeting 289
Listening Practices for Communal Discernment. 292
Spiritual Practices for Communal Discernment 297
Creating a Communal Discernment Process in Your Church
(For Use by a Leadership Team or Church Council). 299

Acknowledgments. 301

Introduction

The Power of Group Spiritual Direction

In a spacious church fellowship hall one late Sunday afternoon in summer, sunlight spills onto the linoleum tile floor. The light illuminates several circles of blue plastic chairs. A gathering of about fifty people has just concluded. People are standing within their circles and conversing. The atmosphere in the room is animated and lively. Some people give each other hugs while others share laughter. A few talk in soft tones, their eyes riveted on one another's faces. Rather than scurrying away to have the typical church "meeting after the meeting" in the parking lot, people linger. Even after an hour and a half together, one participant shares, "I'm not ready to leave! Instead of feeling tired and irritable after a long meeting, I have so much more energy than when I came in. I feel centered and at peace; I feel like I belong with God in a circle of friends. This has been holy ground."

This post-gathering of good vibes happened in a real church with real people. As a part of the church's discernment process around a major decision, the congregation had gathered several times that summer to listen to short presentations on different aspects of the issue and then share with one another what stood out to them and why. They listened reflectively without interrupting. They held space for one another to share their stories of life with God. They sat together on holy ground. They experienced holy listening in community and, as a result, they felt a sense of connection and belonging.

A Proven and Powerful Practice

Those parishioners in that sun-dappled fellowship hall were engaged in an ancient Christian practice known as *spiritual direction*. One description of spiritual direction is "listening to the active presence of God in a person's life."[1] In other words, it is listening to the ways God is moving, working, and speaking in the life of another. Throughout the centuries, people have been drawn to this practice of listening to the Divine in our lives in a space of deep connection and belonging.

The practice of holy listening has roots in the Bible. Moses and the prophets tuned themselves to the voice of God and served in a role of spiritual director for the people of Israel. Jesus provided spiritual direction to his disciples and followers as he asked them open-ended questions such as "Who do you say that I am?"[2] and offered invitations to "Come and see."[3] Through the centuries this practice continued and developed among Christian communities, becoming what we know as spiritual direction today. In its most common form, spiritual direction looks like one person (the directee/storyteller) sharing with another person (the director) about their life with God—a practice called one-with-one spiritual direction. During this process a spiritual director uses prayer, silence, and deep listening to help them hear the one true director, who is the Holy Spirit. Spiritual direction provides companionship on life's pilgrimage of discerning what the Holy Spirit is about in our lives with God (see pages 223–24 in the appendix for guidance on how to find a spiritual director).

> "Spiritual direction is help given by one Christian to another which enables that person to pay attention to God's personal communication to him or her, to respond to this personally communicating God, to grow in intimacy with this God, and to live out the consequences of the relationship."[4]
> —William Barry and William Connolly

When the number of people listening for the presence of God in someone's life increases to three or more, then the practice becomes *group spiritual direction*. Group spiritual direction describes a sacred listening circle of people who pay prayerful attention to their lives in God.[5] Group spiritual direction uses a disciplined structure of sharing, reflective listening, and response, undergirded by prayer and silence.[6] The group offers to each person insight, comfort, and thoughtful, open-ended questions—without trying to "fix," advise, or correct the one sharing their story. The time together becomes holy ground as participants tend to the sparks of the Divine at work in one another's souls. Group spiritual direction provides a deep drink of the Holy. People come away with their spirits quenched, feeling refreshed, renewed, peaceful, energized, and more connected to one another. Having experienced God's grace in the practice, they feel a sense of belonging—to God and to one another.

Years ago, I experienced the power of this communal practice of holy listening for the first time, and it changed me. A wise practitioner taught about group spiritual direction during a session of my certification program to become a spiritual director. She then sent us forth in small groups to practice it. As I sat with that beloved circle of women and shared my story of deep vocational struggle, I felt heard and understood. The shroud of loneliness that had engulfed me in that season fell away. I felt loved as I was and encouraged into a hope I could not yet see. I felt I belonged.

After becoming a spiritual director, I offered one-with-one direction to people in my church, where I also served as their pastor. This practice was life-giving, yet I still longed for the larger communal experience of group spiritual direction. So, I started a pilot group, which met in my home, of neighbors who were also parishioners. As this group flourished, I trained more leaders, and the groups multiplied. Over time and in different church communities, I continued to lead group spiritual direction, and I saw repeatedly how this practice helped people to connect, hear one another, experience God's grace, build friendships, and belong.

I also learned about the power of group spiritual direction to help congregations move through conflict to see where God is leading them as a community—a practice called communal discernment. When a church—the one with the blue chairs described in the opening story—asked me to create a process to help them discern God's calling, I developed a model of group spiritual direction for communal discernment for their context. Through their work together, which I facilitated, the church moved through their conflict and uncertainty to clearly see God's direction for their common life.

Benefits for Your Church

In addition to being a spiritual director, professor, and director of a certification program in spiritual direction at the seminary where I teach, I've served local churches of all sizes and types as a United Methodist pastor for many years. I know how challenging it is to minister in congregations these days. Pastors are often exhausted as they must do more with less and as conflict in their congregations threatens to overwhelm them. Church members are worn out, too—often juggling demanding jobs and caregiving, with little space left to engage in programs or do the work of committees. Many have stopped coming—even as rates of loneliness explode.

People long for holy ground—but don't think they'll find it in church anymore. Church leaders—clergy and laity alike—yearn for experiences of God with others that invigorate and connect them. Group spiritual direction can provide this holy ground by offering a means of God's grace in a practice of Christian friendship that cultivates belonging among people hungry for the Holy, connection, and unity. In a culture and world that can feel lonely, divided, and devoid of God, this practice just might be what your church needs. Consider these four benefits.

1. *A Means of Grace*

As a spiritual practice, group spiritual provides a channel or means through which God conveys grace. It offers an experience of God's love and compassion in a circle with other people. As participants share stories of their life with God, they experience love and acceptance as they are—from God and from those in the circle. At the same time, they are accompanied in discerning where God is leading them to grow or make changes. Group spiritual direction offers people who are longing for grace a profound experience of the Holy through the deep listening of others.

Group spiritual direction as a means of grace has deep roots in the Christian tradition. It offers your congregation a spiritual practice found in scripture, developed in the early church, and sustained first by monks and nuns in monasteries and then by other faith communities. In the Wesleyan or Methodist tradition, group spiritual direction occurred in the small group gatherings known as class meetings. The earliest Methodists in the mid-1700s gathered with ten to twelve others to ask, "How is it with your soul?" and to sustain each other with life in the Holy Spirit—where "truth was spoken in love" and joys and sorrows were deeply shared. By reclaiming group spiritual direction, contemporary Methodists and Christians of all traditions can cultivate a life-giving practice that conveys God's love and grace anew.

2. A Practice of Christian Friendship

We are experiencing a dearth of friendship in the United States. A study conducted by the American Survey Center shows people have fewer meaningful friendships and rates of loneliness have skyrocketed.[7] Christianity offers a robust theological practice of friendship—it's just that we seem to have forgotten how to be good friends—evidenced by the number of best-selling books on the topic of friendship today.[8] Often people can attend a Sunday worship service or a church social gathering without anyone asking how they are doing—without feeling "known."[9] Of course, many people experience true friendships in their church community. Sunday school classes, small groups, and other program ministries offer to many Christians relationships that are life-sustaining. However, enough people, particularly younger people, are opting out of church because they are not experiencing authentic, welcoming, loving community that meets their human need to belong.

By reclaiming the Christian practice of friendship through group spiritual direction, your church can offer people the kind of human and Divine relationships they long for and need. The practice forms people into holy listeners so that others feel heard, seen, and affirmed. Friends created by group spiritual direction can sustain one another through life's sufferings and defeat. As Stanley Hauerwas and Charles Pinches indicate, friends can hold one another's differences while connecting with each other's humanity in the profound love of God.[10] Jesus says in John 15:15, "I have called you friends, because I have made known to you everything that I have heard from my Father." These are the kind of friends that group spiritual direction creates—friends whom we love deeply enough to make God known to them.

3. A Sense of Belonging

We feel belonging when we can show up fully as ourselves—without any pretense, superficiality, or veiling—and know that we are completely loved and accepted. Group spiritual direction creates a group of people who know each other with such grace and love that the powers of loneliness and isolation are resisted. In fact, the practice invites you to be fully who you are in all your wounds and your authenticity. As Diane Millis indicates in her book on storytelling, group spiritual direction provides a way to share our human stories through a practice that connects and heals us.[11] Brené Brown states in her book *Daring Greatly* that connection, along with love and belonging, is why we are here, and this is what gives purpose and meaning to our lives.[12] When we belong in a circle of friends with God, we feel more whole, and we contribute to others' feelings of wholeness in that circle, too. By so doing, we ensure one another's flourishing and well-being according to God's design. In a world of loneliness and strife, group spiritual direction offers your community whole and healing relationships that create belonging.

4. A Practice for Communal Discernment

In some forms, group spiritual direction also provides a tool for a community to discern who they are and what they are to do—even amid conflict. Rather than decision-making, vote-taking, and side-taking, group spiritual direction offers a way to share our stories together on a common issue before us. Through a structured spiritual practice of communal discernment from the Christian tradition, we listen to one another's perspectives and experiences. We drop our defensiveness and rigidity about our own "rightness." As we offer our stories to one another on a particular issue that is before the congregation and develop empathy and insight, the practice of group spiritual direction for communal discernment makes consensus possible. It could be the practice you and your church have been hungering for, and perhaps didn't know existed, to be able to discern together while simultaneously fostering belonging and unity. It's true that group spiritual direction as a means of grace through the power of the Holy Spirit can transform conflict into possibilities for greater growth and mission.

Your Congregation Can Do This!

The need for a spiritual practice that can help us live a common life together in a culture of division and conflict is pressing. The goal of this book is to offer people hungry for authentic spiritual connection with God and others the powerful "holy ground" of group spiritual direction. My hope is that this resource can empower you to begin your own practice of group spiritual direction in your congregation. You can adapt the practice to your context and your people and then give it space to work its wonders of connection, belonging, friendship, and communal discernment among you. I've designed the book to include lots of practical direction plus helpful handouts in the appendix so that you can learn and implement this practice.

Perhaps you're thinking, "But I'm not trained in spiritual practices or spiritual direction. I'm not competent to do this kind of 'holy listening.'" To that, I would say that you are created in the image of God and made as a temple of the Holy Spirit, who is as close to you as your next in-breath and out-breath. You *can* do group spiritual direction because really it is the work of the Holy Spirit, not our own work. You don't have to be an expert or super "holy" to do this spiritual practice. You simply need a heart open to God's presence and the willingness to learn and try. Group spiritual direction is a practice; we do it, we reflect and learn from our attempt, we try again, and we get more adept at holy listening as we live it out.

Perhaps you're questioning whether other people in the church will want to do a practice that involves silence, deep listening, and vulnerability. It's true that some people won't resonate with spiritual direction—and that's okay. All you need is a few people in your congregation who want to try listening to each other with God, and you have a place to begin.

What this book *is not* is another program, curriculum, Bible study, series, or book study. This book is meant to invite you into a spiritual practice—group spiritual direction—that serves as a means of God's grace, cultivates friendships, fosters belonging, and facilitates discernment. I've organized the book according to two key forms, or categories, of group spiritual direction: 1) Christian Friendship and 2) Communal Discernment (see How to Use This Book for more about that). Your congregation could benefit from either or both forms depending upon your needs or desires. Discern the form for your community, practice it, and see where the Holy Spirit leads. You can do this!

A Vision and Blessing

Connecting and belonging through sharing our lives together with God in group spiritual direction can literally make us well! It is a practice that can

- heal people's experiences of isolation, loneliness, depression, and anxiety
- repair strife and divisions and help us to love one another with the love of Christ
- offer connection and belonging
- restore those who feel exhausted and weary
- help us to see the image of God in one another
- enable people from diverse walks of life to hear one another's stories and experience God in one another as a means of grace
- generate friendship
- facilitate discernment (both individual and communal)

When used for communal discernment, group spiritual direction provides a way for congregations to make decisions about their common life other than divisive voting. It offers weary and exhausted clergy the space to be spiritual leaders rather than arbiters of conflict while offering church people a renewing spiritual practice that helps them to hear God in one another's lives, discern where the Holy Spirit is leading them, and become united in mission as the body of Christ.

May God be with you as you learn about and explore the powerful practice of group spiritual direction. May the light of Christ guide you as you discern how to implement group spiritual direction for friendship or communal discernment in your setting. And may the Holy Spirit grant you means of grace and profound peace as you speak the words of Jesus to one another, saying, "I am calling you friend."

NOTES

1. Lucy Abbott Tucker, "Spiritual Direction Supervision" (webinar Spiritual Direction International, summer 2020).
2. Matthew 16:13-16, Mark 8:27-29, and Luke 9:18-20
3. John 1:39
4. William Barry and William Connolly, *The Practice of Spiritual Direction* (New York: Harper One, 1982), 7–8.
5. Lois Lindbloom, *Prayerful Listening: Cultivating Discernment in Community* (Northfield, MN: Ashmore Ink, 2007), 7.
6. Ann Kline, "Raising Holy Sparks," in *The Lived Experience of Group Spiritual Direction,* ed. Rose Mary Dougherty (New York: Paulist Press, 2003), 90.
7. "The State of American Friendship: Change, Challenges, and Loss," American Survey Center, accessed November 12, 2023, https://www.americansurveycenter.org/research/the-state-of-american-friendship-change-challenges-and-loss/.
8. The book *Platonic: How the Science of Attachment Can Help You Make and Keep Friends* (published in 2022) by Dr. Marisa Franco became an instant bestseller, which attests both to the cultural need for friends, and the desire to learn how to be a friend.
9. Of course, many people experience true friendships in their church community as it is now; Sunday school classes, small groups, and other program ministries offer to many Christians relationships that are life-sustaining. However, enough people, particularly younger people, are opting out of church because they aren't experiencing authentic, welcoming, loving community that meets their human need to belong. "Religious Education During the Pandemic: A Tale of Challenge and Creativity," Hartford Institution for Religious Education, accessed September 2, 2024, https://www.covidreligionresearch.org/research/national-survey-research/religious-education-report/.
10. Stanley Hauerwas and Charles Pinches, *Christians among the Virtues: Theological Conversations with Ancient and Modern Ethics* (Notre Dame: University of Notre Dame Press, 1997), 44.

11. Diane Millis, *Re-creating A Life: Learning How to Tell Our Most Life-Giving Story* (Belluvue, WA: SDI Press, 2019), 16. Millis's book is about learning to tell your most life-giving story through group spiritual direction. Informed by narrative therapy, Millis offers that by telling life-giving, redemptive stories through spiritual direction, people experience greater hope, healing, and transformation. "It takes a community to help us learn how to tell a more life-giving story." p.12.
12. Brené Brown, *Daring Greatly* (New York: Penguin Random House, 2012), 68.

How to Use This Book

Any practice of group spiritual direction facilitates friendship and discernment, which makes my two categorizations of Christian Friendship and Communal Discernment somewhat murky. However, I have chosen to address group spiritual direction according to these two categories because each has a unique focus or goal.

I invite you to utilize the descriptions of the two forms of group spiritual direction below to help you determine which kind to implement in your congregation. Then browse the At-a-glance Overview that follows to quickly and easily navigate the book's contents, finding the chapter where you want to begin. If you prefer, you can read the book cover to cover and then return to specific chapters as needed.

Two Forms of Group Spiritual Direction

1. Group Spiritual Direction for Christian Friendship

What: In this form of group spiritual direction, about four to eight people gather regularly (often monthly) for a set time (one to two hours) to share their stories of life with God.

Focus: The focus rests upon each individual member and their own life experience with God, which is shared with the group. Each member offers "how it is with their soul" and has a safe, confidential space to talk about whatever is most present in their life—their griefs, hurts, struggles, and hopes. It is a circle that offers to every person insight, comfort, and thoughtful, open-ended questions that enrich their life and faith journey.

Goal (End): Each member discerns God's guidance in their life with the help of the group. They receive direction on any actions or ways of being to cultivate or practice in their own life. Therefore, the discernment focuses on everyone's life and story with God. As a result of this work together, they nourish deep bonds of connection, friendship, and belonging with one another and with God.

When: Choose this practice to create circles of community for people who long for deep connection to God and others—or when you as a ministry leader feel called to nurture more trusting and loving relationships in your congregation. This practice of group spiritual direction develops friendship with God and with others as people discern the way God is leading them in their individual life. It offers the means of grace of becoming soul friends. It also can help people to love one another, particularly after a time of congregational strife.

2. *Group Spiritual Direction for Communal Discernment*

What: In this form of group spiritual direction, a group of people (could be a church council, staff team, lead team of a ministry area, or the whole congregation) gathers to discern on a commonly held question, issue, or problem. Communal discernment could take place for ten minutes in a council meeting, or it could be a months-long process with a congregation having multiple sessions or even a retreat.

Focus: The focus is on the commonly held story, issue, question, problem, or challenge before the group. Each person's individual stories and experiences matter and can be included in the process, but these aren't the focus. In this form of group spiritual direction, participants gather to listen to how the Holy Spirit is leading them through the issue to an answer, solution, or next step for their group or community.

Goal (End): The goal of this practice is to arrive at a communally held discernment that everyone supports. As we offer our stories on an issue and develop empathy and insight, we arrive at consensus, which is when people agree in heart on a direction to go or action to take. They may still hold different opinions, but they affirm the path the Holy Spirit has led them to walk together.

When: Choose this practice when a group, community, or congregation is facing a key question, issue, or problem. Through a structured group spiritual direction practice of communal prayer and reflection, the community discerns their way to consensus, unity, and a common mission. It offers the means of grace of holy conferencing.

At-a-glance Overview

Part 1: Group Spiritual Direction for Christian Friendship

Chapter 1: Defines what group spiritual direction for Christian friendship is and how it has been practiced in Christian tradition, answering the "What is it?" and "Where did it come from?" questions for your church.

Chapter 2: Explores the means of grace and gifts of grace that group spiritual direction for Christian friendship offers, answering the "Why?" question for your church.

Chapter 3: Helps you to equip participants for the practice of group spiritual direction for Christian friendship, answering the "How?" question for your church.

Chapter 4: Offers detailed guidance for leaders or facilitators of group spiritual direction for Christian friendship groups.

Chapter 5: Describes individual and group challenges for both forms of group spiritual direction (Christian friendship and communal discernment) so that participants and leaders can embrace them for growth.

Part 2: Group Spiritual Direction for Communal Discernment

Chapter 6: Provides a definition and theology of group spiritual direction for communal discernment and describes its practice in the Christian tradition, answering the "What is it?" and "Where did it come from?" questions for your church.

Chapter 7: Explores how communal discernment differs from decision-making and voting processes, serving as a means of grace, while giving guidance on when to choose it, answering the "Why?" and "When?" questions for your church.

Chapter 8: Equips participants for the processes involved in group spiritual direction for communal discernment.

Chapter 9: Resources leadership teams to guide their own group spiritual direction for communal discernment practice.

(Throughout part 2, I integrate the story of one church's discernment process as an example to help prepare participants and leaders for a congregational discernment process.)

Epilogue: Offers a vision of the miracle of belonging offered by both forms of group spiritual direction.

Appendix: Includes resources such as reference sheets, timing structures, covenant guidelines, outlines, and other reproducible handouts for both forms of group spiritual direction.

PART 1
Group Spiritual Direction for Christian Friendship

1.

A Practice of Friendship with God and Others (The What)

Seven of us, ranging in age from early thirties to mid-sixties and with differing vocational backgrounds, settle into a circle in my living room. I've invited everyone from my new church to participate in "group spiritual direction," and these seven have gamely said yes to attend this first session and discern if they want to continue for five more weeks. I've provided snacks (which always helps), we've introduced ourselves, and now I take a breath to teach them this practice that I love so much.

"We're going to do a practice of holy listening—to one another and to God. It's different than a normal conversation—we won't offer immediate feedback or responses after someone shares. Instead of offering advice, solutions, or our own similar story, we will give each other open-ended questions for reflection like, 'I wonder how God is at work in this?' or 'I noticed you said this phrase several times. What does it mean for you right now?' We'll hold space for a lot of silence."

"Wow," said one outgoing and friendly participant. "I'm not sure I even know how or what it means to 'hold silence.' I tend to always hold lots of words to say!" Everyone laughed.

"It's okay," I said with a smile. "This is just a practice. We will each live into it with the fullness of who we are while also learning how to be with each other in spiritual direction. We'll have a gentle structure or process to guide us. Each of us will take a turn as a "directee," when for a short period of time we will share about our life with God in whatever way we feel led to describe it. When not in the "directee" or "storyteller" role, we will serve as "directors"—meaning, we are listening to the Holy Spirit's movement and glimmers in the directee's life."

"As a very logical thinker," said one participant, "I'm not sure I'll know when or how the Holy Spirit is present in someone's life. I don't feel qualified to direct anyone in their spiritual life."

"Yes, thanks for that honesty," I replied. "You are saying what many people feel at first in spiritual direction. It's common to feel unprepared or inadequate for the practice. Listening for God's calling in someone else's life is a sacred, mysterious, and sometimes baffling task. Paying attention to the whispers of the Holy Spirit requires using a different kind of ear—one finely tuned to frequencies of love, wholeness, and presence. It requires both a spirit of humility about our capacity to know God's working and a confidence that God is indeed at work in our lives—all at the same time! Spiritual direction isn't about getting the discernment of God's movement in someone else's life "right" or "wrong"; it's about participating in the Divine love that's already there for us. The One doing the direction is the Holy Spirit—not us. Coming to this practice as beginners every time helps us to listen better and discern more clearly with practice."

"So, I don't have to worry about trying to make an A or to quote the Bible perfectly," the participant said with a laugh.

I grinned with him. "No, there's definitely no grading in spiritual direction. This also isn't like other forms of Christian education or formation, like Sunday school or a Bible study. I might use a Bible verse to center us at the beginning, but we're not reading or breaking down a Bible passage. I'm not imparting information or teaching content to you. In spiritual direction, our lives serve as the 'text.' We trust that God is 'writing' something down for the story of our lives—it just takes others to help us to 'read it.' This really constitutes a spiritual practice and form of prayer, rather than a class or study. I'm here as the facilitator to guide the practice and keep us on track; I trust the Holy Spirit will do the rest. My hope is that you leave here today having experienced a little bit of holiness—time with God in the company of others."

"I'm happy to have some holy time with these people," said one of our church's lay leaders with a laugh.

"Great! Let's open our hearts, minds, and spirits to this practice of spiritual direction. Take a deep breath, settle in, and get comfortable. Let's open our inner ears to become attuned to the presence of God in this place. God is here with us. Now, reflect on these questions: "What has given you joy in the past week? What has given you sorrow?" We'll reflect on these questions for a minute of silence."

I draw us out of the silence by ringing my singing bowl. The first person, the church lay leader, begins sharing for about three minutes about her joys and sorrows. After her sharing, we hold silence and listen for any questions, wonderings, or appreciations God brings to us. Then for another three minutes, we share what we have heard or received with her. We don't try to advise, correct, or fix her sorrows; she doesn't have to respond to anything we say. She simply absorbs this time of deep listening. We then "hold her" in a minute of silent intercessory prayer, before moving to the next person in the circle.

At first, people jitter and shift in their seats, but by the middle of the second person's sharing, people settle into this different way of speaking and listening. In this confidential circle, people speak forth their joys of an adult child's upcoming marriage, and of their longings for a different career. One shares honestly of a sense of God's absence in her experience of grief after a spouse's death. The time begins to shimmer with the "holy" as my living room becomes sacred ground. We leave the time of group spiritual direction with peacefulness in our spirits and a deeper connection of friendship with one another and with God. Everyone decides to continue for the full six weeks of the practice.

What Is Group Spiritual Direction?

As this group discovered in my living room that day, group spiritual direction provides companionship to help you discern what God is doing in your life. It can be hard at times to know what step to take or what path in life to travel; this sacred circle of friends supports you in figuring out how to live well. In group spiritual direction, a small circle of friends listens closely to hear the heartbeat of the Holy in your life. They take the pulse of what gives you vitality (and what doesn't). They prayerfully reflect back your spiritual "vital signs," helping you to see and know your own life force. They serve as a community of love and forgiveness, praying with and for you, so that you may "walk in the way that leads to life."[1]

Here are a variety of definitions of the practice from wise and experienced practitioners:

- Group spiritual direction describes a circle of sacred listening.[2]
- "The group becomes a spiritual director for each person in the group. Through the interceding presence of the group . . . we see more clearly the presence of God in our lives."
—Rose Mary Dougherty[3]
- "The very purpose of the group is to pay prayerful attention to our lives in God and to be together in the prayer of listening."
—Lois Lindbloom[4]

Each member shares whatever they choose—from their life experience to their group of soul friends. The group, which can range in size from four to eight people, listens within a pattern of silence, sharing, and prayer. Group spiritual direction usually lasts for an hour or two, depending upon the number of people and the timing structure used. It's a practice of communal holy listening on behalf of one another that nurtures belonging and binds our hearts together as one.

Where Does Group Spiritual Direction Come From?

Communal forms of listening have existed within the church throughout Christian tradition, offering significant benefits for the body of faith. Yet their history may be unknown to some of us. Like organs in the human body that perform vital functions without being seen, various practices of group spiritual direction have supported Christians throughout the centuries, keeping them alive and attentive to the work of the Holy Spirit in their midst. It's worth remembering these Christian communities and reclaiming their listening practices as a way of restoring the ability of our own "body of faith" to belong to one another in a time of division and strife. I'll offer a quick survey of Christian history and consider some of these important communities and enriching practices.

Jesus, the Early Church, and Monastic Communities

Jesus gathered together a small group of twelve who were drawn to his question, "What are you looking for?" (John 1:38). As they fished, ate meals, ministered to the sick, and prayed together, they formed a community that listened to Jesus and followed his guidance.

The Book of Acts describes the earliest Christian community as they gathered for spiritual and physical sustenance in households. They prayed together, shared the oral traditions of Jesus, and discerned how God was leading them in a time of great uncertainty and liminality. The scripture describes their communal life this way: "They devoted themselves to the apostles' teaching and fellowship, to the breaking of bread and the prayers (Acts 2:42). The experience of holy friendship with God and others made their hearts glad and generous, leading to the spread of a new movement that would come to be called Christianity.

A couple of hundred years later, as the church settled into more status and security in the Roman Empire, people longed for the spiritual community of those first Christians. A gifted holy man named Pachomius heard God calling him to create a dwelling, and sometime between 318–323 AD in Egypt he created a home for seekers of God to live together and pray. Known as a monastery, this dwelling housed people called monks (males) or nuns (females) who lived in a daily rhythm of prayer, work, rest, and worship. They were guided by a document written by Pachomius called a Rule, which provided prayers and precepts for life together.

Monasteries grew, multiplied, and spread from Africa to the Middle East and Europe as they provided an alternative, simple lifestyle of holy belonging. These monasteries were led by abbots or abbesses who exercised their gifts on behalf of the community. One abbess, Brigid of Kildare, led a spiritual community for men and women in Ireland in the late 400s, where they lived in a rhythm of prayer and worship in harmony with the seasons and creation. By the 500s AD, the great monastic leader Benedict of Assisi codified the traditions, patterns, and practices of monastic communities in a written text that became known as "The Rule of Saint Benedict," which created a communal life of listening for those who were seeking God.[5]

Monasteries became communities of spiritual direction that supported each person in a disciplined life of prayer and service.[6] Through their obedience to God, to the Rule of their community, to the abbot or abbess, and to one another, early monastics offered a model of profound communal listening that created belonging to God and to one another.

"Third Order" Communities

As monasteries spread across the Middle East and Europe, they inspired other practices of Christian community among laity, who formed "third orders" based upon a modified rule of life suited for householders—people who lived in the world instead of sequestered in a monastery. Others, like the Sisters and Brothers of the Common Life in Holland in the 1300s, created a community completely outside of church structures that shared a life of daily scripture, study, prayer, work, confession, and reconciliation. Communities for laywomen, called Beguines, formed in northern Europe around this same time, in which women dwelt in common housing while laboring in their cities as teachers and nurses. They used a rule of life and offered communal spiritual direction through their life together.

In the mid-1500s, a soldier turned convert named Ignatius of Loyola gathered a group of college friends, who devoted themselves to poverty, prayer, listening to God, and life together. Guided by Ignatius's text on four weeks of spiritual practices called the *Spiritual Exercises*, the friends listened for God's presence (consolation) or absence (desolation) in their lives—a practice that became known as the Ignatian Examen. They became the Society of Jesus (Jesuits) and developed a focus on spiritual direction and small groups for communal listening and discernment, which became particular gifts of their monastic order.

Protestant Practices of Communal Listening

Monastic practices of communal listening also influenced the earliest generations of Protestants. Philip Jacob Spener, a German Lutheran in the 1600s, created forms of small groups called "colleges of piety" (*collegia pietatis*), which drew from the communal life of monasteries. Spener's small groups read scripture, prayed, and discerned together how God was calling them to carry out Christ's mission to the poor, the sick, and the elderly in their communities. As this renewing movement spread throughout southern Germany, it became known as "pietism"—which included practices of devotion in small groups with a theology focused on the heart.

Another Protestant expression of church called "Moravian," which had developed in the present-day Czech Republic ("Czechia"), found refuge in the 1720s in Herrnhut, Germany. It was influenced by Lutheran pietism's emphasis on the heart and spiritual practices. Moravians organized their members into large groups called "choirs," small neighborhood age-based groups called "classes," and even smaller groups for strict discipline and accountability called "bands." Moravians met in their classes to provide mutual spiritual direction, read scripture, and pray together; they met in their bands to "confess your sins to one another and pray for one another, so that you may be healed" (James 5:16). The bands and classes provided a form of communal spiritual direction that sustained each member on the journey of faith as they developed close bonds of friendship.

Around the same time that the Moravians were instigating a renewal movement in Germany, Church of England pastors and lay leaders met in small groups for what they called "holiness of heart and life" through scripture reading, prayer, daily examination, regular fasting, and the reading of devotional materials.[7] Known as the Society for Promoting Christian Knowledge (SPCK), these monastic-like groups of communal direction also promoted local outreach to the poor and disadvantaged.

Anglican leaders Samuel and Susanna Wesley led a robust SPCK chapter in their town of Epworth, England.[8] Influenced by their mother's spiritual formation and direction of them as children, as well as this SPCK model, John and Charles Wesley, along with their friend William Morgan, began meeting for prayer, Bible study, and worship in their dorm rooms at Oxford University.[9] This communal direction led to social justice work with prisoners and orphans in their community. Though derisively called the "holy club" by their peers for their do-gooding, the Wesleys and their small group of devoted friends remained committed to their practice of "holiness of heart and life," forming a kind of Anglican small group college ministry based in the older practices of early Christian monasteries.[10] The experience of belonging through communal listening, prayer, and social justice work transformed them and formed the backbone of leadership in what would become the Methodist renewal movement.

After a brief mission to Georgia in America, where John and Charles Wesley experienced the piety, faith, and small group communal direction of Moravians, the Wesleys returned to England. Along with their former college friends (now clergy in the Church of England), some English Moravians, and committed lay folk, John and Charles Wesley nurtured large group gatherings called "societies" for worship, hymn-singing, prayer, and communal life. Small groups called "bands"—which were organized by gender, marital status, and age—developed for the purposes of accountability, confession, prayer, and spiritual growth. Bands met weekly, and members would "speak, each of us in order, freely and plainly the true state of our souls."[11]

As Methodist societies continued to grow, more people needed an "entry" small group for spiritual growth that wasn't as stringent and focused on questions of accountability as the bands were.[12] The Wesleys and their friends developed "class meetings," which were small groups of about ten to twelve persons organized geographically by neighborhood and diverse in gender, age, socio-economic status, and marital status; the meetings were open to anyone who wanted to participate.[13] Class meetings would meet "in homes, shops, school rooms, attics—even coal bins—wherever there was room for ten or twelve people to assemble."[14] After singing a song (often with lyrics by Charles Wesley), the class leader, who could be male or female, uplifted their General Rules, which were to do good, to do no harm, and to practice spiritual disciplines.[15] The leader would then offer the question "How is it with your soul?" They would offer the gist of their own life for discernment, and then each member in turn shared their journey with God. Through this practice of communal spiritual direction, people experienced profound friendship and belonging. In addition to spiritual care, class members supported each other with financial assistance and pastoral care through life's crises.[16]

Through the gift of group spiritual direction in the form of a class meeting, early Methodists from all kinds of backgrounds heard each other's sacred stories and experienced communion. Paul Jones in his book *Art of Spiritual Direction,* argues that "[communal] spiritual direction is a central reason for the [Methodist] church's existence."[18] The sharing of life together with God in a sacred circle of friends constituted what it meant to be Methodist, even as it drew from Catholic, Anglican, Pietist, Moravian, and Reformed traditions.

> "Many now happily experienced that Christian fellowship of which they had not so much as an idea before. They began to 'bear one another's burdens' and 'naturally' to 'care for each other . . . advice or reproof was given as need required, quarrels made up, misunderstandings removed. And after an hour or two spent in this labour of love, they concluded with prayer and thanksgiving.'"[17]
> —John Wesley

The Loss and Renewal of Group Spiritual Direction

Unfortunately, the practice of class meetings faded among Methodists by the early to mid-1800s due to the advent of the Sunday school model. As a result of the influence of the Enlightenment and its emphasis on individualism and rationality, prayer became more privatized and transformative practices such as spiritual direction were lost or hidden for both Protestants and Catholics. Christian discipleship for clergy and lay people became more focused on instructional and informational education (Bible studies and curriculum-based studies) and less on spiritual formation and communal prayer practices.

By the time of the Second Vatican Council in the 1960s, the Roman Catholic Church discerned the need for renewal of the rich Christian contemplative tradition of prayer, including practices such as spiritual direction. Catholic priests in the Society of Jesus (Jesuits) took this recommendation to heart and began teaching, leading retreats, and publishing on the practice of spiritual direction—a practice their order had maintained.[19] As the practice of spiritual direction grew in popularity, organizations and leaders across Christian denominations and traditions arose to support and resource it. Training programs for largely one-with-one spiritual direction emerged to train lay and clergy persons in the practice. A wave of Christian writers began publishing books on spiritual direction and the contemplative life, which promulgated the practices to wider audiences across Christian traditions.[20] Influenced by the work of Rose Mary Doughterty on group spiritual direction, other voices began leading and publishing on forms of group spiritual direction, responding to the human need to seek God and to be supported in that search by a loving community of real belonging.[21]

Thanks for making that trek through history with me. As we participate in the renewal of the practice of communal listening, we are reclaiming a form of spiritual community that goes all the way back to the earliest Christians and monastic communities—a practice of prayer that embodies Jesus's own prayer "that they may be one as we are one" (John 17: 22). It's a practice that continues in a world hungry for deeper connection with God and others.

With this background to inspire us, let's turn our attention to five common elements of the practice of group spiritual direction.

Five Common Elements of Group Spiritual Direction

1. A Group of People

Let's begin with the obvious: group spiritual direction requires a group of people. Typically, the group numbers about four to eight people. More than eight can make it difficult for everyone to fully receive and offer direction. Less than three and it becomes one-with-one spiritual direction.

This collective experience of direction means that participants in group spiritual direction can develop deep friendships together. The rich experience of community is a superpower of this practice. Friendship created by group spiritual direction can sustain one another's sufferings and defeats; it can hold one another's differences while connecting each other in the profound love of God.[22]

2. Regular Meetings

The group generally meets monthly but may meet weekly or biweekly at the beginning to learn the practice and solidify the group. These meetings can take place in person, in which case the group usually sits in a circle. Group spiritual direction also functions well over video online platforms, such as Zoom.

3. Leadership

Each group meeting is usually supported by a facilitator or leader. Groups can function without a designated leader if participants bring adequate spiritual direction experience. It helps tremendously if the leader is a trained spiritual director or has contemplative prayer experience. However, a committed person can learn the practice of group spiritual direction and, by God's grace, lead a group. This person may be the same leader each time, particularly as a new group learns the practice, or the role might rotate among the group members. Generally, the facilitator both gives and receives direction from the group, taking a turn as a directee/storyteller; however, the leader also can abstain from receiving direction in some forms of the practice.

4. Mutuality

Although there are models or types of group spiritual direction in which the facilitator or leader serves as the primary provider of spiritual direction to others in the circle, as well as models in which the leader refrains from receiving direction, it's more common for everyone in the group to both receive and give direction, including the leader. (For a comparison of various types or models of group spiritual direction, see Models of Group Spiritual Direction on pages 225–28 in the appendix.) This mutuality of all receiving and giving spiritual direction distinguishes the group practice from one-with-one direction, in which the director and directee usually stay in their roles of provider (director) and receiver (directee).[23] Group members hold equity with one another in their giving and their receiving. Together, the community mediates God's presence, insight, and wisdom for one another.

This mutual and collective spiritual direction also provides for a multiplicity of life-giving responses. While in the role of directee/storyteller, a person might receive lots of different responses from around the circle, each of which could open new insights or growth.

The mutual practice also means that a member might benefit more from another's time as directee/storyteller than even their own. Sometimes an insight or question offered to another is just the one we needed to receive, too. In addition, the different thoughts and experiences shared by group members might generate an awareness of the wide variety and diversity of ways that God is present and working in others' lives.

5. Content: Silence, Listening, Sharing, Prayer

Every meeting usually begins with some silence; the length of silence depends on each group's timing structure. It could be from one minute to twenty minutes! The group facilitator might offer a scripture, quote, piece of music, poem, or other prompt before or after the initial silence to help center and ground the group as they get started. The content of the practice includes a rhythm of sharing by a directee/storyteller, group listening and reflection, silence, and intercessory prayer for the directee/storyteller (not always in that order). At the end, the group reflects prayerfully on their practice and quality of listening together. Group spiritual direction comprises both a contemplative and a communal practice.

Now that we've identified the common elements, let's consider the flow, or steps, of those elements.

The Flow/Steps of Group Spiritual Direction

Group spiritual direction for Christian friendship can be practiced with a variety of different "recipes." The practice invites creativity and contextualization based upon what the individual members of the group bring and the goal of the group spiritual direction practice.[24] In my own facilitation of group spiritual direction, I make adaptations based upon the group, our time commitment for the meeting, and what supports the group's prayerfulness. Within its diversity, though, most group spiritual direction sessions will follow a similar flow, or move through steps, in its process. I'll offer a brief description of some common steps here to give you a better sense of the content of a session, dividing the session into three main "parts." (In chapter 3 on the preparation of participants, we will explore each step in more detail. See also The Steps of Group Spiritual Direction for Friendship on pages 229–34 in the appendix.)

Part 1: Gathering and Beginning (welcome/covenant/prompt/ centering silence)

Group spiritual direction generally moves in three key parts—the beginning, center, and going forth. Part 1, the gathering and beginning, starts with the facilitator/host of the group creating a welcoming atmosphere with comfortable seating, a candle, and pre-gathering prayer over the space, people, and time. Group members then enter a prayed over and prepared space of welcome. After a time of gathering, which could include brief "check-ins" and/or a short time of worship, the group settles into their practice. The facilitator might review the group's guidelines for mutual behavior, often called a covenant, and reiterate the group's way or structure for their practice. Then the facilitator ushers the group into a brief time of centering—either with a short scripture reading, quote, piece of music, or image—and then guides the group into a time of centering silence.

Part 2: The Center

The group now enters the "gist" or main content of their session of group spiritual direction. Generally, this involves a member sharing about their life and the group listening without interruption. In turn, the group members offer to the directee/storyteller life-giving responses—such as open-ended questions or grace-filled "noticings" or life-giving affirmations. The group refrains from offering advice, solutions, or their own similar story in favor of a "holy listening" to help the directee/storyteller hear how God might be guiding them. The directee or the group may move into silence at any time for deeper listening to God; silence serves as a member of the group. At the end of the directee's sharing and the responses of the group, everyone enters a prayerful silence, in which the group members pray silently for the directee. The group also may intercede for any absent group members.[25]

Part 3: Reflection and Going Forth

After everyone has had a turn to share, the group reflects on their practice together. The facilitator may inquire about their practice of prayerful listening, asking if they feel the group got "off track" into possible advice-giving or if they remained focused on the Spirit. The group considers their collective and individual practice without any assigning of blame or shame—it is simply a space for reflection and mutual insight. The facilitator also may check in regarding their faithfulness to the covenant and to their timing structure. In going forth, the facilitator could remind the group of their next gathering time/date/place and take care of any housekeeping details (who might check in on absent members, who is bringing refreshments next time, etc.). The group can close with a short prayer or blessing.

What Group Spiritual Direction is *Not*

Now that we've considered what group spiritual direction *is*, giving us a better understanding of this contemplative listening practice with deep roots in the Christian heritage, let's take a moment to clarify what it's *not*. Because Christians for the past couple of centuries have experienced Christian formation and education as more focused on conveying information and knowledge, it's easy to think of group spiritual direction as just another small group curriculum or study. *It's not.* It's a spiritual practice that serves as a means of grace, connecting people with one another and with God. After you learn the practice, you don't need a book or handout; you simply need to trust the guidance of the Holy Spirit together.

By contrast, adult Bible studies focus on the study of scripture or use other Christian curricula for the purpose of learning about scripture. Adult church classes and groups tend to impart information, often from "experts" or teachers, rather than immerse people in a transformational communal experience of prayerful listening to God and one another. Bible study groups and Sunday school classes generally do not practice discernment, whereas group spiritual direction awakens participants to their own callings in life, in vocation, and in relationships. In group spiritual direction, each person comes to see more clearly who they are to be and what they are to do in the world. The practice helps everyone to participate more effectively in sharing God's love and grace with a suffering world.[26]

Group spiritual direction is a unique and invaluable spiritual practice for our churches. As happened for the circle of people who gathered in my home to try it out for the first time, group spiritual direction can create "holy ground" for people in your church who are longing for an experience of God and beloved community. It is my hope that they, like the earliest Methodists, will keep coming back to "bear one another's burdens" in this beautiful "labour of love."

NOTES

1. "Baptismal Covenant II, *The United Methodist Hymnal* (Nashville: United Methodist Publishing House, 1989), 40. This language comes directly from the congregational promises made in the United Methodist sacrament of baptism to the baptized. Group spiritual direction provides a tangible practice for Methodist Christians to live into their baptismal promises to one another.
2. Group spiritual direction is known by names such as sacred listening circles or prayerful listening circles. For more about this practice, see Patience Robbins, "Group Spiritual Direction," Shalem Institute blog post, March 3, 2017. https://shalem.org/2017/03/10/group-spiritual-direction/.
3. Rose Mary Dougherty, *Group Spiritual Direction: Community for Discernment* (New York: Paulist Press, 1995), 34.
4. Lois Lindbloom, *Prayerful Listening: Cultivating Discernment in Community* (Northfield, MN: Ashmore Ink, 2007), 7
5. Joan D. Chittister, OSB, ed., *The Rule of St. Benedict* (Chicago: Crossroad, 1992), 151.
6. W. Paul Jones, *The Art of Spiritual Direction: Giving and Receiving Spiritual Guidance* (Nashville: Upper Room Books, 2002), 26.
7. Richard Heitzenrater, *Wesley and the People Called Methodists*, 2nd ed. (Nashville: Abingdon, 2013), 44–47. The phrase "holiness of heart and life" was commonly used in the SPCK groups. The SPCK organized out of the programs of small groups of renewal developed by Anthony Horneck in his book *The Happy Ascetik*, published in 1681.
8. Heitzenrater, *Wesley and the People Called Methodists*, 23–24.
9. Jones, in the *Art of Spiritual Direction,* makes the argument that Susanna Wesley served as a one-with-one spiritual director for each of her children. Though she called it instruction, she was really guiding their spiritual lives with prayer, reading scripture, and inquiring into her children's lives with God.
10. John Wesley deeply steeped himself in reading from the monastic tradition of Christianity. Jones, *The Art of Spiritual Direction,* 71, 77 and Heitzenrater, *Wesley and the People Called Methodists,* 39–40, 80.
11. Heitzenrater, *Wesley and the People Called Methodists,* 114–15. Some bands were called "select bands," and were for those leading exemplary lives. Penitential bands were for those who had "backslid" and needed more discipline and support. John Wesley, *The Works of John Wesley*, vol. 9, "Rules of the Band Societies, Drawn Up Dec. 25, 1738," ed. Rupert E. Davies (Nashville: Abingdon, 1989), 77.
12. David Lowes Watson, "Methodist Spirituality," in *Exploring Christian Spirituality: An Ecumenical Reader,* ed. Kenneth Collins (Grand Rapids: Baker, 2000), 181. Watson notes that John Wesley disapproved of the strict monitoring of the Moravian bands in Herrnhut, Germany, and wanted more of the mutual accountability and "watching over one another with love" that the class meetings would provide.
13. Watson, "Methodist Spirituality," 131.
14. David Michael Henderson, "John Wesley's Instructional Groups," Ann Arbor, Michigan: University Microfilms International, UMI 8029228 as quoted in Tracy,

"Spiritual Direction in the Wesleyan-Holiness Tradition" *Journal of Psychology and Theology* 30, no. 4 (Winter 2002), 120.

15. Jones, *The Art of Spiritual Direction: Giving and Receiving Spiritual Guidance*, 86–87 notes that the following of the General Rules in the class meetings was not unlike a monastic "chapter of faults" in which monks meet weekly for feedback around how well they are living the monastic rule. See also on this point Jones, *The Art of Spiritual Discipline*, 79.
16. Every class meeting had a steward, who would take offerings; the class then would often distribute the funds to fellow members or neighbors in need. Class meetings also had a "visitor of the sick," whose job was to call upon those members or their families in need of pastoral care.
17. John Wesley, *The Works of John Wesley*, vol. 9, "Plain Account of the Methodists," ed. Rupert E. Davies (Nashville: Abingdon, 1989), 262. Wesley is quoting from scripture. "bear one another's burdens" is Galatians 6:2, "naturally" is from Philippians 2:20 and "to care for each other" is from 1 Corinthians 12:25 and Philippians 2:20.
18. W. Paul Jones, *The Art of Spiritual Direction: Giving and Receiving Spiritual Guidance* (Nashville: Upper Room Books, 2002), 75.
19. Jesuits such as William Berry and William Connelly published their book, *The Practice of Spiritual Direction* in 1982, which became a classic text in the field of spiritual direction.
20. For an example of the exploration of spiritual direction from a variety of faith communities, including Buddhism, Judaism, Sufism, and Hinduism, see *Tending the Holy: Spiritual Direction Across Traditions,* ed. Norveene Vest (New York, Morehouse Publishing, 2003) and for a volume from people of color see: *Kaleidoscope: Broadening the Palette in the Art of Spiritual Direction,* ed. Ineda P. Adesanya (New York: Church Publishing, 2019).
21. Dougherty, *Group Spiritual Direction*, 13. Alice Fryling writes on group spiritual direction for a Christian evangelical audience, and Roslyn Weiner out of her Jewish tradition—Alice Fryling, *Seeking God Together: An Introduction to Group Spiritual Direction* (Downers Grove, IL: Intervarsity Press, 2009); Roslyn Weiner, *Seeking in the Company of Others: the Wisdom of Group Spiritual Direction* (Bellevue, WA: SDI Press, 2021).
22. Stanley Hauerwas and Charles Pinches, *Christians among the Virtues: Theological Conversations with Ancient and Modern Ethics* (Notre Dame: University of Notre Dame Press, 1997), 44.
23. There are models of group spiritual direction in which the facilitator or leader serves as the primary provider of spiritual direction to others in the circle, or practices in which the leader refrains from receiving direction. However, it's more common for everyone in the group to both receive and give direction, including the leader.
24. I'm grateful to Dr. Amy Oden for this gracious understanding of spiritual practices as having lots of different forms, or places for creativity, through the use of the term "recipes."
25. Fryling, *Seeking God Together*, 26.
26. Fryling, 27.

2.

A Means of Grace
(The Why)

With some good naturing jostling and laughter, six adults nestled into the comfy, overstuffed furniture of my living room. These folk were my neighbors on my street—and members in the church where I pastored (a different church and group than the one I described in chapter 1). I tossed coasters onto the coffee table as Justin and Kyle set down their glasses of fresh green juice. Justin gestured to the window to the backyard, where five of our children were vigorously jumping on the trampoline while one of the high school youth from our church ran around it, tossing in balls. "Sarah is getting quite a workout from our kids out there," Justin said with a grin. "Our kids are too," his wife, Jenny, said. "I love how after our group, our kids go home tired and happy, and I go home centered and at peace for whatever the week holds."

Before settling down in the living room, we'd gathered with our kids and Sarah around the fireplace. Each child lit a candle (with their name labeled on the glass votive candleholder) and placed it on the hearth. The kids, who ranged in age from two to ten years old, took turns sitting on a folded blanket (the "seat of sharing") to respond to the question "How have you seen God this past week?" The two-year-old offered only the word "Mommy," which could have been a request to be picked up or an affirmation of the Divine in his mom. Either way, we responded with smiles. The older elementary children shared about the joy of helping a friend in school or winning a game with their soccer team. One particularly thoughtful six-year-old brought a pine cone from his yard to show his experience of seeing God in nature, placing it in a "jar of wonders" that we kept for any such offerings. Afterward, we stood in a circle and shared intercessory prayer concerns for friends and family. We closed with the Lord's Prayer and a blessing. The whole practice with the kids took less than fifteen minutes, but it attuned them to noticing God in their lives and in the lives of others. Having been spiritually fed, the kids then grabbed a snack from the kitchen and headed outside to play—and jump with wild abandon on the trampoline.

"I'm so glad this practice of group spiritual direction brings you peace," I said to Jenny. "It does that for me, too. So, let's do it—let's get centered!" The adults laughed as I rang my singing bowl, calling us gently to order and drawing our eyes away from the rambunctious play outside the window. As the leader of the group, I briefly reviewed our covenant to hold confidentiality, to listen well, and to be fully present. I invited us into a minute of silence, offering the guidance to "reflect on how your life with God has been this week—how God has been present to you . . . or absent." We settled into silence. I could hear these tired parents audibly drawing in a weary breath and adjusting in their seats for prayerful listening.

I rang the singing bowl to call us out of the silence and invited the first person to share for three minutes. I served as the timekeeper so other members could focus on listening. Kyle began to haltingly share how his work at a large bank felt mundane and without any challenge or life. God wasn't present for him. He offered a dream of beginning his own company, using the years of expertise he had accumulated. It would be an economic risk, but perhaps a chance to have better hours and be more present to his kids. The rest of the group listened without interruption or interjection. At the end of his sharing, we sat in a short time of silence to hear what God's prayer might be for Kyle.

I rang the singing bowl to break the silence. Then I invited the group to offer open-ended responses or questions, using language like "I wonder, I notice, I appreciate." Jenny said, "I hear such joy and energy when you speak of starting your own business. I wonder how that joy feels to you." Kyle nodded his head and then said, "The joy feels way stronger than the fear of losing income. Yeah, the joy feels like making a change will be worth it in the end." Silence fell over us, and then I felt moved by the Spirit to ask, "What do you think God wants for you in this vocational decision?" Kyle paused and listened in silence for a while. Then he lifted his head with a sense of purpose and conviction. "God wants joy for me. God wants life for me. God will give us what we need." Our heads nodded around the circle, and a couple of us gave affirmative "hmms" from deep in our throats. We moved into a minute of silent prayer for Kyle and his vocational discernment. Afterward, I brought us out of the silence and said a short blessing: "May God direct and guide you into the joy that God and you desire for your life. Amen." Kyle looked up from prayer, gave a slight nod, and said quietly, "Thank you."

In turn, each person shared about their journey with God and received prayerful, open-ended questions and responses from the group. At the end of our hour and a half together, we felt a profound sense of belonging to God and one another. We were becoming friends.[1] As a bonus, our kids were tuckered out from all the outdoor play, went to bed easily, and slept well. The peace, centeredness, and unity that we felt (plus the good vibes from the greens juice), made this an invaluable practice in our lives. This experience of friendship with God and others mattered so much to us that amid full lives of raising children and working jobs, we made it a priority. We looked forward to the gathering, and each time we drew from the deep well of God's grace through group spiritual direction, quenching our thirst for connection and friendship with God and others, belonging, and renewal.

Our Loneliness and Longing

Like those gathered in my living room that day, Christians today desire real experiences of God in community with others—rather than church as meetings and additional work. People long for grace—a sense of love, belonging, and peace amid tumultuous and stressful lives. The experience of God's grace describes what the earliest Methodists felt in class meetings—and what my neighbors gathered in my living room received as we listened to one another's lives.

Longing for human connection while feeling its absence has become a pervasive reality. People are desperately lonely. In his book *Together,* Surgeon General Vivek Murthy writes that loneliness is "the subjective feeling that you're lacking the social connections you need and missing the feeling of closeness, trust, and affection of genuine friends and loved ones."[2] According to one international survey, prior to the Covid-19 pandemic, 22 percent of adults said they felt lonely or socially isolated, with one in three over the age of forty-five feeling lonely.[3] After the pandemic, close to 40 percent of Americans feel lonely frequently or almost all the time. Another study revealed that over 60 percent of young adults indicated they feel lonely and that no one in the past few weeks has taken the time to really ask them how they are doing or to express genuine care for them.[4] There are a myriad of reasons for our experience of loneliness, but as Johann Hari writes in *Lost Connections,* the result is that "loneliness hangs over our culture today like a thick smog."[5]

In *Together,* Murthy offers that loneliness is a human condition requiring the consistent, steady love, companionship, and compassion of fellow human beings, rather than an individual prescription for a drug or a surgical procedure.[6] He believes that what is needed to treat the loneliness epidemic are communities that support healthy emotional connection while also protecting individual expression, exploration, and equity.[7] Friendship in a community such as group spiritual direction can heal what ails us.

The Grace We Need

Group spiritual direction serves as a communal practice offering us what we need—a means of receiving God's grace together among a circle of friends to whom we belong. To illustrate this, I'll describe a Wesleyan understanding of "means of grace," which offers that spiritual practices like group spiritual direction are what God uses to save us—to heal us from our loneliness and division and make us whole. Then I will unpack four key practices, or disciplines, that serve as channels or means of grace in group spiritual direction. Through these practices, God works to fill our longings as we experience God's presence, peace, and love in connection with others.

Wesleyan Means of Grace

John Wesley defined the *means of grace* as "outward signs, words, or actions, ordained of God, and appointed for this end, to be the ordinary channels whereby [God] might convey to [all], preventing, justifying, or sanctifying grace."[8] In other words, they are the practices or disciplines by which we experience and know God's presence and direction in our lives. Our ability to practice them comes as a gift of God's prevenient grace to us—the grace of God reaching out first in love. Our response in faith, or *yes*, results in God's justifying grace, which empowers these practices. God's sanctifying grace, or grace in the daily activity of life, sustains us in these spiritual disciplines. They are not works we do to merit God's favor but reminders of God's healing intentions for us and avenues that God has provided for nurturing our responsiveness. As Methodist scholar Randy Maddox states, "Wesley had no reservations about encouraging his people to seek God's grace through the various outward signs, words, and actions that God has ordained as 'ordinary' channels for conveying saving grace to humanity."[9]

> **means of grace—** the practices or disciplines by which we experience and know God's presence and direction in our lives; spiritual disciplines that place us into the heart of God's transforming love; channels for experiencing God's preventing, justifying, and sanctifying grace.

The means of grace name spiritual disciplines that place us into the heart of God's transforming love.

Wesley categorized these disciplines, or means of grace, according to two key types—*instituted* and *prudential*. He recognized five instituted means of grace, which were performed and given by Jesus Christ for his followers: prayer, reading scripture, sacraments, fasting, and holy conferencing. Wesley urged his people called Methodists to practice these means of grace as works of piety that supported God's work of grace. Of the instituted means of grace, prayer and holy conferencing are practiced most in group spiritual direction. However, scripture can certainly be incorporated through a practice of *lectio divina*, meditation on a psalm, or a short reading of the week's lectionary text.

Wesley believed that the instituted means of grace nourished and fed into the prudential means of grace, which he described as "those daily activities that can provide opportunities for a person to experience the presence and power of God in their life."[10] The prudential means of grace, also known as "works of mercy," are expressions of grace and love in the world. As forms of social holiness, Wesley included class meetings as a prudential means of grace as well as acts of mission and service such as visiting the imprisoned and sick and sheltering the unhoused. Friendship also represents a practice of prudential means of grace—we love our neighbor as we support their life in God.

> **Instituted means of grace**—instituted or prescribed by Jesus for his followers; personal or inward holiness (works of piety)
>
> **Prudential means of grace**—from the word "prudence," which means showing wisdom and care in managing our lives and resources; outward or social holiness (works of mercy)

We might say that the instituted means of grace nurture inner holiness and the prudential means of grace express outer holiness and love of neighbor. In group spiritual direction, then, we see both instituted and prudential means of grace—specifically, prayer, holy conferencing, friendship, and mission. Taken together, all these means of grace make us more holy and whole, more loving, centered, and our true selves—strong answers to the "why should we try group spiritual direction" question. Let's unpack each of these practices.

Four Practices of Group Spiritual Direction That Serve as Means of Grace

1. Prayer (Silent, Listening, Intercessory)

God is always willing and ready to be in communion with us. Prayer describes the making of space and time by humans to be in relationship with God. Lots of different ways exist for us to practice "being-with-God." In group spiritual direction, three primary kinds of prayer nurture our friendship with God and with others—silent, listening, and intercessory prayer.

Silent prayer. Group spiritual direction begins in prayerful silence. The prophet Elijah only heard the voice of God after the inner storms of fear, anxiety, and worry quieted enough so that he could hear the voice of God in the stillness (1 Kings 19:11-12). Jesus withdrew to pray in silence (Luke 5:16), instituting silence as a key way for us to connect with God. So too, as a group gathers out of the chaos and breathlessness of life today, the members settle first into silence to be able to hear God speaking. The opening centering silence quiets everyone and shifts our state of being.[11] Trusting, as the Quakers teach, that deep within us all is a holy center, we open the eyes of our hearts to hear the Holy within us. As medieval mystic Meister Eckhart said, "Nothing in all creation is so like God as silence."[12] God meets us in silence as a means of grace.

Entering silence to listen for God, however, is countercultural and makes many of us uneasy. When I lead new groups, I name this discomfort, and the drastic change silence represents in our noisy world. In the first meeting of the group of church members at my home, I acknowledged that getting silent as a group of humans might feel unsettling. I said they might want to wiggle, cough, look around—do anything but tune into the quiet frequency of God. At that, Kyle began coughing dramatically. Humor always helps! God doesn't want us to take the silence too seriously! I then invited the group to silence any devices as I explained that the harder noises to quiet are the personal inner distractions such as a mental list of to-dos, ongoing mind clutter, or a harsh inner critic. I encouraged the group to gently and without judgment turn their attention back to the presence of God and listen anew.

Subsequent silences in group spiritual direction come after each directee/storyteller shares their story and throughout times of offering holy responses to one another. In this silence we listen so that we can truly allow our hearts to hear what God might have us to offer on behalf of someone else. Out of the gifts of silence in group spiritual direction comes this way of listening without any interruption or addition. The silence gives space for the practice of listening prayer—for the grace of being able to hear to the heartbeat of God on behalf of another.

Listening prayer. In her book *Prayerful Listening*, Lois Lindbloom writes that the purpose of group spiritual direction is to unite in the prayer of listening so that we give attention to our lives in God for the sake of each other.[13] When people can share their story fully without receiving advice, suggestions, or corrections, the listening becomes a means of grace for their healing and wholeness. Experienced group spiritual direction leader Anne Grizzle offers these instructive insights:

> Listeners must learn to stifle and still the quick reassurance, the easy identification or telling of a similar story. They must learn to sit in silence together before God . . . to listen into the heart of God for God's heart response and then to softly share. [As] people learn to still reactive responses and sit quietly with each other . . . [this form of listening] becomes a school for a spiritual way of listening in the world.[14]

This prayerful listening can be messy, tattered, unsure, and uncertain. Who knows if what we are hearing is the voice of God for someone else or our own self-deceptions or whims? In listening, what we hear from the silence may be as murky as a creek after a heavy rain. Listening doesn't guarantee that what we hear for a group member is living spiritual water; it could be our own stirred up mud. However, as we practice, we learn to trust more in God's guidance—and in this form of prayer—as a means of grace for one another.

Intercessory prayer. Silent and listening prayer move a group to the practice of intercessory prayer, which is at the heart of group spiritual direction. Intercessory prayer doesn't mean reciting to God a grocery list of items to help feed or fix the directee's life hungers. Instead, it is an "openness to God on behalf of another."[15] Intercessory prayer is holding the person in your heart and lifting that person gently to God for the purpose of God's loving desire and grace for that person—often in silence. For example, when I prayed for Kyle during the time of silence after his sharing, I simply offered him to God's heart. I tend to cup my hands in front of me and imagine holding that person's sharing right there before God—without adding words.

This kind of intercessory prayer might seem difficult—harder than just reciting a list of needs to God. It makes us feel like we are "doing" something to say: "God, please help Linda in her uncertainty. Show her the way she is to go . . . (blah, blah, blah with more holy sounding stuff)." Instead, we offer quietly what might be God's prayer for this person and allow for the Spirit to intercede with "groanings too deep for words."[16]

> "The remarkable experience of God showing up over and over with group spiritual direction makes me think the Holy Spirit delights whenever we listen deeply to God in love for one another."[18]
> —Anne Grizzle

The beautiful grace that comes from our intercessory prayer on behalf of others is that it opens us to God's desire for us. In being courageously and compassionately open to God for someone else, we just might hear God's compassionate love and hopes for our own lives. We may get as much out of others' stories as our own.[17] We, the intercessors, might in turn experience the interceding of the Spirit and feel changed. As we listen in silence and practice intercessory prayer for others, it becomes a means of God's grace for us too.

2. Holy Conferencing

In John Wesley's terminology, "Christian conferencing"—or what also is called "holy conferencing"—is the gathering of Christians for mutual guidance. It's considered an instituted means of grace, as Christ also gathered his disciples for communal discernment. As such, it essentially describes a practice of group spiritual direction (though Wesley didn't use the term "direction" because he felt it put too much power in the hands of the spiritual guide).[19] Early Methodist societies, class meetings, and bands—and eventually quarterly meetings and annual conferences—all represented forms of holy conferencing.[20]

Class meetings embodied holy conferencing's practice of discernment. Class leaders and fellow members listened to how God was at work in their lives and encouraged one another in their lives of faith. A young female participant in a class meeting in England in 1817 wrote this of her experience:

> Then is not Class a *precious means of grace*?
> May we not sometimes thence our blessings trace?
> For when we have our testimony giv'n,
> We really often feel a little heav'n.
> Bound in the chain of our Redeemer's love,
> Our mounting spirits soar the world above:
> The sacred leaven spreads throughout the whole
> Till all th' assembly seems one mutual soul,
> And a rich stream of grace pour's from the skies
> Each true Believer's thirsting breast supplies.[21]

Her testimony affirms the class meeting as a means of grace that was like an experience of heaven—a powerful practice that wrought such belonging they seemed like "one mutual soul." Holy conferencing as a means of grace reveals the impossibility of being Christian alone; we need one another to best hear and understand God's work of grace in our lives.

Communal discernment is the spiritual practice undergirding holy conferencing. Discernment describes the practical wisdom of knowing God's leading and direction in life. The Latin root word *dicernere* literally means to "cut" or "separate"; it means to separate out what is of God . . . and what isn't.

Even then, it can be hard to know for sure if my discernment is what God wants or just what I want—or if I might be confused, fearful, or anxious and offer my own crud instead of the life-giving Spirit. As Rose Mary Dougherty, a wise elder of group spiritual direction states, discernment doesn't guarantee freedom from making mistakes and offering something that lands like the thud of a stone in a shallow stream. Sometimes, we just don't hear the voice of God clearly.[22]

For this reason, discernment isn't meant to be a solo task. Our vision becomes clearer when we are given the clarifying presence of community. The freeing gift of discernment in group spiritual direction is that we all are focused on hearing what God is guiding us to hear for a person or community. If I miss the mark, someone else in the group might discern more clearly. We find our way to God's loving desire for us as we discern together. In this work, holy conferencing becomes a means of grace.

3. Christian Friendship

Friendship is a Christian practice. Jesus established a community in which people could become friends with God and one another in communion with the Holy Spirit. He called together disciples of different backgrounds and life experiences to become one Body together. In sharing God's love, story, ministry, meals, travel, and service, he said, "I have called you friends" (John 15:15).

As described in the Book of Acts, the church continued in Jesus's example and gathered unlikely people to be in community as friends together. Groups of people from a range of socio-economic and cultural worlds met in homes to break bread together, worship, preach, pray, and share their stories of life with God (Acts 2). They overcame—though not without struggle—their differences by telling stories of the Hebrew Scriptures and the oral stories of Jesus Christ, and by placing their own communal and individual life stories within those sacred narratives. In the breaking of bread and sharing of wine, the earliest Christians found purpose, meaning, and friendship. They found healing for what ailed them from Jesus, who said, "Your faith has made you well," and who ushered them into deep friendship with people they never would have chosen. Then and now, as theologian Willie James Jennings offers in his commentary on Acts, the Spirit creates joining.[23]

Throughout its history, the church's teachers have reflected theologically on the practice of friendship they saw embodied in Christian life. Aelred of Rievaulx, an English Cistercian abbot from the twelfth century, understood friendship as patterned after the Gospel of John's words: "You did not choose me, but I chose you. And I appointed you to go and bear fruit, fruit that will last" (John 15:16). Friends bear fruit, he said, by enjoyment of each other and their mutual pursuit of good habits and character. He noted that true friends are a medicine that make "favorable circumstances even more splendid and adverse circumstances more bearable by sharing them." Aelred believed that friends in God support us in all of life's turns, showing their faithfulness and love in our times of need, praying for us, and rejoicing with us in times of good.[24]

Thomas Aquinas, a Catholic priest and theologian from the thirteenth century, understood friendship with others to be an essential part of a life of flourishing with God.[25] As we learn and practice good lives together, friends lead us to the possibility of a life of virtue with God that sustains real happiness. What's more, we enter suffering for and with our friends because we are to "love one another as I [Jesus] have loved you" (John 15:12). Our struggles, suffering, and hardship are made bearable by the sharing of them with others who are unafraid to sit with us in the dark. By participating in Christ's love for us, we return that love to one another in the profound gift of friendship.[26] For Aquinas, we practice God's love with and to one another, and this practice renders a life of great goodness, even and especially during hardship. He thought that the church provides a practice ground for friendships that sustain us, no matter what life dishes up.

Like Aquinas, John Wesley understood friendship to be a moral practice that required discipline and commitment.[27] With his view of friendship formed mainly by scripture, Wesley saw friendship as a practice of social holiness whereby friends could help each other to know and love God more deeply.[28] He believed that as a means of grace, friendship required discipline and commitment, a regular practice for accountability, and growth in grace.[29] In particular, he saw class meetings as a place for the practice of friendship, noting that "many now happily experienced that Christian fellowship of which they had not so much as an idea before. [They began to] "bear one another's burdens" and "naturally to care for each other."[30]

As a practice of friendship, group spiritual direction teaches us how to be friends with God and with one another—a skill that many of us may need to learn or revitalize in our lonely culture. In group spiritual direction we learn how to listen—deeply and with full presence to God and to each other. We develop comfort with sitting in silence with God and others. We practice offering open-ended responses without any attempt to fix, change, correct, or advise. By hearing the humanity and the divinity in one another's stories, we experience empathy for one another. We develop the ability to walk in each other's shoes, even if the path those shoes take is very different from our own. These skills make for a good friend—someone who listens, is fully present, empathizes, welcomes us as we are, and trusts that we have inner wisdom from God. This is the kind of friendship that creates "joining" through the Holy Spirit—which, in turn, becomes a means of grace for all involved.

4. Mission: Love for the World

As Lois Lindbloom describes so beautifully, the contemplative practice of group spiritual direction draws people into God's loving, compassionate presence and then compels them to extend God's love and mercy out into the world that needs it so much.[31] This was certainly true for participants in the Methodist class meetings, whose experience of inner holiness extended outward into social holiness for the needs of the world. Early Methodist societies, of which classes were a smaller part, supported orphanages, schools for the poor, medical clinics, prisoner visitation, and housing for the unhoused. As Paul Jones puts it, "These prudential means of grace are a way of insisting that sanctification involves more than personal cleansing. Sanctification embraces the whole social order."[32] Group spiritual direction within class meetings led to grace-filled care for the needs of society's vulnerable people.

The deep inner work that happens in group spiritual direction provides such love and joy that God then invites us to desire to share that intercessory love out in the world. Prayer leads to participation in sanctification. Healthy inner spirituality is always interconnected to outward social witness. As the practice of group spiritual direction transforms and heals us inwardly, it opens our eyes to how we are called, in Rabbi Abraham Joshua Heschel's words, to "dream in league with God, to envision His holy visions."[33] As Anne Kline states, people formed by the means of grace in group spiritual direction are called to be a part of God's holy sparks, to "repair the brokenness of the world", and to love creation for God's sake.[34] The inward contemplative practice of group spiritual direction can lead to outward practices of justice and mercy for the sake of the world.

Three Gifts of Group Spiritual Direction

Through these four means of grace, or spiritual practices, that are part of group spiritual direction—prayer, holy conferencing, friendship, and mission—we put in the work or discipline of the holy life. They become the means of God's grace that enable us to experience three beautiful gifts from group spiritual direction—gifts that, I believe, provide us what we most need in a lonely and anxious world: belonging, unity, and renewal.

1. Belonging

Belonging describes being fully heard, seen, and loved as you are among a circle of people. When we belong, we can show up with all our vulnerabilities, wounds, gifts, and stories, knowing that we are fully welcomed and affirmed. Belonging means that when we aren't there, the circle isn't the same. When we belong in a circle of friends with God, we feel whole—and we contribute to others' feelings of wholeness in that circle too.

God created humans with the need to belong; it is woven into the fabric of what it means to be human. Simply put, God created us for connection with God and with each other (Genesis 2). As theologian Willie James Jennings teaches, as embodied creatures we are formed to share, taste, touch, see, and hear the goodness of God in one another as members of a community.[35] Reflecting on this aspect of being human, sociologist Brené Brown writes, "We are psychologically, emotionally, cognitively, and spiritually hardwired for connection, love and belonging. Connection, along with love and belonging, is why we are here, and it is what gives purpose and meaning to our lives."[36] When we don't have belonging, we struggle. The healing antidote for loneliness, and its resulting rampant illnesses of depression, anxiety, and addiction, is belonging.[37] God made us to belong, and by creating small communities of care, such as those found in group spiritual direction, we ensure one another's flourishing and well-being.

Jesus healed by creating belonging. He offered the well-being of belonging for people who were excluded and on the "outside" of human community. To a woman with an issue of blood who was prohibited from associating with others (Matthew 9:20-22, Luke 8:438), to people with incurable disease (Luke 17:19), and to a person with a visual disability (Luke 18:42), Jesus says, "Your faith has made you well." How amazing that must have felt to people who were desperately lonely and ostracized because of conditions over which they had no control—to be made well by being restored to human connection and belonging with God! This is what Jesus, the great healer, does. Christ opens arms wide and brings in the lonely and the lost, the broken and the depressed, the outsiders and the marginalized, saying, "I have called you friends (John 15:15)." Jesus's healing creates belonging and friendship.

Time and time again as I have facilitated group spiritual direction, I've witnessed and experienced this beautiful, graced gift of belonging. The group of church members who met in my living room became true friends to one another—neighbors who, instead of talking about superficialities (weather, events, yard/housework) when they encountered each other, could say, "I'm holding you in prayer." You don't have to update me or report, but just know I'm with you and God in your discernment." That's the kind of relationship in which you feel like your life and what's happening in it really matter to another human. That's what it means to belong. When I facilitated a group of clergywomen by Zoom, that visual space of squares on a screen became a place where women could be vulnerable with their struggles in ministry and could feel fully understood and accompanied That's what it means to belong. One participant in another group said she felt a connection there she hadn't felt in years of adult Bible studies and Sunday school. She could show up in her broken and tattered self and feel loved, whole. That's the graced gift of belonging.

In group spiritual direction, belonging means that you show up as you are for yourself and for one another—without any pretense, superficiality, or veiling. In fact, the practice invites you to be fully who you are in all your wounds and authenticity. This kind of belonging holds the capacity to keep loneliness, anxiety, and depression at bay as people are buoyed by being loved fully as they are—held in the love of God and others. As Diane Millis has observed, group spiritual direction provides a way to share our human stories through a practice that connects, heals, and brings our desires for God alive together.[38]

2. Unity

Out of this gift of belonging that comes from group spiritual direction, people experience an inner communion. As each person draws from the common Source, which is God, they touch an interconnectedness with one another. As Ann Kline so beautifully expresses, the members of the group become like spokes on a wheel, all drawn to the center, which is God.[40] This drawing to the center opens participants to experience their common humanity; people feel a unity with one another—in and through different personalities, ethnicities, socioeconomic backgrounds, and racial experiences.

> "The love that develops among strangers in group spiritual direction feeds and nurtures all our loving."[39]
> —Tom Adams

The commonality of human struggle and suffering in all its varieties and forms binds people together into a oneness. I often have a physical sensation of my heart opening in my chest to another person as they share in a circle; it's as though on a cellular level I am connecting to the story and longings of the other person. I become fully "with them"—perhaps in the way that Jesus is with us in the Incarnation.

Patience Robbins, an experienced leader in group spiritual direction, describes the qualities of unity that come out of the practice: openness, receptivity, mutuality, reverence, and compassion.

First, she names an *openness* to each person, to all of life experience, and to the deeper unknown. We open to what another person's life might be like.

Second, group members practice a *receptivity* to each other—to receive the other as they are without a need to lecture, fix, change, or judge. We pay attention closely.

Third, the group practices *mutuality*, giving all an equal turn to share and to listen; there is no hierarchy or "expert" in the group. Everyone receives and gives equally. Everyone appreciates fully what everyone else is offering.

Fourth, group members learn *reverence*, coming to deeply appreciate the sacred mystery within every person. In receiving one another with reverence, group members offer space for difference and unfamiliarity within each person.

Lastly, group spiritual direction cultivates *compassion* for one another, honoring each person's struggle, pain, and suffering by accompanying them through it. In listening to group members' stories, each participant opens a space for God's love and wisdom to come in and work healing. All these qualities together create a profound experience of Oneness with each other and with God.[41]

This unity with God's heart and with others generates the capacity for people from very different backgrounds to see the humanity and divinity in one another. As Nan Weir, director of the Group Spiritual Direction workshops at Shalem Institute, says, there is a kind of bonding formed by spiritual care that transcends different theological backgrounds, political affiliations, and personality types.[42] Together people begin to see through to the true voice of God in their life situations. As people share authentically and honestly about their journey with God, they discover that, in the words of Tom Adams, "we are more alike than different."[43] They also find their hearts are more open to issues of justice as they begin to love those who have different life experiences and stories than their own.

> **A Caveat on Unity**
>
> It's important to acknowledge the harm and exclusion done by the church and the lack of belonging it has perpetuated. Christians, particularly those with power and privilege, have made the church in their own broken image rather than in the image of God, often discriminating against people based upon their gender, sexuality, race, and ethnicity. This profound sinfulness inhibits the practice of beloved community in group spiritual direction.

> Group spiritual direction cannot, in and of itself, heal the entrenched racism, sexism, and abuse found in the church. In fact, listening circles could be misused, particularly by those with dominant identities, to foster a token kind of proximity with people in minority groups. True friendships made in group spiritual direction, however, could lead to outward works of justice and healing in the community.

3. Renewal

The final gift of group spiritual direction is renewal—a sense of revived faith, hope, love, and peace. People experience this personally, as Jenny did in my living room circle. She left our group spiritual direction gathering with a spirit of peace, renewed for the week ahead. Even with years of experience, I often go into a circle consumed with all the things I need to do, thinking I don't have time for this group today. I leave feeling that it was the most significant experience of my entire week. I gain perspective, connection, peace, love, belonging, calm, centeredness, and presence. I'm revived again for life. It comes fully as gift.

This graced gift of renewal can come collectively to the church through circles of group spiritual direction. By reclaiming and practicing this means of grace that has deep roots in Christian history and practice, churches can receive God's renewing work. The experience of belonging and friendship developed by group spiritual direction can draw newcomers and revive long-time church members. It is a practice the church needs—perhaps as never before.

Belong Groups: A Means of Grace the Church Needs Today

My neighbors and I, and our trampoline-bouncing kids, were practicing means of grace. We sat with one another in my living room to pray and discern together how the mystery of God's love was at work. Among the easy, mundane, and the hard details of our lives, we discovered and named for one another the threads of the Holy at work. We practiced holy friendship in a space of belonging that imparted God's grace such that we left, in Jenny's words, centered and at peace.

I decided to call our group, and other groups that we formed in that congregation, "Belong" groups. The name describes what the groups fostered: a way to belong. Besides being much easier to say than "group spiritual direction," Belong helps people easily connect the name of the group to the longing in their own hearts for connection to others and God.

The Belong groups gathered in homes located in neighborhoods around the church. I trained leaders for each group who, in turn, recruited others for participation. Chapters 3 and 4 in this book teach how to participate in and lead Belong groups. I want to be clear, however, that these groups aren't a program, a new curriculum, or the latest trendy fad your church can try. The church doesn't need more programming, curriculum, or consultants.

Instead, Belong groups represent an ancient Christian practice—a practice of group spiritual direction that is a means of grace. As Andrew Root explains, these groups immerse people in a form of prayer in which they experience God and others in friendship.[44] This is a beautiful thing—and what the church needs, because what the church needs is God. In a culture based on an "attention economy" that leaves us addicted and lonely, the church needs to offer a life-giving practice that helps us pay attention to God.

Through the grace of God, the church can remember, practice, and attend to who we are as a healing community of belonging and friendship. We can be a body of Christ that includes in our midst the anxious, depressed, suicidal, and lonely. We *all* can receive the life-giving means of grace that comes through the "holy conferencing" of group spiritual direction.

NOTES

1. As I was the pastor of the people in this group, I moderated my own sharing and held appropriate and healthy boundaries with parishioners. The other group members developed friendship that was of a different quality than the kind I could develop with them.
2. Vivek Murthy, *Together: The Healing Power of Human Connection in a Sometimes Lonely World* (New York: Harper Collins, 2020), 8.
3. Murthy, *Together,* 10, citing Bianca DiJulio et al., "Loneliness and Social Isolation in the United States, The United Kingdom, and Japan: An International Survey," The

Henry J. Kaiser Family Foundation August 30, 2018, https://www.kff.org/mental-health/report/loneliness-and-social-isolation-in-the-united-states-the-united-kingdom-and-japan-an-international-survey/.
4. "Loneliness in America: How the Pandemic has Deepened Loneliness and What We Can Do About It." Making Caring Common Project, Harvard University February 9, 2021 https://mcc.gse.harvard.edu/reports/loneliness-in-america.
5. Johann Hari, *Lost Connections* (New York: Bloomsbury Publishing, 2019), 79.
6. Murthy, *Together*, 6.
7. Murthy, 70, 96.
8. John Wesley, *John Wesley's Sermons: An Anthology*, eds. Albert Outler and Richard Heitzenrater (Nashville: Abingdon, 1991), 160.
9. Randy Maddox, *Responsible Grace: John Wesley's Practical Theology* (Nashville: Abingdon, 1994), 163.
10. Richard Heitzenrater, *Wesley and the People Called Methodists* 2nd ed. (Nashville: Abingdon, 2013), 239. Heitzenrater utilized this text to make his assertions. John Wesley, *The Methodist Societies: The Minutes of Conference*, "The Large Minutes of 1763," ed. Henry D. Rack, vol. 10 of *The Bicentennial Edition of The Works of John Wesley* (Nashville: Abingdon, 2011), 855–56.
11. Anne Grizzle, "Group Spiritual Direction: Offering Spiritual Depth and Community Building in Diverse Settings," *Journal of Spiritual Formation and Soul Care* 11, no. 2 (November 14, 2018): 220. In this article, Grizzle offers the steps of hushing/quieting, listening deeply, and being.
12. Matthew Fox, *Meister Eckhart: A Mystic Warrior for Our Times* (Novato, CA: New World Library, 2014), 64.
13. Lois Lindbloom, *Prayerful Listening: Cultivating Discernment in Community* (New York: Paulist Press, 1995), 7.
14. Anne Grizzle "Prayerful Listening for Life," *Shalem News* (Summer 2002), 7.
15. Lindbloom, *Prayerful Listening*, 9.
16. Romans 8:26
17. Ann Kline, "Widening the Lens: The Gift of Group Spiritual Direction," *Presence: An International Journal of Spiritual Direction* 10, no. 2 (June 2004): 40.
18. Grizzle, "Group Spiritual Direction," 227
19. Wesley Tracy, "Spiritual Direction in the Wesleyan-Holiness Tradition," in *Spiritual Direction and the Care of Souls: A Guide to Christian Approaches and Practices*, eds. Gary Moon and David Benner (Downers Grove, IL: IVP Academic, 2004), 118. Tracy notes that though Wesley didn't use the term "direction," Christian conferencing as Wesley understood it is undeniably the older and more ancient form of Christian discernment in community known as group spiritual direction.
20. W. Paul Jones, *The Art of Spiritual Direction: Giving and Receiving Spiritual Guidance* (Nashville: Upper Room Books, 2002), 87.
21. "A Description of Class-meetings in an Epistle from a Young Lady of the Methodist Connexion to a Female Acquaintance," in David Lowes Watson, *The Early Methodist Class Meeting* (Nashville: Discipleship Resources, 1987), 243, emphasis added.
22. Rose Mary Dougherty, *Group Spiritual Direction: Community for Discernment* (New York: Paulist Press, 1995), 30.

23. Willie James Jennings, *Acts* in the Belief series (Louisville: Westminster John Knox Press, 2017), 28–29. Jennings' profound insight in this commentary is that God called together disparate people with the intention of binding them together with love for each other into God's people and God's body.
24. Aelred of Rievaulx, *Spiritual Friendship*, trans. Mark F. Williams (Cranbury, NJ; London: Mississauga, Ontario: Associated University Presses, 1994), 35–37, 44–45, 70–72, 77–81.
25. Aquinas draws heavily from Aristotle's account of friendship in the *Nicomachean Ethics*. For an in-depth discussion of Aristotle's understanding of friendship, see chapter 3 in Stanley Hauerwas and Charles Pinches, *Christians Among the Virtues: Theological Conversations with Ancient and Modern Ethics* (Notre Dame: University of Notre Dame Press, 1997).
26. Hauerwas and Pinches, *Christians Among the Virtues*, 49.
27. Jason Vickers, "On Friendship: John Wesley's Advice to the People Called Methodist," *Wesley Theological Journal*, (January 1, 2007): 47. Wesley was most dependent on Scripture, such as 1 and 2 Corinthians and 1 and 2 Timothy on his views of friendship. Vickers argues that Plato and Cicero could also be classical sources for his view of friendship. His understanding of friendship as a means of grace, and therefore, a spiritual discipline, is more in keeping with the virtue ethics of Aquinas—even if Wesley doesn't indicate any direct sourcing from him.
28. Vickers, "On Friendship: John Wesley's Advice to the People Called Methodist," 42.
29. Maddox, *Responsible Grace: John Wesley's Practical Theology*, 211.
30. John Wesley, *The Works of John Wesley*, vol. 9, "Plain Account of the Methodists," ed. Rupert E. Davies (Nashville: Abingdon, 1989), 262.
31. Lindbloom, *Prayerful Listening*, 20.
32. W. Paul Jones, *The Art of Spiritual Direction: Giving and Receiving Spiritual Guidance* (Nashville: Upper Room Books, 2002), 91.
33. Abraham Joshua Heschel, *Moral Grandeur and Spiritual Audacity* (New York: Farrar, Straus & Giroud, 1997), 353.
34. Kline, "Widening the Lens: The Gift of Group Spiritual Direction," 40.
35. Willie Jennings, *After Whiteness: An Education in Belonging* (Grand Rapids: Eerdmans, 2020), 11.
36. Brené Brown, *Daring Greatly* (New York: Penguin Random House, 2012), 68.
37. Hari, *Lost Connections*, 76.
38. Diane Millis, *Re-creating A Life: Learning How to Tell Our Most Life-Giving Story* (Belluvue, WA: SDI Press, 2019), 16.
39. Tom Adams, "Spiritual Intimacy: The Power of Group Spiritual Direction" Shalem Institute blog post June 6, 2018, https://shalem.org/2018/06/15/spiritual-intimacy-the-power-of-group-spiritual-direction/.
40. Kline, "Widening the Lens: The Gift of Group Spiritual Direction," 40.
41. Patience Robbins, "Group Spiritual Direction: Overview" Shalem Institute workshop on Group Spiritual Direction (Zoom), October 2020.
42. Nan Weir, "Group Spiritual Direction: Overview of Group Spiritual Direction," document for Shalem Institute's Group Spiritual Direction workshop, Feb. 2003 (revised March 2009), 2. Unpublished.

43. Adams, "Spiritual Intimacy."
44. Andrew Root, *The Pastor In a Secular Age* (Grand Rapids: Baker Academic, 2019), 273, 275, 277. Thanks to Root for his insight that people in a secular age need to be formed around the practice of prayer. He offers that it is in fact the pastor's vocation in a secular age to form people's lives around the practice of prayer (273). This book represents my offering to help pastors and other leaders to do just that.

3.

Preparing Participants for Group Spiritual Direction for Christian Friendship

When beginning group spiritual direction for Christian friendship, you are embarking on a grace-filled spiritual practice that holds the promise of real belonging, unity, and renewal. It is not necessary for participants to be spiritual giants or super holy; the only requirement is a desire to be with God and others in a circle of friends. Together you have all you need because the Holy Spirit is with you; that Spirit will bring alive this ancient contemplative Christian practice in your midst.

This chapter serves to support what the Spirit makes possible. It describes ten steps of group spiritual direction and equips you to prepare participants for group spiritual direction in a Belong group (or whatever name your group might hold or choose). For every step, I include a story or details about a group I facilitated to help make the process come alive for you. (If you or others in your group learn best with a chart or handout, see The Steps of Group Spiritual Direction for Friendship on pages 229–34 in the appendix. You even might use these tools during your group time for guidance.)

We'll journey now from the first gathering of the group to the closing prayer at the end of the meeting.

Step 1: Gathering

Once you have discerned the call to begin a group spiritual direction—what I have called a Belong group—you then invite participants through a prayerful process. Those who say yes to the group likely are responding to a stirring in their own hearts to know God and others in a beloved community. This gathering is a communal response to God's prior action of prevenient grace, calling each of you to fill the longing in your heart by nestling more closely with the Divine.

As participants prepare for the first and subsequent gatherings of your group, encourage them to be in a spirit of prayer. Perhaps when they are washing dishes or walking the dog or driving in the car, they may recall by name each member of the group. Invite them to hold each person in loving intention with God, explaining that words are not necessary because prayer can simply be connection with God on behalf of another in silence.

Encourage participants to pray for themselves as well, being open to what the Holy Spirit might be leading them to share from their lives during the group meeting. You might offer them some questions to guide their prayer, such as:

- Is there a question or issue in your life in which you are trying to discern an answer or response?
- Is there a decision before you that you would like to bring before God?
- Is a relationship in your life in a place of difficulty, transition, or loss, in which you are seeking a faithful way forward?
- Do you sense God calling you in a new direction, whether vocationally or personally, that you would like more clarity for the next good step?
- Is there a desire, longing, or dream that you want to bring before God?
- Is there something in your life you are giving thanks for or celebrating?
- How have you seen or sensed God present (or not present) in your life recently?

Invite participants to simply hold any of these questions, or others that come to them, in prayer before God. Perhaps the Spirit might lead them to what they need to share in the group time, or perhaps not. Either way, holding key life questions in prayer will hold them close to God.

As group members gather, the story each person brings is woven together in a holy alchemy that comprises God's healing purpose for the group. In the gathering, group members listen for God's true word to them, so that they can offer those words of life to one another. The gathering provides the holy space in which postures of hope, trust, and discernment can be fostered and people can experience belonging.

As participants cross the threshold into the group's gathering space, whether virtually through an online video platform or through an actual door, they are invited to open their hearts to the possibility of the gathering. Encourage them to offer a warm welcome to others and to themselves—just as they are. Greet one another as those made in the image of God and beloved, and trust that God is with you.

> Noticing a longing in my heart for a circle of close friends, I began praying for whom I might invite to a Belong group. I received a clear invitation from the Holy Spirit to invite clergywomen of diverse denominational and racial backgrounds. Names of people I admired and respected came to mind, and I prayed over their possible participation in the group. After a month or more of prayer, I reached out via email and invited each person. Thankfully, after their own prayer and discernment, many replied yes to my invitation! I offered them the question "How is God present (or not) in your life?" for their sharing at our first meeting.
>
> After some scheduling work, we finally gathered for the first time in a cozy and spacious room on the seminary campus where I teach. This first gathering started with hot tea, coffee, fresh fruit, and snacks—and a hubbub of excited introductions and greetings. We shared briefly about our churches, ministries, lives, and families before settling down onto the couches and chairs. I lit a candle and invited us to reflect on guidelines that would support a healthy practice of group spiritual direction.

Step 2: Covenant Making

A covenant represents a set of sacred guidelines or agreements made by group members with one another and with God. We see the practice of covenant-making in God's covenant with Abraham in Genesis 17:7: "I will establish my covenant between me and you and your offspring after you throughout their generations." The covenant provides a structure of accountability for God and Abraham's relationship; they made promises to each other that they committed publicly to uphold. Similarly, as Ruth Haley Barton explains, covenant-making in group spiritual direction includes creating a structure of public accountability for the practice and setting expectations for everyone's behavior toward one another and God.[1]

These agreements guide the group's behavior to support healthy group dynamics and to prevent harm. The covenant holds people accountable to the practice of spiritual direction and provides a way to "check in" after a session to make sure the covenant is upheld. I recommend always including the guideline of confidentiality for your group. I also recommend upholding the practices of being present, honoring the process, listening prayerfully, speaking truthfully, offering life-giving responses, and turning to wonder when things get rough. You'll find the handout Covenant Guidelines for Group Spiritual Direction, culled from extensive experience and some great organizations, on pages 239–40 in the appendix.[2] My suggestion is to start with these seven guidelines and revise or amend them as suits your group's needs and context.

> In my first meeting with the clergywomen group, I gave them the Covenant Guidelines handout and invited them to select the one that was most important to them. This selection process generated the three or four guidelines that were most important to us, which we put checkmarks beside. The clergywomen affirmed confidentiality, prayerful listening, and the offering of life-giving responses as the most important guidelines to them. At the beginning of each subsequent gathering, I handed out the guidelines, we reviewed them, and we affirmed our agreement to uphold them. The women stated that the guidelines created a space they could trust and could therefore share more vulnerably.

Step 3: Timing Structures

A unique feature of group spiritual direction is the disciplined use of time. This practice of time provides a safe structure so that people can begin to unpack the question "How is it with your soul?"—a vulnerable question to answer. The patterned use of silence, sharing, listening, responding, and intercessory prayer helps participants stay centered in God's presence so they can answer this profound question. The structure frees people to listen more fully and be more fully present. Group members don't have to worry if one person will receive more time than another. As experienced spiritual guide Diane Millis indicates, specific time allotments also help them to focus on what is most important to share when they are in the role of directee/storyteller. People tend to speak in a more mindful way when the time is limited.[3]

Depending upon the number of people in the group and the total time commitment for each group meeting (one hour, one and one-half hours, two hours, etc.), the timing structures for the different elements within the meeting can be shortened or lengthened. Likewise, various elements can be combined or dropped. Play with it to determine what structure works best for the culture and context of your group. Make it your own! Whatever elements and timing structure you choose, it's important that group members agree to both the total amount of group meeting time and the specific timing structure used within the meeting. The group covenant also can include an affirmation of upholding the group's timing structure. (See the appendix for several handouts outlining various timing structures based on the total amount of time focused on each person, found on pages 241–51.)

> My clergywomen's group uses a 3-1-3-1 structure, in which a directee/storyteller shares for three minutes (3), the group listens for a minute of silence (1), the group shares responses for three minutes (3), and then the group has a minute of silent intercessory prayer for the directee/storyteller (1). Then we repeat this process for every other group member. This allows the six of us to have time to share and finish in our hour and a half time commitment. The efficiency of the structure encourages

> us to be focused and clear in our time of sharing. My group likes for me to set a timer on my phone with an audible chime that goes off when the time is up, which helps us to uphold the timing structure; sometimes I might use my singing bowl or a bell to sound the end of the time.

Step 4: Prompt and Centering Silence

After affirming the covenant and timing structure, your group may choose to do a brief check-in (one to two minutes), as Alice Fryling suggests, so that each member has space to offer any updates on significant life events before practicing group direction.[4] Then you can ring a bell or bowl or otherwise invite the group into the time of prayerful listening.

Begin the time of prayerful listening by offering a "prompt" for a common focus, which could be a scripture, poem, a visual image, a photo on your phone, a brief reading, or a musical piece. The prompt also could be a question, such as those offered here.

> **Example Prompt Questions**
>
> - "What do I want to hear from God?"[5]
> - Where do I experience God in my family and/or friends?
> - When have I last felt really, fully alive?
> - When have I recently felt discouraged, frustrated, angry, or upset?[6]

Invite participants to listen for what speaks to them in the prompt. This reflection could inform your sharing time, or it might just help with your centering.

After (or before) the prompt, guide the group into silence. For one to five minutes, depending on your timing structure, the group sits in silence. In this centering silence, group members offer their hearts to God and dedicate the time to God's direction. If participants are unsure how to do this, tell them they can say silently in their minds something like this: "God, I am offering to you this time of group spiritual direction. (pause) I ask you to free me from anything that is distracting or burdening me right now. Help me to be fully present however I am showing up today—in my hopes, fears, doubts, failures, joys, and successes. Help me to listen to your still voice. Amen."

Silence is not easy for many people, particularly at the beginning. We live in a world addicted to noise and distractions. This noise distracts us from hearing our own inner voice and the voice of God. Silence makes space for us to hear God. It cuts through our habitual ways of responding and our biases—and therefore can be unsettling. Let participants know that if silence makes them feel uncomfortable or brings up difficult memories, they may simply ask God to be with them in that. Even if it doesn't feel good to them now, they can trust that God is working in the silence whether or not they can sense or know it. Paying attention to their breath—to their inhale and exhale—or gazing at a lit candle can help individuals to focus. Encourage everyone to trust that the silence is making space for the group to listen to God together.

> The members of our group come to our meeting time from busy, hectic lives in which they are constantly giving to others. A couple of days before one meeting, I heard a beautiful arrangement of orchestral music by the Kyiv Symphony Orchestra, based in Kyiv, Ukraine. Russia had just invaded Ukraine a few days before, and I knew this war would be heavy on all our hearts. During the time of the prompt, I simply played the music from my phone for a few minutes. In the time of silent prayer afterward, I invited them to be in prayer for Ukraine—and whatever else might help them to center. When I rang my singing bowl to gently nudge us out of the silence, we had a brief time of sharing our feelings about the war and for the people of Ukraine and Russia. This space of addressing a critical issue happening in the world cleared the way for us then to have space to listen to each other.

Step 5: Holy Listening to the Directee/Storyteller

After the centering time, the group moves to the "gist" of group spiritual direction, in which the directee or storyteller verbally shares an important aspect of their life and the other group members listen for God's presence and action in the life of the directee.

The Directee/Storyteller's Practice of Holy Listening

Before or after the centering silence, you may establish with the group the order of sharing (who will go first, second, third, fourth, etc.). The group then opens their hearts and spirits, maybe taking a breath together, as they prepare to receive the first story.

At this time, the directee/storyteller may begin sharing the recent story of their life with God. If the person finds words difficult or feels unsure, they may begin by saying, "I'm not sure what to say." Invite them to be silent and listen for the Lord. Assure them that God moves in the silence too. There is no "right" way for the directee to do their sharing. They may listen to what is true and let their life speak—or hold silence.

Group Members' Practice of Holy Listening

While the directee/storyteller shares, the rest of the group enters the practice of holy or prayerful listening. The group doesn't offer any verbal response. They don't interrupt or interject. No one begins telling their own similar experience. Instead, the group remains silent, listening with focus and attention. The group holds space for the directee/storyteller to share throughout the allotted time—even and especially if that sharing includes silence. Learning to listen to the Holy in someone else's life requires both intentionality and a willingness to be open to mystery. As Henri Nouwen observed, we listen with attention and care to the Voice speaking in each person's center.[7]

This kind of empathic listening, which shows reverence to another person's story, differs incredibly from the factual listening common in Western culture—which is focused on solving problems, determining solutions, and showing what we know. We're not used to listening without verbally responding or "fixing" something. Empathic listening feels strange to many of us, particularly if it is new to us.

Because we are formed in a world of factual learning, impediments to empathic, holy listening often arise in us. At times we might feel any of the following:

- *Anxiety.* We can feel uncomfortable with silence or rush to speak to ease our own discomfort. We might worry about not hearing God.
- *Roles.* Those of us in helping professions, particularly clergy or counselors, might feel we need to be "experts." But in group spiritual direction, all are in the role of "listener."
- *Overidentification.* We listen through our own experiences and might rush to overidentify with another person's storytelling that resembles our own—and so not hear them fully.

These impediments to our listening *will* arise; it's important not to judge or criticize ourselves or others but simply to note when one of these happens within us, offer it to God, and commit anew to empathic listening.

Given that holy listening is so countercultural and impediments are real, here a few suggestions for how to empathically listen:

- *Step into another's shoes.* Imagine yourself in the multiple dimensions of another person's experience.[8] Enter into another's story and pain without answers, approval, or agreement.[9]
- *Connect and separate.* Connect with what the storyteller might be feeling, while also differentiating your own feelings and emotions. Make a deep investment in connection without overidentification.
- *Empathize, don't sympathize.* Empathy is feeling *with* another; sympathy is feeling *for* another. In empathy, you feel the emotion of another's life experience. Sympathy stays aloof from another's feelings and can move into paternalism without care.
- *When listening, be intentional to notice, appreciate, and wonder.* *Notice* what happens in someone as they share their story, *appreciate* the aspects of their story to which you are drawn, and offer *wonder* for places filled with mystery or possibility.

Because these practices of noticing, appreciating, and wondering are so critical to holy listening, let's explore them in more detail as we sit in the role of a group member.

1. Noticing

Noticing involves the gift of paying attention. Notice what the directee/storyteller conveys in their body language, tone of voice, and facial expressions as they share. Listen for feeling instead of just content. Notice what stirs their heart. Attend to a softening of their voice as they share griefs, or animation in their voice as they share joy. Observe their formulation of words: Do they search for words to say, or speak slowly or quickly, or repeat a word? All of these signs offer insights into how God might be present.

Notice also what stirs *your* heart as you pay attention. Diane Millis has observed that the place where your heart felt stirred, enlivened, or softened might be the very place where God is at work in the sacred text of the directee/storyteller's story.[10] If you already know that you will put pressure on yourself to offer something "wise" to the directee/storyteller during the response time, the practice of noticing might be the antidote to that pressure. Being deeply noticed may be what the person needs most. Attending to someone else's humanity by giving them space to share their story is a profound offering.

2. Appreciating

In this practice, we appreciate the aspects of a person's story that move us. Diane Millis suggests we listen for aspects of courage, perseverance, strength, humanity, and heartfulness in the one who is sharing. How did they continue to endure through daily challenges? How did they pursue dreams despite limited resources? How did they seek joy, even when others around them were discouraging? In short, how does the directee/storyteller inspire us with the working of Holy Mystery in their life?[11]

Another way of appreciating someone's story is through the questions, "What shimmers for you? What stands out to you as significant or holy or beautiful?" Hold these observations gently. A nugget of a story that shimmers or shines to you might indicate the Holy Spirit's work.

3. Wondering

Wonderings are questions that arise for us as we listen to the directee/storyteller's story. These wondering questions are not to satisfy our curiosity or to offer thinly veiled advice. They are open-ended questions that we can't answer and that offer no attempt to fix, change, judge, or correct. Contemplative questions offer space for the directee/storyteller to explore their own story and perhaps discover something new. An example might be: "I wonder how God is loving you in this?"

Hold on to these noticings, appreciations, and wonderings gently as they come to you while listening to the directee/storyteller's story. You might be led by the Spirit to share them during the response time, or you might not. I sometimes take notes on what I notice or appreciate and pray over them during the silent intercessory time. In the end, our listening becomes a means of grace through our attention to God on behalf of another.

> When I share as a directee/storyteller in the group, I'm usually sharing what I've been led to offer from prayer during the week. For one group meeting, I shared about feeling overwhelmed with my work as a teacher and needing God's guidance in what to do and what to let go of. Even though I was clear on what I was to share, I still struggled to formulate the words around the stress I felt. I paused at times, gave spaces for silence, and kept listening for what to say. No one interrupted the silence, and I felt heard and held as I shared.
>
> When I listen to others in the role of directee/storyteller, I pay attention to body language and anything that "lands" in my heart or shimmers. As one member of the group shared about her need for rest, I **noticed** how she rubbed her temples while she talked, as though she had a headache. I **appreciated** just how much amazing and prophetic work she was doing through the nonprofit she led. I **wondered** if she was able to take a Sabbath time of rest—to take a break. As she spoke, I simply held all these insights in prayer and kept listening.

Step 6: Silence to Hear God (Intercessory Prayer)

After the directee/storyteller finishes their allotted time of sharing, the group moves into a second planned time of silence (the first being the centering silence at the beginning of the meeting). This silence might be one to five minutes, depending on the group's timing structure. During this silence of intercessory prayer, the members of the group listen for the Holy Spirit's guidance on behalf of the directee/storyteller. As we saw in chapter 2, this kind of intercessory prayer is not reciting to God a grocery list of items on someone's behalf but holding the person in your heart and lifting them gently to God for the purpose of God's loving desire and grace for that person.

Lois Lindbloom offers the following series of wonderful questions to support this silent intercessory prayer time of listening:

- "God, what is your prayer for this person?"
- "What do you want my prayer to be?"
- "Is there anything I need to surrender to you to join your prayer for this person? What in me stands in the way (my judgment, my curiosity, my need to solve the problem or to try to make someone happy)?"
- "Is there anything you want me to say to this person on your behalf?"[12]

Through listening to God's answers for these questions on behalf of someone else, we participate in the Spirit's work in the depths of our own hearts.[13] We are listening for God's word to the other person, which also might be a word of life and love to us as well. In the silence, we immerse ourselves in the ongoing stream of God's grace. We might receive a life-giving drink of the Spirit for the storyteller, or we might not. No matter what we hear or do not hear, it's always worth wading into grace in silence on behalf of someone else. Keep the silence as if silence is a member of your group, too—because in effect, it is.

> We listen for just a minute of silence in our group, which often feels too short for me! During this time, I'm actively praying for what God's prayer is for the person who just shared. On this day I sensed that God

was offering the practice of Sabbath as a time of rest and renewal for my fellow group member. After receiving the word "Sabbath," I prayed over whether this was something I should say to her. As I listened in the silence, I felt God indicating that my mentioning of Sabbath wouldn't be advice-giving but, perhaps, a life-giving practice for her. I held this "nudge" in prayer until the timer went off.

Step 7: Life-Giving Responses and Questions

The group now moves to the practice of offering to the directee the thoughts or questions they sense that the Holy Spirit is giving them on behalf of the directee.

The Directee/Storyteller's Practice of Response

During this time, the directee/storyteller doesn't have to answer the questions asked by group members. They may choose to reflect on a question later or simply note internally that the question isn't helpful. For example, the directee/storyteller may say, "That gives me something I want to reflect on later," or "Thank you." Or they simply may remain in silence. As Alice Fryling notes, "In group spiritual direction, the goal is not to answer life's questions (or every question a group member poses). The goal is to draw closer to God in the midst of the questions. Many times, it is in embracing our questions that we move more deeply into God's love."[14]

Group Members' Practice of Response

Out of such attentive listening comes the capacity to offer life-giving, open-ended responses and questions. The guidelines of noticing, appreciating, and wondering used during the listening step now provide a helpful prompt for a group member to offer during this response time. For example:

1. *I notice . . .* (body language, tone of voice, facial expressions, speech patterns, breathing patterns, repetition of words or phrases, questions of noticing God in daily life)

2. *I appreciate* . . . (aspects of the directee/storyteller's story that inspire or draw you; qualities of courage, perseverance, strength, heartfulness in a person; what "shimmers" for you)
3. *I wonder* . . . (open-ended, life-giving questions; can't predict an answer; refrain from "telling," advising, fixing, or other conventional questions)

Many group members struggle with how to ask a wondering, open-ended, life-giving question. Our culture teaches us to ask questions for information only or to satisfy our curiosity. Discerning the difference between a wondering question and a conventional question takes practice. Here are a couple of examples:

> "As we listen, we discern: what can I ask this person, in such a way, that will help them listen more deeply within and give voice to more of their story?"
> —Diane Millis[15]

1. <u>Conventional</u>: I wonder if you felt exhausted in seeking mental health care for your son?

    <u>Contemplative</u>: I wonder what felt supportive to you during your son's experience of mental health challenges?

2. <u>Conventional</u>: I wonder if a spiritual director or a therapist might help you with this part of your story?

    <u>Contemplative</u>: I wonder how you sense God is present in this part of your story?

The first conventional question assumes a feeling for the storyteller: exhaustion. It "tells" the presenter a way that she might feel. In contrast, the contemplative question invites the discovery of a source of support during a difficult time.[16]

The second conventional question offers thinly veiled advice—get a spiritual director or therapist. The contemplative question, on the other hand, invites reflection on the presence of God in the storyteller's life.

Conventional questions tend to . . .

- be answerable with a yes or a no.
- show or reveal what the questioner knows or thinks.
- start with a "why," such as, "Why is God doing this?"
- imply or tell the directee/storyteller what they "should" do.
- offer advice.
- be about the questioner's curiosity (center on the questioner).
- ask questions already known to the directee/storyteller.

Open-ended or life-giving questions tend to . . .

- invite a loving focus on the directee/storyteller.
- allow for exploration and the directee/storyteller's curiosity.
- help the directee/storyteller hear their own inner teacher.
- start with a "how," "when," or "what," such as, "How do you want God's help?"
- appreciate the directee/storyteller's story as full of wonder and discovery.
- invite encounters with the Holy.
- sound like Jesus: "Who do you say that I am?" (Matthew 16:15)

Open-ended Questions[17]

1. What is bringing you energy, joy, or life?
2. What is bringing you sorrow, weariness, or apathy?
3. What in your life is drawing you to God or away from God?
4. When have you felt God's presence or God's absence?
5. What is your prayer in this? What is prayer like for you?
6. What is your soul longing for today? How would you like for God to satisfy that soul's longing?
7. How would you describe your relationship with God now?
8. How would you like God to help you in this?
9. How are you being changed by what is happening in your life?
10. How might the Spirit be whispering to you in this situation? (See Elijah's listening to God's whisper in 1 Kings 19:11-13.)

Group members also do not have to offer a response or question. A Quaker guideline can be helpful here: "Be neither determined to speak or not to speak. Be willing to remain silent and continue holding the person's story in the presence of God"[18]—unless you sense that the Holy Spirit gave you words to offer.

Silence During This Time

Be sure to allow for silence between questions and responses. Group spiritual direction goes slowly—at the pace of grace. The person in the role of directee/storyteller and the other group members are listening for God's voice in the silence. At first, it might feel profoundly uncomfortable; hold the awkwardness, breathe through it, and keep listening for God above all. Silence belongs as a member in group spiritual direction.

As Alice Fryling says, "Spiritual direction is an art, not a science. It is a charism, a gift from God."[19] As a means of grace, group spiritual direction enables us to practice silent prayer. Over time, silence becomes holy rather than uncomfortable as we learn to trust in the reality of the Spirit's direction of us in the silence.

> I rang us out of the silence with a singing bowl. I felt the Holy Spirit inviting me to let others share responses first as I listened. A group member spoke up and offered, "I noticed how you mentioned needing rest. How might God be inviting you into holy rest?" The directee took a deep breath, reflected in silence, and then said, "That's a good question for me. I might need to reflect on that further. What comes to mind initially is play. I haven't played in so long that I don't know what that is. Maybe a massage? (laughs) I'll need to keep praying on God's invitation to me to play."
>
> I discerned that I didn't need to ask her about God's invitation into Sabbath at this point. She resonated with the language of "holy rest." I let my offering go, taking comfort in the way that the Holy Spirit led the other group member and I to a similar question for her. I continued holding silence.

In the silence, I felt the incredible appreciation I had for her and for her work rising up in me. I prayed silently over this—"God, am I to offer to her this appreciation?" I took a deep breath, still unsure if I was to share, and said, "I appreciate so much the work you do in our community. Your work shines out in the world. I admire your courage and your dedication. What a light you are!" Then I added, almost under my breath, "And you are so well deserving of a week's worth of massage!"

The timer went off, and I invited us into a time of silent prayer over her. I wondered if I had gotten overly exuberant and had distracted from her prayerfulness. Had I given advice about getting a massage? I wasn't sure. I just had to go to God in prayer and say, "Give me grace if I got off-track."

Step 8: Intercessory Silent Prayer for the Directee/Storyteller

To intercede for another is to hold them and all that they are experiencing within the heart of God through prayer. The group offers this sacred gift to one another with the powerful offering of wordless presence.

The Directee/Storyteller's Role

The group prays silently for the directee and over what was shared. To be held in the loving prayer of others can be life-giving; it's a holy form of belonging. The directee/storyteller might open their hands as a physical sign of receiving prayer. Focusing on their in-breath can be a way of literally breathing in grace. They also might want to jot down a note during this time to remember what they have received. Encourage them to receive this time of silent intercessory prayer as God's and your group's gift to them.

Group Members' Role

During this time, all other group members are to share with God their prayer and their hopes for this person. As Rose Mary Dougherty puts it, they are to keep on looking at God for the directee.[20] Group members might hold their palms in front of them, mentally placing the directee/storyteller and their needs there and offering the person to the heart of God.

A group may choose to offer spoken words of prayer over the directee. Words can be powerful—particularly if the person just shared something deeply personal or vulnerable. However, spoken words of prayer can sometimes become attempts to advise, correct, or fix . . . disguised as words to God. We can start preaching to the presenter in our prayer, as Alice Fryling says, "God, help this friend to do . . ."[21] Discern carefully if words or silence offer the best form of intercessory prayer for the directee.

After the last group member has shared, be sure to give prayerful attention to any absent members. Any known needs for the absent member can be named. Then pray in silence for the absent member. You are nourishing an interconnectedness with God and the absent member, even when apart. True belonging is cultivated when we are missed and prayed for when we are not there.

> As a clergyperson who has offered so many spoken prayers of intercession over people's needs, I love the alternative of simply holding someone in silence. It feels life-giving. I mentally placed my tired group member in God's love and light. Then I imagined her receiving a refreshing massage. My group has learned to connect to each other and to God in silent prayer with the gift of presence. There is such deep belonging there.

Step 9: Reflection on Your Time Together

At the end of the meeting, move the group to reflect on how you have been present to God together. This step is an analysis of your practice. It isn't meant to critique anyone. It's also not a review of material shared in the meeting. Instead, it is a gentle noticing of the group's attentiveness to God, and to each directee/storyteller during their turn. The focus is on the experience of prayerful listening.[22] Whatever is shared in this time is to be done in the spirit of prayer and grace.

Questions to Guide Your Reflection

- Were we prayerful during this session?
- How well did we keep silence?
- How attentive were we to God? When did we lack attention?
- How did we stay focused on the spiritual life of the directee?
- Where did we veer off course (offering advice, telling our own story, problem solving)?
- When I was the directee/storyteller/presenter was I vulnerable? Did I share what the Spirit was leading me to share? Was I
- open to hearing responses? Were there times when the response of another was really helpful, or when a group member's response was unhelpful? Do I need to offer any feedback about this?
- As a group member, did my words or my silence stay centered in God? Was there a time when my words or silence may have come from a place of competition, insecurity, or ego? Did I hold on to an agenda for the directee, or really listen to my other group members?
- Is there an awareness that I take away from our time together about our practice? Is there any way the group needs to pray for me?

Adapted from Rose Mary Dougherty, *Group Spiritual Direction*[23]

This time of reflection will help the group dwell in love and grow in the practice of group spiritual direction. You don't need to cover every question listed above; the Holy Spirit will lead you to select the appropriate questions and guide each person to what is most important to share in this time.

This reflection time is also when you can do a brief check-in regarding the group's upholding of the covenant. You can literally look at a copy of your covenant and review your faithfulness to it. Again, this isn't the space to call people out or be accusatory. Reflection on the practice of upholding the covenant keeps everyone accountable and reminds people to maintain confidentiality.

I opened our time of reflection by asking about the quality of our prayerfulness and attentiveness to God. One person commented that she is learning that group spiritual direction is a different way of being together than she has experienced in other church groups—she reminds herself to keep focused and not tell a joke or get derailed from the time structure. I offered that if God leads her to tell a joke, then that is fine. Group spiritual direction can have humor and joy too!

We then reflected on our experience as group members. One member said, "I'm concerned I might have moved into advice giving in suggesting that Rachel needed times of holy rest." Rachel quickly piped in that she felt like that question on how God was inviting her to holy rest was helpful and open-ended. I also spoke up and said that I felt like I might have been too enthusiastic in affirming Rachel, which could have been distracting to her or to the group. Rachel laughed and said, "It's always nice for me to hear that a friend admires me." She didn't offer any other feedback, but I felt the Spirit nudging me to be more attentive to my energetic outbursts for subsequent meetings.

We closed by reflecting on our covenant; everyone thought we had practiced the covenant well and affirmed that we would hold confidentiality.

Step 10: Closing Prayer and "Housekeeping"

After this time of reflection is over, the group might conclude with a closing prayer. This can be a minute of silence, a space for journaling what members want to remember, or a blessing. You also might pose a question for group members to reflect on in silence, such as, "What invitation is God offering you to take with you from this time?" (See chapter 4 for additional questions.)

Participants might take a moment to notice how they feel at the end of the group meeting in comparison to how they felt at the beginning. Whatever stress, anxiety, or worry they carried with them at the start most likely has shifted, changed, dissipated, or even been transformed into the gifts of belonging, union, renewal, calm, and peace. By taking note of this change, people reaffirm their commitment to this practice.

Group housekeeping details come last. Remind the group of your next meeting time and place, which is usually about a month later. Finalize any details of who might bring what refreshments for the next meeting, and who might check in on absent members. Have someone offer a brief blessing or benediction. Then disperse with hearts full and spirits nourished with belonging to God and one another until you meet again.

> I invited the group to reflect for a minute of silent prayer on what seed God was inviting them to plant from our time together. I sensed that God was inviting me to let go of the stress I put on myself to be a "good teacher" and to cultivate a sense of joy in my teaching. As the bell on my timer chimed, I invited us out of that time of prayer. "May God bless you in whatever invitation God has given you and may the seed that you have been given from this time today be planted in the good soil of your soul to take root and begin growing until we meet again." We took a deep breath together, sighed it out, and opened our eyes. We stood up, hugged one another, and said our goodbyes.

A Final Word

At the beginning of almost every group spiritual direction session, I don't feel like I really have the time. At the end of every group spiritual direction session, I feel like that was the best hour and a half in my week (and maybe in my month). I always feel gentler, softer, less stressed, more focused, more peaceful, and centered in God. I think, "This is what life is about. This is beautiful and wonderful and such a deep and powerful connection. My heart always feels full, and sometimes even on fire (as John Wesley famously described) after time in the Holy Spirit in group spiritual direction.

Saying yes to an invitation to group spiritual direction is a yes to a means of grace. May God be with you in your yes. May God be with you in your group's beginning and as your group practices the art of prayerful listening. May God bless you in this holy, hard, wonderful work of group spiritual direction. May you know that you belong.

NOTES

1. Ruth Haley Barton, *Pursuing God's Will Together: A Discernment Practice for Leadership Groups* (Downers Grove IL: Intervarsity Press, 2012), 154–55.
2. I draw from Nan Weir of Shalem Institute's guidelines for group spiritual direction, the Center for Courage and Renewal, and Diane Millis's book *Re-creating a Life: Learning How to Tell Our Most Life-Giving Story* (Bellevue, WA: SDI Press, 2019).
3. Millis, *Re-creating a Life*, 154.
4. Alice Fryling, *Seeking God Together: An Introduction to Group Spiritual Direction* (Downers Grove, IL: Intervarsity Press, 2009), 129. Fryling allows for a two-minute check-in per participant in her model. This can serve to address the "stuff" of life, so that then people let go of life updates to better listen for how God is at work in their lives.
5. Rose Mary Dougherty, *Group Spiritual Direction: Community for Discernment* (New York: Paulist Press, 1995), 49.
6. The last two questions in this list (When have I felt alive? When have I felt discouraged?) are adapted from the Ignatian Examen practice, in which we reflect on what in life is bringing us joy and what is not as a way of discerning God's work in our lives.
7. Henri Nouwen, *Reaching Out: The Three Movements of the Spiritual Life* (Garden City, NY: Image Books, 1986).
8. Karen Scheib, *Pastoral Care: Telling the Stories of Our Lives* (Nashville: Abingdon, 2016), 64–65.
9. Greg Ellison, *Fearless Dialogues: A New Movement for Justice* (Louisville: Westminster John Knox, 2017), 102.
10. Millis, *Re-Creating a Life*, 148. "Pay attention to what stirs in our heart as we listen to the sacred text of a person's story, and to note what seems to stir their heart as they speak."
11. Millis, 149.
12. Lois Lindbloom, *Prayerful Listening: Cultivating Discernment in Community* (Northfield, MN: Ashmore Ink, 2007), 10.
13. Romans 8:26
14. Fryling, *Seeking God Together*, 45.
15. Millis, *Re-creating A Life*, 151.
16. Parker Palmer, *A Hidden Wholeness: The Journey Toward an Undivided Life* (San Francisco: Jossey-Bass, 2004), 132–34.
17. These questions are common in spiritual direction and are informed by the practice of the Ignatian Examen. See also Alice Fryling's questions in *Seeking God Together*, 50–51.
18. Lois Lindbloom, *Prayerful Listening: Cultivating Discernment in Community* (Northfield, MN: Ashmore Ink, 2007), 13.
19. Fryling, *Seeking God Together*, 54.

20. Dougherty, *Group Spiritual Direction,* 37, quoting Margaret Dorgan, D.C.M. *Guidance in Prayer from Three Women Mystics: Julian of Norwich, Teresa of Ávila, Thérèse of Lisieux* (Credence Cassettes, 1986). This saying is attributed to Julian of Norwich.
21. Fryling, *Seeking God Together,* 94.
22. Lindbloom, *Prayerful Listening,* 14.
23. Dougherty, *Group Spiritual Direction,* 55.

4.

Equipping Leaders for Group Spiritual Direction for Christian Friendship

Here's some encouraging news worth repeating: the Holy Spirit is the one who leads group spiritual direction. Your role as group leader or facilitator is to follow the active, real, and live presence of the Spirit, trusting in the Divine guidance of the group. The Holy Spirit will support and sustain you as a leader; you are never alone in this work. The more you can "empty" yourself of ego or insecurity, the more God can "fill" your group's practice of holy listening with grace, love, and presence (Philippians 2:7).

Even so, learning how to listen well to God's guidance and how to support a group takes discipline and practice. The purpose of this chapter is to equip you with practical guidelines and training to help you lead others in group spiritual direction, perhaps starting a Belong group in your own community. Remember, God is with you!

Spending Time with God in Silence: Contemplative Spiritual Practices

The best preparation for leading a Belong group is intentional time with God—also known as prayer! The practice of listening for God in silence prepares you to hear God's voice speaking in your life and in the lives of your group members. Contemplative prayer describes this kind of quiet listening to God. By contemplative, I mean a form of attention to God without lots of words. Contemplative prayer gives space for silence. Pope Gregory the Great from the sixth century called this form of prayer a practice of "resting with God." The ability to rest in prayer comes as a gift of God's grace, and it involves opening our minds, hearts, and spirits to God.

Examples of contemplative prayer include centering prayer, the Ignatian Examen, practicing the presence, and gentle awareness. (See the handout Contemplative Spiritual Practices to Support Listening to God, pages 252–58 in the appendix, for descriptions of each practice.) Consider praying in one or more of these ways for at least a few weeks prior to the beginning of your Belong group. Pay attention to how you find yourself listening differently. Hearing God's voice isn't "woo-woo magic." The ability to discern God's voice from the noise of life comes from the means of grace of disciplined prayer. Notice how these practices of prayer open space for you to be more aware of God's voice back to you and keep listening.

Contemplative Prayer Is . . .

- Quiet listening to God
- Attention to God with few or no words
- Allowing space for silence
- "Resting with God" (Pope Gregory the Great)

Facilitating the Group

In chapter 3 we walked through the ten steps of the practice of group spiritual direction in detail. Now let's focus on some key points for the role as leader/facilitator. (Be sure to read chapter 3 carefully if you have not already done so.)

Attending to Logistics (Day/Time/Duration/Location)

Whether you are starting one group or launching multiple Belong groups at your church, having clarity on logistics facilitates a successful beginning. In some cases, you might invite group members first and then determine the details of your meeting by coordinating schedules. However, in the complicated world we inhabit, I find people often appreciate knowing the logistics in advance so they may discern their ability to participate without having to complete online Doodle polls or respond to scheduling emails.

Day/Time

Discern what day and time will work best for you as the leader. When are you consistently available in your schedule? If, for example, you are regularly available on Sundays in the late afternoons, set Sundays at 4:00 p.m. as your group's meeting time. Stay consistent in your day, meeting time, and meeting place throughout the length of your group spiritual direction commitment; any changes tend to confuse people and dampen their commitment and participation.

Duration

Establish how long and how regularly your group will meet. Clearly state the dates when the group will begin and end. For example, for beginning groups you might meet weekly for six weeks during Lent, or for a six-week block in the fall after school starts. Another option might be to commit to meet monthly from September to May (perhaps with a break in December). Clear start and stop times help people to know the commitment level they are making and to plan their schedules accordingly.

Location

The last important logistic to determine is location. Group spiritual direction functions wonderfully in person but operates well in online spaces, too. A hybrid option of both in person and online can also accommodate people's needs. Consider which location option works the best for your group members' ability to participate consistently.

Meeting in person. Group spiritual direction works well in a home environment. Home spaces can be cozier and less intimidating than a church building. The person offering their home is called the "host," and by providing a meeting space, they share a gift of hospitality with the group. The host arranges a simple circle of seating and could provide some refreshments at the beginning. Alternatively, a room in your church that accommodates a circle also works fine. You might decide to meet at the church because of your schedule or group members' commuting patterns. Or you might choose a community space where you won't be interrupted and where there is a guarantee of confidentiality (a room with a door in a coffee shop or library, for example). With in-person participation, people experience the fullness of incarnational spiritual direction. You can more easily read body language, stay present, feel someone's energy, and give someone a hug. In our increasingly virtual world, the power of human touch and embodied presence makes a difference.

Meeting online. Group spiritual direction also can function quite well in online platforms such as Zoom, Google hangout, or Microsoft Teams. Online groups provide access to people who might live at a distance from the church, or for whom time constraints or caregiving responsibilities make it difficult to meet in person. If you normally meet in person and a member will be out of town for one of the sessions, online platforms provide access so they don't miss.

As leader, be attentive to having good sound—the use of headphones can make a difference. Good lighting from a ring light or a desk lamp placed behind the screen helps with visibility. Enhance your screen presence by having a candle lit in the background. Close doors and limit interruptions.

Consider preparing slides (Google slides, PowerPoint, etc.) with your covenant and the timing structure you will use. If you are using scripture or text for a prompt, put those words on a slide. The slides help provide visual direction and to hold focus, which is important since people can experience more distraction while online (their dog barking, a family member coming in, etc.). You also can choose to stream music into your session by sharing your screen and then sharing a music file.

As leader, one of your roles is timekeeper. When meeting online, you can set a timer on your cell phone and hold it up to the screen when it goes off so that the directee/storyteller and other group members see and hear it. Or you might use a countdown timer in your online platform or through Google timer.

Invite people to mute themselves during silences and as the directee/storyteller is sharing. The group might choose to be unmuted during the response times. You also can choose to use the chat feature—or not—during the response times. Offering holy responses can be a little more clunky online, as people have a harder time reading body language when someone might share; acknowledging this and offering grace when people talk over each other is important in online groups.

After a while of practicing, the technology tool you are using drops away and simply becomes a space to hold the group together as you listen together to the Spirit. The Holy Spirit knows how to move into Zoom squares to connect us to God and one another in profound ways. After an initial first or second session that might have some technical awkwardness, you'll settle into the gift of the online practice.

Invitations to Belong: Recruiting Members

In your prayer practices, ask God to reveal potential group members. Participants could include fellow church members, friends, neighbors, or even coworkers who desire to foster their connection with God and others. Who is already practicing a contemplative life, or who would be interested and open to learning? As people's names and faces come to you, pray over their lives and whether group spiritual direction might meet their longings for discernment, friendship, and belonging. Seek diversity in age, gender, race, marital status, ability, and ethnicity to reflect God's diverse creation. Ask God to confirm for you if you are to extend to these persons an invitation to your group.

When I'm starting a new group, I pray over a potential member for several days or even weeks. I pay attention to a sense of calm peace or confidence or even joy that comes to me about this person in prayer. When I have this inner confirmation, I reach out to the person with a text, phone call, or email and invite them to the group. I give them the dates, times, and place of meeting in writing/text and let them know when I will need confirmation of their participation. I let them know that I was guided to them in prayer and invite them to pray about their potential participation. If they say immediately that the time/date doesn't work for them or that they don't have space in their life for this for whatever reason, I accept their own insight and boundaries and invite them to keep their hearts open for a future opportunity. Many times, though, if asked through personal invitation and prayer, people will pray about the opportunity, make space in their lives, and commit to participate—even if they've never heard of group spiritual direction.

You and/or your church or community might publish the upcoming opportunity for group spiritual direction in all the usual avenues of communication (social media, email, newsletter, bulletin, pulpit announcements, etc.). Interested participants can then sign up through the church's website or registration system (such as Realm), a Belong group administrator, or directly with you. This opens the opportunity to everyone and ensures inclusion of all interested people.

The combination of personal invitation and your church's usual publicity/recruitment for small groups ensures the best and broadest participation. Trust that God will guide new members to sign and that your group will fill as it needs to. Prayer plus some effort usually yields a group through which God will work to create belonging.

Creating a Covenant

As group leader, be sure to discuss and create a covenant in the first meeting and then refer to it in each subsequent meeting (see the information on covenant in chapter 3). Or, you could simply select the covenant agreements important to your group from the Covenant Guidelines for Group Spiritual Direction (pages 239–40 in the appendix) and show this list at each gathering, making amendments or additions as you like. After the group agrees to a covenant, send those guidelines in a text or email for reinforcement and have a paper copy or electronic version (a photo in each group member's phone, for example) at each meeting to help you remember and uphold it. With your guidance and the group's input, you'll develop a covenant that provides a safe and solid boundary for behavior and practice in your group.

Choosing a Timing Structure

Since the timing structure determines how many members you can accommodate in the meeting's duration, you can decide the timing structure in advance so you know how many group members to invite, or vice versa (see pages 241–51 in the appendix for various timing structures). For beginning groups, I recommend the 3-1-3-1 timing structure, which allows eight minutes of direction total per participant. So, a six-member group could meet for an hour and fifteen minutes meeting (6 people x 8 minutes each + 27 minutes for gathering/covenant/check ins/prompt/closing reflection and prayer/housekeeping =75 minutes). Regardless of which timing structure you use, the important thing in group spiritual direction is to use one; it provides a safe "container" for the process, invites people into a pattern of spiritual direction, and keeps the focus on listening for God in a contemplative practice. Without a clear time structure, participants can go overly long in their sharing, lose a prayerful focus, or feel anxious about how long their group will take.

Usually, the leader serves as the timekeeper for the group's structure. As the group becomes more comfortable with the practice, you could delegate timekeeping if a group member is willing. Most smart phones have a timing device on them. Other free apps such as Centering Prayer from Contemplative Outreach and Insight Timer offer sounds such as singing bowls, chimes, and bells, which gently bring people out of times of storytelling, silent listening, and offering life-giving responses.

Leading the Prompt and Centering Silence

Now allow space for any brief check-ins—one to two minutes when participants may offer very concise updates on what is happening in their lives. Next, you might invite participants to decide who wants to go first, second, third, and so forth, in the sharing—or you might have a group in which you leave the order of sharing open. Another option is to determine the order of sharing after the prompt and centering silence. This movement from gathering to covenant to timing structure to check-ins to prompt should only take a few minutes. Try to keep the group moving so the focus remains on spiritual direction. Because some groups require "nudging" to get started in a timely manner, you might clearly indicate when the group spiritual direction practice begins (for example: gathering at 4:00 p.m., practice begins at 4:10) to prevent latecomers, which is disruptive.

The prompt serves to focus the group members on God and offers some content for communal reflection. As mentioned in the previous chapter, the prompt can be a small portion of scripture, a reading, poem, piece of music, or an image or icon (see the handout Prompts for Leading Group Spiritual Direction, pages 259–64 in the appendix, for descriptions of various prompt practices). Be open in the time prior to your group meeting to anything God might lead you to use as a prompt.

Often in the week prior to a group I'm leading, I'm attentive to any music, scriptures, quotes, or images that come my way—whether during my own prayer time or through other worship or learning experiences. I pray, "God, could this be what I am to use during my group's centering time?" I wait for a sense of confirmation from the Spirit. Many times, I simply use the portion of a psalm or scripture that comprise that week's lectionary texts. When leading groups online in a Zoom space, I like to use the resource *The Work of the People* (theworkofthepeople.com) or to play a song from one of my online music accounts (Spotify, Pandora, Apple Music, etc.). Or sometimes I opt for silence, without any prompt, especially if people in the group are experiencing deep griefs or trials and need space of silence to settle.

The time of centering silence might come before or after the prompt, depending upon the group's energy and needs. If a group is chatty during the gathering and review of covenant/timing structure, I might offer a minute of silence, then the prompt, then a longer period of centering silence. You can invite the group into silence by saying something such as, "Now, we open our hearts, minds, and spirits to the presence of the living God, who is always with us." The centering silence should be at least a minute, and might go as long as five minutes, depending upon the timing structure. You can invite the group out of the silence by using a chime on your phone or a singing bowl or bell—or just your voice, with words such as, "We give thanks for the Holy Spirit's listening presence with us and ask the Spirit's guidance as we now listen to the first person's sharing."

Leading the Practice of Holy Listening

As leader, you participate in listening to each person's sharing just as the other group members do. You might direct your group to the handout Group Spiritual Direction Process for Friendship-Based Groups (pages 235–38 in the appendix) as a gentle reminder. Practice listening for what you notice, appreciate, and wonder in the directee's sharing. If a person stops sharing and goes silent with more time to go, you can simply hold the silence, or you might say to the directee, "As you listen in the silence, is there anything else that God might be nudging you to share?" Many times, I've experienced that this gentle invitation leads someone to share the true, deepest thing that is on their heart. On the other hand, if a directee continues sharing past their designated time, you can interject words such as, "We appreciate so much the story you are sharing of your life with God. We will uphold our covenant and our commitment to our spiritual direction process and invite you to bring your sharing to a close in the coming moments."

Leading the Practice of Silence to Hear God

As the timekeeper, you (or your phone timer) can indicate the end of the time of sharing and invite the group into "silence to hear God." For example, you might say, "Thank you to our group member for her sharing. We will now listen for a minute of silence to hear God's prayer for her and to be open to anything the Holy Spirit might guide us to offer." You might refer your group (particularly beginners) to the handouts Group Spiritual Direction Process for Friendship-Based Groups and Guidelines for Holy Listening and Lifegiving Responses (see pages 235–38 and 265–68 in the appendix).

In this time, you too are listening for what God's prayer is for this person and if there is anything God is nudging you to offer on this person's behalf. Honestly, sometimes I don't clearly receive something I'm to share. I trust that I am to hold silence in the coming time of holy responses, and that other group members have received what the person needs to hear. At the end of the time of intercessory prayer, you can invite the group into a time of offering holy responses by saying something such as, "With thanks for the Holy Spirit's intercession, we now move to a time of sharing holy responses."

Leading the Practice of Life-Giving Responses and Questions

During this time group members share what they have noticed, wondered, or appreciated about a person's sharing. As leader, you are free to speak into this space if you have received something from the Spirit on the directee's behalf. However, you don't have to show up as some kind of holy guru or wise one. Often, when leaders "try" too hard, they move into offering advice or opinions instead of providing a life-giving statement or question. Simply be you and be honest with whatever you have—or haven't—received. You can be a role model for others, showing that they don't need to feel a compulsion to share a response for each person.

Sometimes another group member offers the same response that I was going to share, and I might (or might not) note to the group that the Holy Spirit led us both to the same response and then go into silence. Allow the time of "holy responses" to be a time of grace for you as leader, too. Trust that God will guide you to what you need to say or prompt you to remain silent.

Group members often struggle most with how to offer life-giving responses. Again, you can refer them to the Guidelines for Holy Listening and Life-giving Responses (see pages 265–68 in the appendix). Encourage them to use the pattern "I notice, I appreciate, or I wonder" or the spiritual life questions: *What is your prayer in this? How would you like God's help?* Note for them that a one-sentence question or response might be a sufficient offering. If they find themselves talking for a long period, they've probably moved into advice giving, fixing, or telling their own story. Use humor when people do overshare! Expect that beginners will have a learning curve on how to offer life-giving responses and offer them the grace we all need.

Leading Intercessory Silent Prayer for the Directee

When the time for offering holy responses is over (either your timer on your phone goes off, or you sense that the fullness of sharing is over), transition the group into a time of silent prayer for the directee. You might say something such as, "Now that we have offered what we have received from the Holy Spirit for (name), we lift her/him/them up to God in silent prayer." This time of intercessory prayer is for the group to hold the directee/storyteller in God's loving presence. You might discern that instead of silent prayer, the individual might need words of prayer spoken over them. Keep any spoken prayer short and free from advice-giving or assignments—and free from any pressure for every group member to say something. In general, resting in silent intercessory prayer can bring the greatest balm to the directee. You can bring the prayer to a close by a chimer/bell and/or by offering a brief blessing for the person. I might say something like, "God, may you bless (name) as she lives into your love and grace." Often, I'll integrate in the blessing a few words that reflect the fruit of the time of direction. For example, "God, may you offer all that (name) needs to live into the calling for rest that she is receiving."

After everyone has had a turn as a directee/storyteller, give space to pray for any absent members. If any known prayer requests have been offered by the absentee person, these may be mentioned. Give at least a minute of silence per absent member to offer them up in silent prayer by the group. As the leader, email, text, or call the absent member after the gathering to let them know they have been held in prayer and to check in on them.

Leading Reflection on Your Time Together

As leader, you guide this process of reflection. As Lois Lindbloom says, the purpose of this time isn't to analyze or critique the practice or to rehash members' sharing.[1] The intent of this time is to reflect on the experience of prayerful listening and what the group can learn from it. There is no judgment, shame, or "calling out" during this time. Instead, invite group members through an open-ended question to reflect on their practice. As Rose Mary Dougherty teaches, it is a space of "gentle looking" with God at how the time together went and an honest sharing of what group members "see" about their practice. The group might address their human dynamics together, their practice of silence, or their offering of words—all of which is to be examined through a spirit of prayerfulness.[2] Choose one or two questions (see chapter 3 or Group Spiritual Direction Process, pages 235–38 in the appendix) to offer to your group, asking God for guidance as to which questions might be most pertinent.

Receive whatever reflections are offered with a spirit of grace and compassion. You don't have to fix or change anything. Remember, God is in charge and is the true leader; you are only the facilitator. Trust that God will guide your group during this time of reflections to the insights you need to stay healthy and functional as a group. At the end of the reflection time, you can guide the group's attention back to the covenant and check in on how the group upheld the covenant. Then offer a gentle reminder of confidentiality.

Leading the Closing Prayer and Housekeeping

After the reflection time, invite the group into a time of closing prayer. You might offer any of the following questions for your group's reflection:

- What invitation is God offering you to take with you from this time?
- What is the "seed" that you received that God is inviting you to take and plant in your soul until we meet again?
- How would you like to experience God in the next week/month/until we meet again?
- What do you see as a step on your spiritual journey because of our time together?[3]
- What is the gift or insight that you received during our time that you want to hold in your heart?

Almost always I use silence for this time of closing prayer. However, be attuned to the Spirit. You might be led to offer verbal prayer on behalf of the group or invite group members to offer their own prayers. As with everything else in group spiritual direction, there isn't a "right" or "wrong" way of doing the closing prayer; it is simply a practice of listening with God. Whatever brings you and your group closer to the heart of God and to one another is a good practice of closure.

After bringing the group out of the time of closing prayer, remind the group of the next meeting time, date, and place. You might talk about who can bring refreshments next time and who might check in on absentee members with a text, email, or call.

On the meeting days when you plan to do a midway or ending evaluation, move into that after the closing prayer time. This brings us to the discussion of evaluations.

Evaluating How It's Going

Evaluations solicit valuable feedback from members to shape the group's practice to be the most beneficial and healthy for everyone. I recommend doing an evaluation midway through and at the last session. These check-ins don't have to be complicated or extensive. Simply ask a few questions and allow space for group discussion and discernment.

Midway Evaluation

The midway check-in provides a boundary in which people know they can share their experience and give feedback. Here are some questions you might ask:

- What are your thoughts about our practice of group spiritual direction?
- How does it confirm or challenge your expectations?
- How are we doing with our prayerful listening and open-ended responses? Are there any changes we need to make?
- Are we fixing, advising, correcting, Bible quoting, or telling our own stories too much?
- Is there anything about our group that you would like to see changed?[4]

Receive whatever is offered during the midway evaluation with an open heart and implement any changes that have resonated with the whole group. You might ask other Belong leaders and/or your church's Belong organizer for any prayer or support. Then, go forward in faith.

Ending Evaluation

At the end of the appointed commitment time for the group (e.g., six weeks, six months, etc.), create an intentional space at the end of the last meeting for evaluation. You might need to schedule more time for that last meeting to have this evaluation and a time of holy closure.

Here are some possible questions for the ending evaluation:

- How did we do in our practice of group spiritual direction?
- What did we receive from this time together?
- Is the Holy Spirit guiding us to continue as a group (if that is a possibility within the church system)? If so, when might we start again? For how long? When would our stop date be?
- How would we like to have holy closure of our group (e.g., a short liturgy, prayer, offering of what each member has received)?

If group members discern they want to continue, determine together the logistics for the next sessions of meetings. If the group does discern that this will be their last gathering, honor the time you have had together. It's okay if the group doesn't continue—it has served its time and intention. God will bring fruit from the practice even after it ends. Give space for participants to offer what they have received from the group and any closing prayer requests. Keep the closure simple. Trying to craft an elaborate liturgy or "goodbye" can overwhelm both you and the group. Close with gratitude for the time together and a prayer of blessing for God's continued guidance in each person's life. God is always with you.

Planning a Multi-Group Launch

This section is for leaders who are launching multiple Belong groups for friendship in your church or community. I'll offer tips for recruitment of leaders and hosts, several launch models, and a descriptive outline of a sample training session. As you read and discern what makes sense in your context, allow God to direct you in the planning, preparation, and launch of group spiritual direction and multiple Belong groups in your community!

Recruitment of Belong Leaders and Hosts

Recruitment of Belong leaders for a multiple group launch takes a measure of the Holy Spirit's grace and a measure of the recruiter's heartful effort. If someone in the congregation has training in spiritual direction or is practicing as a spiritual director, this person would be great at leading a group spiritual direction group. People who serve as Stephen Ministers also would make ideal leaders because they've learned to listen well. Other good leaders are those who already have a rich practice of spiritual disciplines including contemplative prayer. Experienced small group leaders of Companions in Christ, Disciple, or similar small group studies make for good candidates as well. Who in your congregation is sought out because of their wisdom and listening skills? These "wise ones" in your midst would make good Belong leaders.

Pray over your potential leaders. I'm always enlivened by whom the Holy Spirit brings to me to ask to be group leaders—the youth director, the quiet woman with an unofficial ministry of visitation in care facilities, the recovering alcoholic who understands suffering. Once clarity arrives, extend a personal invitation and ask the person to have a discerning conversation with you about leading a Belong group. If you and the person mutually confirm a calling to leadership of a group, invite them to an upcoming training session.

Another role in a Belong group is that of the "host," who offers their home for meetings. The host is someone with a gift for hospitality, who enjoys welcoming people into their space and helping them feel at home. The host also might be the leader if these two roles fit well with a person's gifts. Usually, it works best if the host is also a member of the Belong group. The host's participation fosters their own understanding of the practice and further supports the practice of confidentiality within the group. If you are doing a home-based version of Belong groups, recruit hosts and leaders at the same time. The recruitment will take time and prayer, but this process will bring the leaders you need.

Different Models for a Multi-Group Launch

Here are several different models you can choose from when planning a launch of multiple Belong groups in your church or community. Discern with your leadership team which model will serve your context and community best.

1. Home/Community-Based

In this model, Belong groups meet in different host homes in neighborhoods. Groups also could meet in a community space that offers a quiet room/space and the possibility of a door or closure for confidentiality (e.g., coffee shop or public library). Church members/participants who live in the neighborhood of a host home could be invited to participate in their closest Belong group. Church software programs or resources such as Realm or Mission InSite can provide people's home addresses and contact information on a map of neighborhoods to aid in recruitment.

One gift of this model is that it closely resembles the practice of the earliest Methodist class meetings, which met in neighborhoods in eighteenth-century Great Britain—often in homes, but sometimes in local businesses (even a coal bin!). Also, this can be a more evangelistic approach by inviting people who might not otherwise enter a church building. What's more, it can be convenient for people who live at a distance from the church to participate in a space closer to their own home.

The downsides of this model include that it necessitates people with gifts of hospitality to open their homes, requiring the coordination of more spaces than just meeting at the church building. Childcare needs to be arranged, and most church insurance programs won't cover the provision of childcare at settings other than the church building. It also diffuses the sense of participation in the Belong experience because everyone in the church community who is involved in Belong groups is not gathering in the same place on the same night.

2. Church/Campus-Based

Another model for the launch of multiple Belong groups is to have everyone meet at the church campus. In this model, the church might offer an orientation session to group spiritual direction first, with the head leader/coordinator providing teaching and a "workshop" practice so that participants are better prepared for their Belong groups.[5] The orientation could include time for each group to sit together, introduce themselves, and meet their leader.

Then the Belong groups would meet for a set duration at the same time—six weeks on a Wednesday evening in the fellowship hall, for example. The space could be arranged with circles of chairs for each group and their designated leader. Every week, one of the group leaders could begin the session with a collective covenant, centering silence, and prompt (this leadership could rotate week to week). The groups then could practice group spiritual direction in the fellowship hall or disperse to different rooms on the campus.

Alternatively, all Belong groups could meet at the church but at different days and times. This allows for more flexibility with people's lives and schedules. This practice also might be more familiar to typical small group planning in many church communities (e.g., Disciple Bible studies, curriculum/book-based small groups).

The benefit of this model is the collective sense of participation and the greater ease of coordination. The church can more easily provide childcare on the campus for children, and children and youth could be incorporated into the opening centering and prompt if it is a collective gathering. Youth could then disperse to meet in groups in their space—or integrate intergenerationally with the Belong groups.

3. Zoom Groups

If travel to the church or to a host home isn't possible for some, offering Zoom-based groups can expand participation. Select a Belong leader comfortable with online facilitation. Simplify log-on by establishing one Zoom link that is used the entire time. Just as for in-person groups, meet the same day/time for each meeting and keep the same group members for the duration of the practice, rather than allowing people who can't make their in-person group to drop in, so that trust and confidentiality build.

A Training Session for Belong Leaders

A training session equips all leaders with the same skills and language for the Belong groups, bringing equity and consistency to the groups' practice. The training also builds camaraderie and community among the leaders. A training session for Belong group leaders could include the following elements. Feel free to rearrange, add, or drop elements as fits your setting and context.

- Introductions and Opening Worship
- Logistics (date/time/duration/place of Belong groups)

- Invitations to Belong: Recruiting members
- Inclusion of children and youth (as applicable)
- Teaching on group spiritual direction and history
- Discussion of group covenant and timing structures
- Teaching on holy listening and responses
- Addressing challenges
- Practice of group spiritual direction
- Establishing evaluation times/meetings
- Blessing and Benediction

I'll briefly explain each part of this sample training session, encouraging you also to peruse the Belong Leader Training Session: Sample Agenda on pages 269–70 in the appendix.

Introductions and Opening Worship

Prepare the space for the training as a group spiritual direction space, with a circle of chairs or seating. You might have refreshments available. Nametags are always helpful. Place a packet of information—agenda, worship service, group covenant suggestions, timing structures, logistics information, holy listening guidelines, and so forth—on each seat; you might email this information to them after the session as well. Consider gifting each leader with a large candle that they can use with their groups.

As your leaders settle into the space, invite them to introduce themselves. You might offer an open-ended question for them to answer, such as, "Why did you say yes to leading a Belong group," or "What are you hopeful about and/or worried about related to leading the group?" Invite them to light their candle and offer silent prayer over them and the members of their groups. You also could lead a short worship service including space for prayer and silence (see Opening Worship for Use in Belong Groups and Belong Leader Training, pages 271–72 in the appendix, for a sample worship service).

Logistics (date/time/duration/place of Belong groups)

After an opening prayer or worship, move to the logistics of how Belong will function in your context. Clearly communicate about start and end dates for your Belong practice, duration of each meeting, and locations for meetings. This information might include how you would like leaders to use the church's database system to register participants, take attendance, and send email or text reminders and follow-ups when people miss a session. (Provide training on the use of the church database system if that is necessary.) Share how the church will handle publicity and enrollment of the new Belong groups and what role Belong leaders have in recruitment. If you have more than one Belong group and you're using the home-based model, you might name each group after the neighborhood in which the group is meeting; for example, Belong Sherwood Forest, Belong Green Acres, and so forth.

Invitations to Belong: Recruiting Members

In advance of training, decide your Belong groups' membership size and the timing structure you'll use. In general, four people would be a minimum and eight people the maximum for group membership. During the training, Belong leaders could pray over whom they might invite to join their group; they could even write down the names of potential group members. Neighborhood maps with church members' addresses and contact information plotted on them can spark Belong leaders to invite neighbors. Some group members may come because of the church's publicity/announcements about the launch of Belong groups. Let the recruitment be a combination of prayer, resourcing, and effort.

Inclusion of Children and Youth (As Applicable)

Children and youth can easily be incorporated into a practice of Belong groups. The head Belong group coordinator could decide how to welcome children and youth in consultation with church staff in advance, or the group of leaders could discuss the following options and make decisions together. One possibility is to include young people in an opening worship practice (see my story on page 3 and a sample opening worship service on pages 271–72 in the appendix). Then children can be excused for a playtime supervised by a caregiver, perhaps one or two of the church's youth.

If the Belong group meets in a home, outdoor play is ideal, or in a playroom if there is inclement weather. The parents can then focus on their practice of group spiritual direction. If there are a handful of adolescent children, they can have their own Belong group in a different room in the house, facilitated by two adults (youth leaders, adult volunteers, etc. Two adults uphold Safe Sanctuary policies). If the Belong group meets at the church, children can play on the church playground while youth meet in a youth group space.

The coordination and planning to involve children and youth is completely worth it. Families experience bonding through the initial worship time; children receive recreation and play; youth have deep connection with each other; and parents have time to tend to their own spiritual, emotional, and social lives—all at the same time. Everyone goes home filled, at peace, and in deeper harmony.

Teaching on Group Spiritual Direction and History

Since leaders might bring varying levels of understanding or practice of group spiritual direction, adapt the training content to who they are. You might offer a simple working definition of Belong groups in the agenda, such as: "Belong is a small group practice that is based in the Christian tradition of spiritual direction. For those in the Wesleyan tradition, the early Methodist class meeting is an example of group spiritual direction." As is appropriate for your context, the training can utilize chapters 1 and 2 of this book to offer an introduction to group spiritual direction and its basis in Christian history and tradition.

Discussion of Group Covenant and Timing Structures

An important part of the training of Belong leaders is to cover the element of a group covenant as essential for providing healthy guidelines and expectations around behavior. Instill in your leaders their own capacity and strength to uphold the covenant. Encourage them to check in with their group in the reflection time at the end of the meeting on how they have upheld the covenant—and to name where the group has growing edges or learning in the covenant.

The training also should include teaching on the timing structure you decide to use for your groups, while allowing some freedom for experimentation. You can use the handouts on timing structures (see pages 241–51 in the appendix) to help you explain and discuss timing structures.

Teaching on Holy Listening and Offering Life-giving Responses

You might want to include attention to the guidelines on how to listen well to others and ask open-ended questions (see Guidelines for Holy Listening and Life-Giving Responses on pages 265–68 in the appendix), particularly if the leaders haven't had training in spiritual direction. Belong leaders tend to feel most uncertain about guiding their group through the response time, being afraid that they or their group members won't be contemplative or "get it right" with open-ended questions. During the training, reinforce that this practice of spiritual direction is always guided by the Holy Spirit, not our own skill or expertise. The wisest Belong leaders rely on the Spirit and not their own ego.

Addressing Challenges

Give some space in your training to address the group and individual challenges that might arise (see chapter 5). You might invite them to reflect on which challenge could be the most difficult for them personally and discuss how each of them might address their greatest challenge. This group brainstorming and reflection will benefit everyone, giving space for both naming fears and offering how they might move through them in their leadership. Acknowledging and addressing challenges and conflict with a spirit of curiosity, empathy, and compassion will go a long way toward supporting groups through conflict and into God's transformative peace.

More than anything, offer to your leaders the reassurance that God is with you in your challenges and in your growth, and that you are resources for one another. Provide clear guidance for how Belong leaders can contact the Belong group coordinator and arrange one-on-one consultations. No leader is alone in this work. The Holy Spirit is with you, guiding you to the next wise step together.

Practice of Group Spiritual Direction

The most significant, memorable, and impactful part of the training is the actual practice of group spiritual direction. You can set up the practice like a workshop, with Belong leaders free to interrupt with questions or wonderings during the process. Some learners might appreciate seeing the process before them. It is helpful if the participants have handouts of the spiritual direction process and timing structure you are using (see pages 235 and 241–51 in the appendix). Remind them that we all are learners in this work; this is a practice, not a perfection. No one needs to impress with their insight and wisdom; everyone is encouraged to listen to and follow the Holy Spirit's guidance.

Give space to process the practice afterward with one another—what responses or questions were helpful and which ones were not, and why? Leaders will learn far more by practicing and workshopping in a grace-filled training space than by merely hearing about it, and they will leave refreshed, calm, and inspired. The training itself becomes emblematic of the practice, which is the best gift to you and to the leaders!

Establish Evaluation Times/Meetings

Establish with your Belong leaders a midway check-in time for all of the leaders to gather; set the date, time, and place of the gathering at the training. Keep this gathering to an hour or less, mainly giving space for questions and concerns. Also schedule a celebration and evaluation time for the end of your Belong groups. Learning from your leaders what worked and what didn't is invaluable to the next launch of Belong groups.

Blessing and Benediction

End the training by offering a benediction and blessing on the leaders. You might invite them to offer their prayer requests or "asks" from the Holy Spirit for leading a Belong group. You could close with each person offering a silent prayer for the person to the left of them in the circle. Then close with a spoken blessing, such as this:

> May the Lord bless you and keep you,
> May the Lord shine upon you and upon your Belong group,
> May the Lord lift up your group, and may you sense God's gracious
>   Spirit already with you, guiding you as you lead your group.
> May you live in that peace. Amen.

Trust that the Holy Spirit will guide you into what you most need as you lead your Belong group. You are ready. Keep listening. God is with you.

NOTES

1. Lois Lindbloom, *Prayerful Listening: Cultivating Discernment in Community* (Northfield, MN: Ashmore Ink, 2007), 14.
2. Rose Mary Dougherty, *Group Spiritual Direction: Community for Discernment* (New York: Paulist Press, 1995), 53
3. These questions are common in spiritual direction. See also Alice Fryling's questions on page 53 in *Seeking God Together: An Introduction to Group Spiritual Direction* (Downers Grove, IL: Intervarsity Press, 2009).
4. These are common questions for assessing the practice of group spiritual direction. See also Alice Fryling's questions in *Seeking God Together,* 124.
5. You could also do an orientation at the church for all Belong participants for home-based groups—it just requires more planning and communication.

5.

Addressing Conflict and Challenges

Clergy and lay leaders were sitting in small circles of four or five people on a retreat weekend. I'd taught them the basics of group spiritual direction, and we were practicing offering life-giving responses to a directee. In one group, I heard a person start with an appreciation of the directee's story and then veer into advice-giving mode. I heard phrases such as, "I think that you ought . . ." and "As it says in this scripture, we should . . ." This participant spoke for most of the three minutes of response time, leaving little time for others or for silence. The directee was hunched over and looked anxious; the other group members fidgeted in their seats. I rang the singing bowl to end the time of holy responses and then guided the groups into silent intercessory prayer for the directee.

Before I moved the groups to the next directee, I sensed a nudge from the Spirit to provide guidance. I said gently, "Thank you for participating in that first practice with a directee. Remember that you don't have to fix, correct, or change any situation or person here. You can let that go! Instead, offer where you see God in the person's life. What shimmers? What do you appreciate or notice in their sharing? Practice care to refrain from language such as 'you ought, you should, you could'—these words often proceed advice giving. Be thoughtful with any sharing of scripture; if God seemed to bring a verse of the

> Bible to mind, consider offering just the verse or phrase, without any commentary. Be attentive to the length of your sharing—one sentence or a few words is often enough. Several group members should have time to offer holy responses in the three-minute window. Okay—let's try this again!"
>
> As I led them in the process of listening to and then offering holy responses to the second directee, I noticed that the "dominator" in the first round offered only a few words this time and listened to others. Throughout the rest of the rounds, he continued to listen more and talk less. I offered quiet thanksgiving to God that he self-corrected the common issue of being an "advice-giver" with only a little bit of direction.

Challenges like this in group spiritual direction are normal and to be expected. Humans trying to engage in the countercultural practice of contemplative holy listening might struggle at times! Beginners (and sometimes longtime practitioners) can feel nervous, scared, or uncertain about doing a new spiritual practice, particularly in a group of people they don't know. Everyone deserves kindness and the understanding that this is a practice, not a perfection. We're going to make mistakes, frustrate each other, and lose prayerfulness. We're going to have issues in group spiritual direction, and for that, we all deserve grace.

This chapter addresses the conflicts and challenges common to *all forms of group spiritual direction*—including spiritual direction for friendship (part 1) and spiritual direction for communal discernment (part 2). After normalizing conflict in the practice, I'll describe how conflict functions through different stages of group development in spiritual direction. I'll also offer information on conflict styles so that you can better identify how you and your group members function and react in times of conflict. Then, together we will explore some common challenges that emerge both in groups and individuals participating in any form of group spiritual direction. Whenever we encounter these and other challenges, the important thing is that we respond in a loving and nonjudgmental way so that group spiritual direction can live into the fullness of its grace-filled possibilities for healing and renewal.

Conflict Is a Normal Part of Group Development

Challenges and conflict are a normal part of group formation and help the group to form and deepen. Expect that issues will arise in your group, but also expect that the God who guided you to this group will also guide you through any challenge. Get curious rather than reactive when there is conflict. Stay in the liminal space of the challenge long enough for God's grace and strength to direct your group, so that you emerge stronger and in deeper friendship together.

Often we view conflict as something to be avoided, yet normalizing conflict can help you to move through it in a way that benefits the group. Conflict is one of the five stages of small group development that every group moves through, as described by Bruce Tuckman in *Developmental Sequence in Small Groups*—forming, storming, norming, performing, and adjourning.[1] Let's walk through each stage briefly.

Forming. In the first meetings, as the group is *forming*, participants will experience the normal emotions of curiosity, anxiety, and excitement that are common to any beginning. They also will begin to gain clarity on who they are and what a Belong group is when establishing a covenant together. As they practice group spiritual direction, they'll learn the timing structure and process and begin to become more comfortable.

Storming. As the group settles into the covenant and practice, different views, opinions, wishes, desires, and needs around group spiritual direction will emerge. People will frustrate each other with advice giving or overtalking. Conflict or friction might emerge as people's ways of being and thinking might clash—or as people might veer from the covenant. It's important to directly address the conflict or tension and invite the group into prayerful ways of evolving together. Group members also have a role in upholding the covenant and being honest in addressing conflict. The covenant serves as a strong boundary during the "storming" to hold people accountable. You might meet with individual members one-on-one to address an issue, or if it is a group issue, give space during a gathering to directly discuss and pray about the issue.

Norming. In this stage, people resolve their differences, appreciate one another's gifts and strengths, and respect the Belong leader's presence and leadership. They share an even stronger trust of one another and commitment to the practice after having gone through the "storming" stage. Their practice is gaining "norms"—how they gather, how the practice unfolds, how they listen and respond to each other. Leaders and members are becoming accustomed to one another and building trust and holy habits together.

Performing. In this stage, the group is in the flow of group spiritual direction, having gained experience and trust. Now they can really do profound work of listening to God together. People know each other and the practice, and in this knowing they can be open to the working of the Holy Spirit. This is the most rewarding and "holy ground" stage of group spiritual direction.

Adjourning. Eventually, though, all good things come to an end. For example, the six-week practice during Lent ends. The Belong leader leads the group in an evaluative conversation and people prayerfully offer thanksgiving for each other. The last stage of ending comprises a natural part of any small group. Though there may be some sadness associated with the ending of the group, group members will take with them the gifts and memories they have received through the practice together.

Though these stages appear to be linear, we know from experience that conflict is not limited to the early stages of a group's development. Whenever conflict might arise, remember that how we approach interpersonal conflict is part of our spiritual practice. As Jes Stoltzfus Buller writes in the *Peaceful Practices Curriculum,* "As image-bearers of Christ, how we engage in conflict reflects a certain picture of Christ that either demonstrates the values of the kingdom, or perhaps doesn't, depending on our actions. Inviting God to wrestle with us as we work toward healing and reconciliation is a necessary step on the faith journey. Conflict is not to be separated from our spiritual life."[2] Conflict can be excruciating and painful, but it also creates the potential to receive the Divine in new ways. Sometimes, a difficult experience with another can create a space of greater welcome and blessing in relationship—but it requires approaching conflict as a spiritual practice guided by God's presence. If we are to approach conflict in this way, it can be extremely helpful for us to recognize and understand different ways that people tend to respond to conflict.

Five Conflict Styles

Each member of the Belong group has their own way of responding to conflict, which often stems from how they've learned to survive or get along as children. Just as we have our gifts in the body of Christ (1 Corinthians 12:12-31), so too we have our own conflict styles. Social psychologists Kenneth W. Thomas and Ralph H. Kilmann developed a widely used model for conflict styles called the Thomas-Kilmann Conflict Mode Instrument. This model describes five different styles on a continuum from cooperativeness to assertiveness: accommodating, avoiding, competing, compromising, and collaborating.[3] Though our personalities, the context of the conflict situation, and the relationships involved all impact our approach and responses to conflict, generally we have a predominant style out of which we function. Each style has its benefits and challenges—no one is better than another!

Understanding and appreciating our own conflict style, and that of others, supports a healthy process of group spiritual direction. You might find it helpful to discuss these styles in your group, including which one each person thinks is their predominant style (be sure to acknowledge that these styles serve as helpful tools for understanding one another, and aren't meant to be used as labels, limitations on our wide ways of being human, or wielded against one another). Consider using the road sign or animal metaphors included in the following descriptions to describe your styles—and insert some humor!

1. Accommodators

Accommodators try to keep the peace no matter the cost, putting the relationship and the other person's goals before their own. This style fears conflict and often yields to the other party, denying their own needs to reach what seems like peace. An accommodator might say, "Our relationship is more important than what I want." They hold a high concern for relationships in the discernment process and a low concern for accomplishing the goals. The benefit of this style is that it upholds group spiritual direction's emphasis on relationship and respect of others; the downside is that this emphasis often is at the cost of the accommodator's own viewpoint or experience. It also can reduce creativity and may signal disinterest. The road sign that signifies this style is a "yield" sign, as an accommodator yields to another. The animal metaphor would be that of a sheep (following along with the flock).[4]

2. Avoiders

Avoiders withdraw from conflict. They may not attempt to respond or engage, most often out of fear or because they don't think engagement will bring any fruit. They appear nonassertive or uncooperative and often engage in procrastination, diversions, denial, or postponement. An avoider holds low concern both for the goals of the discernment process and for the relationships. Their disadvantages are that they seem disengaged or uncaring. Avoiders reinforce the idea that conflict is negative, thereby often preserving or intensifying conflict. An avoider's gifts or advantages are that they offer the group time to process and reflect, and they can protect others from harm by ending the process. An avoider also differentiates between what is significant conflict and what is trivial. Their road sign is an "exit," and their animal is a turtle (hiding in its shell and withdrawing).[5]

3. Competitors

Competitors in conflict think they have the right position and will go strongly after its defense, even at the sacrifice of the relationship. In this style, people think there is a solution, and they will not hesitate to use their power to go after their answer to the problem. They hold a high concern for the goals of the process and a low concern for relationship. The advantages of competitors are that they are quick, decisive, energetic, and generative of creative ideas. They get things done. The disadvantage is that sometimes what is "getting done" isn't true discernment but the person's own perspective. Competitors can reduce complex issues to "either/or" options to "win" and can escalate situations with aggressive behavior and coercion. The road sign for this style is a "one-way" and the animal is a shark because of the insistence on "my way" and use of force to gain solutions to problems.[6]

4. Compromisers

Compromisers understand conflict as a mutual difference that can be solved by everyone sacrificing a bit and meeting each other halfway. They are highly practical and tend to take on the role of a facilitator in a discernment process. Compromisers are moderates who don't get emotionally or personally invested in conflict but, instead, see it neutrally as an issue that can be resolved through a fair "give-and-take" model. They occupy a middle ground of valuing relationship and goals in the process. The advantages of compromisers are that they accomplish goals efficiently, uphold an equal balance of power, and achieve agreements in difficult situations. The disadvantage is that they may skim the surface and not address the deeper issues out of a desire to get to the compromise. Neither party may be happy with the compromise, and so the conflict really remains because there isn't consensus. Their road sign is the "two-way traffic arrows" and their animal is the fox due to their willingness to go either way on issues and their practical cleverness for solving problems.[7]

5. Collaborators

Collaborators commit lots of time, energy, and effort to discerning the resolution of the conflict. They want to get everyone involved, uncover everything about the issue, and respect each person's voice and contribution. Collaborators understand conflict as normal and natural, and as offering potential for creative, yet-unknown solutions. They hold both high concern for relationship and for the goals. Their advantages are that they are generative of new, creative ideas: they foster full inclusion of everyone, and relationships flourish through their work as they find a solution that really satisfies everyone. The disadvantages of a collaborator are that they use significant time and energy, they can get bogged down in the process, and can be manipulated by the more competitive members. Their road sign is a "merge," and their animal is an owl because of their wise collaboration with different parties in an issue to come to a solution.[8]

Understanding and appreciating your own conflict style and those of others will support a healthy process in both group spiritual direction and practices of communal discernment. The combination of self-awareness and group awareness in recognizing, evaluating, and valuing different ways of engaging conflict can help your group or community to "invite out" the best in yourselves so that you might be a Spirit-filled body, engaging in the holy work of group spiritual direction.[9] God's "more excellent way" (1 Corinthians 12:31) of communal discernment includes *all* the conflict styles of the interdependent body of Christ!

Common Challenges in Group Spiritual Direction

Let's focus now on specific challenges that are common in group spiritual direction for friendship and for communal discernment, looking first at group challenges and then at individual challenges.

Group Challenges

1. Fears of Leaders and Members

Our fears and insecurities about the practice of spiritual direction impact the group collectively as well as each group member individually in their own inner psyche. You might consider giving space in the beginning meeting for people to name their fears; when we name our fear, the power of it begins to lessen so we can live more freely into our true selves with courage. Here are three common fears.

The fear of being unfit. Both you and the members in your group may feel insecure about your own fitness for this work. You may feel that you aren't "spiritual" enough, don't have sufficient (or any) experience with spiritual direction or communal discernment, or aren't close enough to God. The way to treat these feelings of "unfitness," as Gregory C. Ellison observes, is to build proximity to others in the group.[10] As you build bonds of closeness, you will realize that most people feel somewhat unfit for this holy work, but that together as the body of Christ, you are more than enough for God to use you as God sees fit as you practice group spiritual direction.

The fear of being unprepared. It's natural to feel unprepared or unready when beginning new things. Naming this reality helps people to not feel alone. Contemplative prayer practices prepare people by forming them in habits of holy listening to God and others. Though not required for group spiritual direction, working one-on-one with a spiritual director is another way for both leaders and members to grow more comfortable in holy listening.

The fear of being unseen or unvalued. Jane Vella uses the the term "plopping" and says it describes the moment when a person says something in a group and the words splat on the "floor" of the conversation without any response or affirmation.[11] This experience of being unheard or invalidated often causes feelings of shame, invisibility, or what Kipling D. Williams calls ostracism.[12] The huge gift of group spiritual direction is that the intentional structure of sharing, silence, and holy listening enforces a deep respect for and honoring of what each person says. Your words—and even the feelings and meanings behind the words—matter in group direction.

In light of these fears, remember that you are called for this work of group spiritual direction. Your own trust in God's equipping of you through your prayer practices and openness to the Holy Spirit will go a long way to provisioning you for a healthy practice. As Alice Fryling advises, "Give space for the Holy Spirit to be the guide."[13] Enter into the space of group spiritual direction with confidence that you have what you need—which is God and a heart open to listening to others.

2. Loss of Prayerfulness

Group spiritual direction's emphasis on prayerful listening and open-ended, Spirit-guided responses make it a distinctive small group practice. Because many Christians haven't had much training or experience in a contemplative practice based upon listening to God, it's easy for groups to lapse into advice giving, problem solving, and attempts to "fix" people. Belong members also might struggle with maintaining silence—both during the intercessory prayer times and in giving silent spaces between offerings during the response time.

When you experience the loss of prayerfulness in the group, first take a breath and name to yourself what happened—someone interrupted the directee during their sharing, someone started telling their own story, a member began talking over another during the response time, and so forth. Then, welcome God's grace for the group and for the persons involved. Remember that we all are learners in this practice. Ask God to guide your response as a leader and group member. You might pray in the moment, "God, how might you guide us back into prayer with you? What is needed currently for the benefit of the group?" You might be led to say something in the moment or to wait until the check-in at the end. Don't ignore serious breaches of prayerfulness when they arise. For the sake of the group's own health, well-being, and sustainability, it's important to address issues so that the Holy Spirit can help the group to be the nourishing place it is meant to be.

3. Superficiality

The practice of group spiritual direction is for those seeking authentic belonging and deep connections with God and others. However, group spiritual direction invites a level of vulnerability to God and to other humans that can be challenging. The easier path can be for some individuals to skim across the surface of their life, sharing something "light" because sharing the real thing feels too tender or difficult emotionally. Often, then, the whole group adopts this kind of superficiality, which prevents anyone from receiving true guidance from the Holy Spirit.

Superficial sharing and responding also can occur when there are power dynamics at work in a group. For example, if a senior pastor and her associate pastor are in the same group, both might feel uncomfortable offering their struggles with God. Be aware of possible power disparities when assembling groups and try to avoid them. If there are couples, some might elect to be in the same group while others might benefit from being in different groups. A conversation with each partner before the Belong groups start can help clarify needs.

When you experience surface level sharing in your group—which often can lead to a loss of prayerfulness as well—pray about the best response. If your group is in the beginning stage, it's understandable that sharing will be less deep until people build trust and relationship with one another. Begin each group with a reminder of the covenant and conclude each group with a check-in on the covenant; this is integral for the cultivation of confidentiality. Model appropriate sharing yourself, both in your own "directee/storyteller" time and in the response times. Again, use the check-in time at the end to see if the group is remaining prayerful and listening to God.

Questions to Help a Group Examine Their Level of Sharing

- Have we moved from being present to God for one another to just sharing our lives, with only a passing reference to God?
- Are our responses and sharing focused on the purpose of listening to God's presence and guidance in our lives?
- Might we be avoiding or staying absent from God in this practice?
- Are we living into our covenant fully with each other?[14]

—Rose Mary Dougherty

In her book *Group Spiritual Direction*, Rose Mary Dougherty suggests that group members might examine what they want from the group and how they might wish to continue from a place of prayer.[15] If the group is able to recognize that they want to shift focus and reclaim the purpose of group spiritual direction, they'll derive much greater benefit from the practice. If they decide they would rather be a more social "prayer request and check-in" kind of group and you are the leader, you should discern if you want to continue to facilitate.

Keep in mind that many groups are just learning the practice and how to go deeper. A Belong group that I facilitated took a while to feel comfortable with the practice and one another before they could do deeper. As the facilitator and leader, I needed to stay with them and remain present to where they were, while gently guiding them to continue in the process.

4. Diversity and Inclusion

In group spiritual direction, everyone shows up fully as who they are and is fully welcomed.

This is a space of hospitality for diverse life experiences and understandings of God, fostering a sense of inclusion for all people regardless of cultural, ethnic, racial, ability, or sexuality differences. However, diverse experiences of God and life sometimes can lead to tension in the group. Such tensions and differences need to be acknowledged as they happen. Anyone's experience of exclusion from the group must be directly addressed and processed; the Belong leader's role is to facilitate this discussion and ask God for direction on healing practices for the group and for the person who experienced exclusion.

It also might be the case that a group member discerns they might fit better in another group. Just as not every spiritual director is for each directee in one-with-one spiritual direction, so not every Belong group might be the best for a person. Someone might feel they don't belong in their Belong group! If you are the leader, offer support to the person, and if there are more Belong groups gathering in your congregation, you can work with other Belong leaders to initiate a transfer to that group.

5. Inconsistency

Groups benefit from meeting at the same time and place on the same day of the week for every gathering. Unpredictable or shifting times or locations will diminish people's commitment level and usually result in someone being confused or showing up at the wrong house. People will drop out because they forget when the meeting is or aren't sure where to go—especially if they have lost the leader's phone number to text questions. I've had groups where members have kindly offered to rotate hosting to their homes and I've declined because consistency matters so much for a small group's success. I've encouraged those with gifts for hosting to volunteer to host the next six sessions of meetings. Meeting at the same time and place and with a consistent schedule strengthens participation.

6. Continuity Questions

People appreciate a firm sense of the time frame for a Belong group. Especially for beginning groups, it's important to establish dates for when it starts and ends. Without firm boundaries and time frames, groups can spend lots of time spinning around when, where, and how long they will continue meeting. If your church has more than one Belong group going, decide as a team if groups will have the space to discern if they want to continue meeting after the set season for the Belong group (six weeks, three months, etc.) is over. Clear expectations and time frames ensure greater success and continuity.

Individual Challenges

People show up in group spiritual direction with all their past survival skills and communication or conflict styles within them; sometimes these ways of being, particularly when unexamined by the group member, can interfere with the prayerfulness of the practice. When this happens, the Holy Spirit might be giving the person and the group opportunities for growth and learning. The naming of the challenges below isn't meant to label or accuse people but to indicate behavioral tendencies that commonly happen in order to better empower everyone for healthier group dynamics.

1. The Dominator

This is the person who always has a response to offer and sometimes might consume the response time. The dominator often tends to be the one who can fall into advice giving, fixing, and correcting. A dominator may quote too much from the Bible and proof text or talk too much about themselves. Often, this person is well-meaning and intentioned and sometimes unaware of their own loss of prayerfulness.

Another form of a "dominator" is the group member who is going through an intense time of crisis, whether through grief, loss, health challenges, or other emergencies. They might talk over their sharing time by several minutes or extend the response time. They may divulge way too much intimate information. You might step in to share, "Thank you, (name), for sharing. We have come to the end of your time and want to uphold our covenant so that all receive and give direction. It may be that in someone else's direction time, you receive just what you also need." While it is understandable to give a little more space to someone going through crisis, when this time-sharing becomes a pattern, it can create tension in the group and inhibit the life-giving nature of the group for everyone else. The group is not to replace therapy and counseling.

For both kinds of dominators, the reflection time at the end remains important. Losses of prayerfulness can be insightful for both the person and the group. If the problem remains, you might want to check in with the dominator one-on-one and explore how the Spirit might be at work in their life on this issue. Again, remember that we are to be a conduit of God's grace and that we all are beginners in this practice.

2. The Reluctant

The reluctant one might elect to "pass" and not share anything during their directee/storyteller time—not just for one session but for multiple ones. This person also might elect to share very briefly and very little of any specificity or depth—or to share more about others than about their own journey with God. A Belong member in one group of mine would only take one minute of her time and would only share in a large "paintbrush" kind of way. She might say, "I have a big challenge that is taking a lot out of me. I pray that God will direct me, and I read my Bible every morning." Then she would stop, and not share any more, remaining silent during the rest of the time. It left the group little to work with when listening for the Spirit and offering responses. She also didn't change or adapt this form of nonsharing over time. While personal sharing as the directee/storyteller is always invitational and no one is required to share the "guts" of whatever they are going through, consistent surface-level sharing prevents the person and the group from really engaging in the practice.

On the other hand, many reluctant ones may need a greater feeling of trust and safety with the group before opening up. Some might be going through deep places in their journey and need time to process on their own with God before bringing it to the group. A middle-aged man in one of my Belong groups was going through a difficult job change and was seeking God's direction in a new vocation. For the first few practices, he didn't share as much, but gradually he revealed his discernment on a new job as he became comfortable with the group and the practice.

Some group members may be reluctant to engage in prayerful sharing and listening and may engage in distracting behaviors out of discomfort. They may ask for advice or tell funny stories for humor or lapse into socializing. This kind of reluctance often hints at a fear of vulnerability with the spiritual intimacy of the practice. Group spiritual direction can take time to adjust to and requires us to have grace and patience with those completely unaccustomed to and perhaps scared of it. Often this reluctance comes from fear of rejection or hurt. Be gentle and invite this reluctant one to stay focused on the practice and open to the Spirit.

If you are the Belong leader, continue to use the reflection time to check in. You might also want to have a one-on-one conversation with the reluctant one. Often other things are going on under the surface that are inhibiting them from sharing. Compassion and caring might be just what they need to feel safe in opening to the practice.

3. The Absentee

Regular, committed attendance is essential for forming the trust and covenanted practice of group spiritual direction. Of course, life happens, and inevitably group members will miss a session. However, if a pattern of absenteeism emerges from a Belong member, check in with them. This may not be the right time for the person to participate in the group. Perhaps after one session they felt that group spiritual direction wasn't the right practice for them but are too afraid of offending you or others in the church by withdrawing. Maybe the person genuinely has a lot going on in their life and needs prayer and pastoral support. Yet again, receive God's grace for this person and reach out as one who will share that grace with them, giving them space to affirm their commitment or to withdraw.

Conflict and Challenges as Invitation

Any challenges or difficulties in group spiritual direction are possible invitations into deeper growth and intercessory prayer. Conflict invites us into deeper trust of God's presence with us. By remaining in the grace of God's presence in prayer, we can more readily extend that grace and peace to others. Conflict and challenges can be an entryway into a richer practice of listening and being present to one another. As Christians, we all are interdependent and interconnected in the body of Christ (see 1 Corinthians 12 and Romans 12), and we are called to be in community with God and one another. This practice of being in community necessarily involves learning and growing through our disagreements, differences, and perspectives. When we learn to see the way someone else sees life, with different vision than our own, we expand our own horizons, strengthen our relationships, and grow the body of Christ in the world.

NOTES

1. Bruce Tuckman, "Developmental Sequence in Small Groups," *Psychological Bulletin,* 63, no 6 (1965).
2. Jes Stoltzfus Buller, *Peaceful Practices Curriculum,* ed. Kirstin De Mello and Ed Nyce (Mennonite Central Committee, 2021), 7. This curriculum is a great resource for spiritual practices that engage in conflict transformation.
3. https://kilmanndiagnostics.com/. Accessed Feb. 7, 2023.
4. Ron Kraybill, "Approaches to Conflict," *Conflict Transformation and Restorative Justice Manual* 5th ed., eds. Michelle F. Armster and Lorraine Stutzman Amstutz (Akron, OH, Office on Justice and Peacebuilding, a program of the Mennonite Central Committee US, 2008), 39, and Steve Thomas, "Approaches to Conflict," *Peacemakers Empower Teacher Manual* (Creative Commons License, 2012), 145, as used in Buller, *Peaceful Practices,* 34–35.
5. Buller, *Peaceful Practices* 34–35.
6. Buller, 34–35.
7. Buller, 34–35.
8. Buller, 34–35.
9. Buller, 32–33.
10. Gregory C. Ellison II, *Fearless Dialogues: A New Movement for Justice* (Louisville: Westminister John Knox Press, 2017), 88–90.
11. Jane Vella, *Learning to Listen Learning to Teach: The Power of Dialogue in Educating Adults* (San Francisco: Jossey-Bass, 2002), 10. This theory has prominent influence in Gregory Ellison's practice of "Fearless Dialogues," 68.
12. Kipling D. Williams, *Ostracism: The Power of Silence* (New York, Guildford Press, 2001), 1–2, as cited in Gregory Ellison, *Fearless Dialogues,* 69. Williams, a social psychologist, notes that everyone has had these experiences of feeling excluded, shunned, or rendered invisible.
13. Alice Fryling, *Seeking God Together: An Introduction to Group Spiritual Direction* (Downers Grove, IL: Intervarsity Press, 2009, 121.
14. Rose Mary Dougherty, *Group Spiritual Direction: Community for Discernment* (New York: Paulist Press, 1995), 69.
15. Dougherty, *Group Spiritual Direction,* 70.

PART 2

Group Spiritual Direction for Communal Discernment

6.

A Practice of Seeking Consensus Together with God (The What)

Parishioners in a congregation I worked with on communal discernment were reacting intensely to denominational tumult and conflict on the issue of human sexuality. Social media posts of all sorts were flying out from people's fingers into the ether, generating more consternation. The pastors were receiving a high volume of emotional communication.

The church council wanted something that would lead to everyone feeling heard across the spectrum of positions. They wanted a decision-making process that would promote unity rather than the divisiveness of voting—something from Christian roots rather than from secular business practices. They wanted a space of courageous conversation and discussion but didn't know how to structure it or keep it from going "off the rails" into even deeper conflict. Might there be something—a process for prayerful decision making, and guided by the Holy Spirit, that could move them through this conflict and into who God was calling them to be?

What this church council longed for, even if they couldn't articulate it, was a Christian practice of communal discernment. This process, which is rooted in scripture and the history of the church, helps congregations and communities hear how God is calling them to live. Instead of post-meeting "parking lot recaps" and disgruntled people leaving the church, churches that practice communal discernment can experience greater belonging, unity, and mission. Communal discernment transforms conflict into a means of grace and creates connection to one another as a form of "holy conferencing." Though it may sound miraculous, when we trust in the Holy Spirit in our discernment together, wonders can happen.

In this chapter we will come to understand communal discernment and its goal, which is consensus-building. After considering definitions of each and some theological underpinnings for the practice, which have roots in scripture and church history, we'll look at different types of communal discernment—from the monastic, Ignatian, Quaker, and Wesleyan traditions. Your community might choose one of these historical types or mix elements of several to create your own process. By the end of this chapter, you'll see that there is indeed *something* that can support your congregation through a difficult issue and move you into God's mission and heart for you—and that *something* is communal discernment.

What Is Communal Discernment?

Elizabeth Liebert offers that discernment is "the process of intentionally becoming aware of how God is present, active, and calling us as individuals and communities so that we can respond with increasingly greater faithfulness."[1] Another source describes it as a gift of the Holy Spirit that works through the human intellectual capacity to judge, test, and weigh God's word and to faithfully respond to it.[2] Leibert says it's the Christian practice of seeking God's call in the midst of life's decisions.[3] As Rose Mary Dougherty explains in *Group Spiritual Direction*, discernment guides us to what actions, ways of being, or steps will lead to fullness of life.[4]

When a congregation's leadership team commits to discerning God's call, they are opting for a prayer-filled practice that will guide them to what the Holy Spirit might be doing in their midst.[5] In communal discernment, a congregation practices listening to God's heart and purpose in the tough decision, issue, or problem before them.[6] "Communal discernment is a consensus-building process to help individuals listen for, or discern, what it is God desires from the community of participants."[7] Communal discernment helps congregations to see the path they might walk—together. As New Testament scholar Luke Timothy Johnson comments, "Discernment enables communities, finally, to decide for God."[8] In the midst of a confusing and conflicted world, spiritual discernment—which is guided by the Holy Spirit—enables Christians to know God's heart for their communal life.

This goal of knowing what God desires for a congregation's or group's communal life differentiates the practice of group spiritual direction for communal discernment from group spiritual direction for friendship, in which participants share about their life. People may share some of their personal experience in a practice of communal discernment using group spiritual direction, but any personal storytelling is directed to the aim, or goal, of determining God's will for the community. The end or goal of group spiritual direction for communal discernment is to come to clarity together about an issue of congregational or community concern as you seek to discern God's will. It is to come to consensus.

What Is Consensus?

The clarity that comes from group spiritual direction through communal discernment describes consensus. According to Susan Beaumont, consensus indicates group solidarity in heart, mind, and soul around a decision or issue.[9] Business consultant Larry Dressler defines consensus as occurring when "all group members develop and agree to support a decision that is in the best interest of the whole."[10] Consensus is reached, he says, when every person can honestly say, "I believe this is the best decision we can arrive at for the church at this time, and I will support its implementation."[11] The superpower of consensus is that all group members commit to enacting and supporting the decision. Instead of passively, or passive-aggressively, acquiescing to a decision they might not like, group members become champions for it. People carry out and implement what they champion.

Consensus doesn't mean that everyone agrees. Some may still hold a different position. In consensus, however, they've let go of their sense of "rightness" because they've wholeheartedly accepted the collective vision. As the World Council of Churches (WCC) teaches about their practice of communal discernment, consensus doesn't create "winners" and "losers" because in the end the community affirms the direction they all have discerned God is calling them to go. Everyone "wins" because the community continues together to seek God's will in their work and ministry.[12]

A Theology of Discernment

As Amy Oden plainly clarifies, discernment is not a "special hot line to God," a guessing game for God's will, or a kind of "decoder ring" to read God's mind. It is an attending to God's movement in our daily life.[13] It involves listening for God's calling in our communal decision-making because we believe God is participating with us in our life together. For a community to practice communal discernment well, both participants and leaders need to discuss and understand a commonly held theology about the process. For practices of discernment to work well, it matters how we think God communicates with us; having theological touchstones can ground a group, particularly when the discernment seems murky or confusing. What follows are some significant elements of a theology operative in a communal discernment practice. Discernment as "faith seeking understanding" draws people closer to God and closer to one another as the Holy Spirit works to guide their community to a decision they mutually support.

God at Work in Communal Discernment

When we consider God's part in communal discernment, it can be helpful to view it through a Trinitarian lens of God's will, Jesus's revelation, and the Holy Spirit's gift.

1. God's Will

Some participants may think of God's will as fixed, predetermined, and something that humans must live with. Another stream in the Christian tradition understands God's will not as a set plan of right-or-wrong but as God offering us choice (free will)—with the understanding that the choices we make matter to God. This is theology that upholds discernment—that God cares about the decisions we make and longs for us to come freely into life with God. We practice discernment because we believe God is active in our lives while offering us complete freedom to determine the way we are to go. God desires for us to live into God's love but will not coerce or force us into that embrace, nor will God abandon us.[14]

2. Jesus's Revelation

Discernment assumes that God is revealing and self-disclosing God's self to us. This revelation is evident in creation and seen in the person of Jesus. As wise teacher Amy Oden describes it, in discernment, this revelation might occasionally appear like bolts of lightning in our midst, but most often it is a series of nudges, hunches, and glimpses.[15] In my own practice of communal discernment, when I experience a sense of calm spaciousness and peace in the group, I have a glimpse of Christ among us. Christ can also appear in a spirit of joy and laughter as we encounter our unity together.

3. The Holy Spirit's Gift

Jesus promises us, "The Holy Spirit . . . will teach you everything and remind you of all that I have said to you" (John 14:26). The Holy Spirit reminds us of Jesus's teaching when we need it most. This is a gift given to help us know through our human intelligence the way God is calling us to go (see 1 Corinthians 12:10). Since it is a gift, we can't manipulate or predetermine the outcome of the Holy Spirit's work or timing. We trust that God has indeed given us the Holy Spirit and that the Holy Spirit will lead us in the fullness of God's time into the clarity we long for and the hope of our calling. Through the guidance of the Holy Spirit we are led into peace—into consensus when we are at dispute with each other. Jesus said, "My peace I give to you" (John 14:27), a peace that comes to us when we rely on and listen to the Holy Spirit.

> **Guidelines for Communal Discernment Through the Holy Spirit**
>
> 1. Many spirits exist, and they are not the Holy One. False spirits can lead people astray and can engender destructive prophets within a community; they don't support godly discernment. Instead, the true Holy Spirit testifies to Jesus Christ. (1 John 4:1-3, see also 1 Corinthians 12:1-3).
> 2. The Holy Spirit always ushers us into God's love. When we are abiding in the Holy Spirit in discernment, we know the love of God in our own hearts and experience that love and peace in community (1 John 4:13-21). As we abide in love together, we become more confident and clearer in understanding the way God is leading us to go (1 John 4:17).
> 3. The Holy Spirit will continue working through our reading of scripture and prayer to reveal congruence and to develop a spirit of consensus among us.[16]

Humans at Practice in Communal Discernment

When we humans seek to follow God's call in our life together through reliance on the Holy Spirit in prayerful practices, we live more fully into God's vocation for our community. The following elements comprise this prayerful, communal work of discernment:

1. Discernment Happens in Community

God's will and desire for us as a community is revealed to us *together*. We need one another to test our discernment and see it is bringing peace, gratitude, union, love, belonging, hope, and liberation. I may receive one thing, others might receive something else, and together we discern the surprise that God has for us that we never could have seen on our own. We are one body with many members, and we need all parts to see the wholeness of God's calling (see 1 Corinthians 12). Together we seek common ground.

2. Discernment Is a Habit or Discipline

Discernment is a habit of virtue that requires time, attention, and practice. As we commit to a discernment process, we cultivate the habit of prudence—a form of practical wisdom as we live into God's will for our life together. Discernment as a discipline means we can't just do it once as a leadership team or have one "quick" congregational meeting. It takes time and commitment to "let the same mind be in you that was in Christ Jesus", (Philippians 2:5). Instead of parliamentary rules (Robert's Rules of Order), discernment requires practices of prayer and silent listening to God, as well as holy listening to everyone's voice.

3. Discernment Requires Relinquishment

When we practice communal discernment, we must be willing to relinquish our own starting position. This means we must give up our cherished ideas and opinions—a letting go that is helped by the group spiritual direction process. By relinquishing our ego attachments to an outcome, we open space for the movement of God in our personal hearts and in the group. Though the process of shedding our attachments isn't always perfect, the practice makes room for greater clarity for God's will, rather than our own.

4. Every Voice Matters

Because every person is made in the image of God, every voice matters. Vigorous dialogue, debate, challenge, and disagreement often accompany processes of consensus precisely because everyone's contribution is valued. Communal discernment is characterized by respect, support, mutual empowerment, and a commitment to fellowship based in a deep practice of the *Imago Dei*—seeing everyone not as enemy but as made in the image of God and a mutual member of the body of Christ.[17] When I'm in a discernment process with people I know have a different opinion than I do, I intentionally remind myself that this human is my sibling in Christ, that they are beloved by God, made in God's image, and that God is working through them and me to bring us together to God's will.

5. Disagreement Is Seen as a Positive Force

Churches often avoid conflict, which only drives the conflict deeper—or out into the parking lot for post-meeting discussions. In communal discernment, everyone welcomes legitimate concerns and critiques. The community understands conflict as normal in human relationships and as generative of new, creative possibilities through prayerful discernment. Rather than conflict engendering fear or anger, conflict can propel us into deeper understandings of God's plan for our life that we couldn't have foreseen without the "spark" of the disagreement (see chapter 5 for more on conflict transformation).

Discernment as theological reflection and practice keeps us grounded in our Christian identity and open to the ongoing work of the Holy Spirit in our midst. As we hold on to a spirit of discovery and combine our collective wisdom and discernment to come to a decision that is in no way predetermined, we step into the unknown together with the Spirit and discover with surprise and delight what the Spirit is doing among us.

Where Does Communal Discernment Come From?

The practice of discernment undergirded the people of Israel and the Early Church's search to understand God's presence and will in their lives and has edified communities throughout Christian history. We'll examine this story of discernment in the Bible and church history in order to better ground our own practice.

Scripture

A clear example of the practice of communal discernment in Israel's life was the tent of meeting. Moses set up this tent outside of camp after the people of Israel complained vociferously about conditions in the wilderness (they were sick of manna!). Moses needed more help and support than his own voice. God commanded him to gather seventy elders in the tent of meeting and God rested the Spirit upon them. These elders prophesied and shared in leadership, offering communal wisdom and discernment for individuals and for the people of Israel (see Numbers 11:1-30).

At the end of Moses's life in Deuteronomy 30, Moses commends the people of Israel to keep practicing discernment together: "Choose life so that you and your descendants may live, loving the LORD your God, obeying him, and holding fast to him, for that means life to you and length of days" (Deuteronomy 30:19b-20a.) Moses transfers his practice of discernment to the people, so that they might continue following God's divine plan for Israel. People such as Queen Esther, who courageously listened to God and stood up to the king, exemplified discernment on behalf of her people. The prophets, such as Isaiah, Elijah, and Micah, continued Moses's tradition of discernment as they spoke forth God's will for Israel, often at great personal risk. As Elizabeth Leibert points out, Israel as a people determined that these prophetic discernments were true by codifying them as scripture; the veracity of an individual prophet's discernment was affirmed by communal discernment.[18] The Old Testament holds many stories of discernment of the will of God and the human struggles and holy efforts to follow that will.

In the New Testament, a prime example of communal discernment of the disciples and early Christians comes in Acts 15. New converts who weren't Jewish struggled with whether they had to be circumcised and keep Jewish food rituals to follow Jesus. In general, they preferred to not keep these customs. Jews who believed in Jesus as the Messiah, however, thought that these Judaic practices were part of the emerging faith. The hard question for the earliest followers of Jesus centered around what new, non-Jewish (Gentile) people needed to do to belong.

As the Book of Acts narrates it, the leaders in the church gathered in Jerusalem and listened to personal testimony from Peter, Barnabas, and Paul. They kept silence afterward, listening for God's heart in this significant issue. Out of that silence, James was able to affirm that God loved new people, too, and that they didn't have to uphold Jewish ritual practices. Non-Jews, or Gentiles, needed to respect the Jewish kosher practices so that they could all eat together, but they didn't have to practice the laws themselves. This discernment out of prayerful listening and sharing provided space for all non-Jews to be welcomed into the family of God.

Through the so-called Jerusalem Council of Acts 15, the earliest Christian leaders came to consensus on a significant issue through discernment: "We have decided unanimously . . . for it has seemed good to the Holy Spirit and to us to impose on you no further burden than these essentials" (Acts 15:25, 15:28). This work of discernment in the Council of Jerusalem shows God's people seeking God's calling for their life together—and discerning by faith through the work of the Holy Spirit that God called them to welcome everyone without requirement.

Church Tradition

We also see communal discernment throughout church tradition. The Early Church discerned important matters of doctrine and theology through the guidance of the Holy Spirit as they read scripture together and tested its meaning for their community. Monks and nuns, first in solitary prayer in the desert and then in monasteries, advised church leaders out of their times of silence and listening to God. Eastern Christianity's emphasis on the relationship in the Trinity shaped its leaders to seek insights from others in making important decisions. After the church split in 1054 AD into the Roman Catholic Church and Eastern Orthodox Church, the Orthodox retained some of their practices of communal discernment while also maintaining a hierarchical structure of leadership.[19]

The Western Church, influenced by the Roman Empire's emphasis on law and reason, abandoned practices of prayerful discernment as seen in Acts 15. Early Church councils argued over issues of doctrine by presenting arguments, citing authoritative evidence, and taking votes. In doing so, the church councils modeled themselves more on the deliberative body of the Roman Senate than on the prayerful discernment of the Council of Jerusalem. Duplicating Rome's practice of hierarchy and status, the church's decision-making became ensconced in the Roman Catholic Church's authority figures of popes and the cardinals, rather than by the church community.

Though monastic communities in Western Christianity maintained a hierarchical structure of authority for discernment, with the abbot or abbess retaining ultimate decision-making authority for the community, monasteries in the West have maintained a communal practice of discernment that sets them apart from the larger Roman Catholic Church. Abbots seek the consensus of the community in making their final decision. According to the Rule of St. Benedict, the abbot calls the community to meet in the chapter room and explains the issue at hand. The brothers have space to ponder and pray over it and then express their opinions with humility. Once the abbot makes the decision out of discernment with the community, everyone must obey it. Yet their obedience flows from love of Christ and the abbot is constrained to provide leadership that shows faithful care of the souls in the community, shepherding in a way that resembles Christ. True communal discernment in a monastery means that the abbot or abbess is simply confirming the discernment of the community.[20]

Another significant contribution to communal discernment came through Ignatius of Loyola (1491–1556), founder of the Society of Jesus order (Jesuits), who emphasized the practice of discernment in his book *Spiritual Exercises*. His "Rules for the Discernment of Spirits" called upon the use of imagination, reason, experience, reading the Bible, and examination of conscience (the Examen) to know God's way.[21] The Examen called for reflection upon both God's presence and absence in an issue in order to make a prayerful discernment about God's will.

The *Spiritual Exercises,* and particularly the Examen, helped Ignatius and his society innovate a form of communal discernment, which they utilized frequently for significant decisions.[22] Known as "the Deliberation," this process incorporated a form of group spiritual direction as the community reflected on different aspects of an issue. Ignatius and his friends used this process to discern that they were indeed to become a new order in the Roman Catholic Church.[23]

The Quaker expression of Protestantism, which arose out of the Anabaptist movement in the seventeenth century, cultivated a silent listening to the Holy Spirit as a key aspect of their communal worship. This worshipful practice of communal discernment extends into their form of governance.[24]

Out of their own experience of persecution as pacifists during the Reformation, Quakers distrusted the State and disavowed forms of church governance (boards, councils, assemblies) that too closely resembled national government—which was often copied in other Protestant churches. Quaker preacher Edward Burrough (1634–1663) invited Friends to decide their business "not in the way of the world as a worldly assembly of men, by hot contests, by seeking to out-speak and overreach one another in discourse" but "in the wisdom, love, and fellowship of God, in gravity, patience, meekness, in unity and concord, submitting to one another in lowliness of heart and in the Holy Spirit."[25] Instead of parliamentary processes or "hot contests," Quakers humbly claimed a New Testament practice of communal discernment that led toward the unity and upbuilding of the faith community.

For Quakers, inward yielding and waiting for a spirit of unity to grow undergirds the spiritual discipline of communal discernment. It is always preceded by worship, so that the Friends are centered in God's presence and quiet listening before beginning any aspects of business. When they do turn their effort to the issue before them, they don't hold votes or use any parliamentary procedures. Instead, the practice of decision-making includes the elements of wisdom, the Holy Spirit, and the meeting. These three elements come together in a process that leads to unity on the issue, task, or question before them.

In the Wesleyan tradition, we see communal discernment in the first conference of Methodist preachers in England in 1744, when John Wesley invited clergy and lay preachers to discern on the questions of "what to teach; how to teach; and what to do" in shaping the emerging Methodist movement. Wesley had drawn up the agenda and questions, but everyone was invited to speak freely in discussion. There were no votes taken; the goal was to arrive at a consensus that everyone could affirm with their own conscience. In ways similar to a monastic chapter house meeting, Wesley served as the abbot in a clear and decisive leadership role while ensuring that the clergy and lay preachers had an important voice. This conference led to the development of annual conferences and quarterly meetings in which important matters of doctrine and polity (church organization) were discussed. These practices of "holy conferencing" served as a means of grace because the early Methodists experienced God's love and harmony in their gatherings for discernment.

Quakers and Consensus

Quakers tend to not use the word "consensus" because it is seen as the work of human reason, whereas the sense of the meeting is a commitment of faith. They understand consensus as requiring human compromise or shaving off objectionable positions. My use of the word consensus is more of a sense of oneness from mutual discernment, which does more closely parallel the work of Quakers in their business meetings.

Four Types of Communal Discernment

As we've seen in our review of church tradition, there are four historical communal discernment practices that can inform our practice today—the monastic practice of group spiritual direction, Ignatian Deliberation, the Quaker "Sense of the Meeting," and the Wesleyan Quadrilateral. Let's consider how each of these functions. (You will find a brief description of each type in handout form in the appendix.)

1. Group Spiritual Direction (Monastic Tradition)

All forms of communal discernment practice group spiritual direction as people listen together for God's voice in directing their life. In this type, a community might sit in small circles. After hearing the clear statement of the issue and a prompt for their discernment (a Bible passage, theological content, or teaching on the issue), each participant reflects and prays in silence, listening for the guidance of the Spirit. Each person then receives the same amount of time to share, without interruption, how they hear God's presence or work in the issue. Silence generally follows each person's sharing as a way for listening to God. The process could allow open-ended responses after each person's sharing in the circle, or the responses might come after everyone has shared as a way of noticing common preferences or leadings. The circle then could offer their experience and responses to the larger group as a way of moving to consensus. The group also could pray in silence after their collective responses as a way of discerning God's leading in the issue. Whatever way the circle or the whole group practices group spiritual direction, the structure and form of holy listening and life-giving responses offers a significant way for people to hear together how God is moving them.

2. Ignatian Deliberation: A Practice of Pros and Cons

As one source explains, the Jesuit practice of Deliberation, which includes wisdom, the Holy Spirit, and the congregation, focuses on the pros and cons of a particular discernment.[26] Practitioners find that focusing first on the "cons" or the negative of a position, as did the earliest Jesuits, clears the ground of intense emotions and aggression. As Jesuit Gervais Dumeige puts it, the "no" makes room for the "yes."[27] After sharing their "cons" and then praying over them, the group reassembles to share their affirmations of a position and then prays over those. In the evaluation step, the community discerns the movement of the Holy Spirit among them, which brings them to a place of consensus that they couldn't have foreseen at the start.[28]

This prayerful practice of communal discernment by the Jesuits brings consolation—the real gladness and spiritual joy of which the *Spiritual Exercises* speak.[29] Those who had opposing opinions at the start often find their differences incorporated into the final outcome. Even more wondrous, those whose initial position didn't make it into the consensus decision often decide to soften their views and adhere to the decision of the community. This sacrifice comes because they value the mutual discernment more than their own opinion. As Dumeige reflects, the resulting unanimity comes from the gradual approach to mutual agreement and the relaxation of tension as people recognize the work of the Holy Spirit among them—so that they may ultimately flourish and glorify God.[30]

3. Quaker Practice of the Meeting

In this Quaker practice, a facilitator, called a "clerk," gathers the meeting together and offers the issue before the body for consideration. As they sit in silence, people rise up to speak out of an inner "leading" they've received to share on the issue. Others listen; if anyone doesn't feel at ease with someone's leading, they voice their concerns, which are called "considerations." The Friends make adaptations to the decision based upon considerations until it aligns with everyone's inner Light. Quakers let go of their own attachment to any outcome as they seek God's guidance for their community together. Their unity comes from calm and steady attention to the "Light" within and the understanding that all members are actively seeking the leading of the Spirit. When the clerk determines there is unity, she or he offers the "sense of the meeting." The community then affirms it, and it is recorded as the decision of the body.

4. The Wesleyan Quadrilateral and Holy Conferencing

The Wesleyan tradition offers additional help for a practice of communal discernment. Though, to be clear, while the early Methodist conferences were intended by John Wesley to comprise mutual deliberation (as described above), in reality John Wesley served in a rather domineering role, so his conference leadership doesn't offer the best model. However, his Anglican (Church of England) tradition's practice of finding a *via media* (middle way) amid conflicting theology and opinions provides a resource. In particular, Anglican theologian Richard Hooker created a theological method that incorporated scripture, church Tradition (the theology and history of the church—Catholic and Protestant), and human reason to discern God's leading in turbulent times.[31] Influenced by Hooker, Wesley upheld the primacy of scripture for the church's life, employed the Christian heritage, and utilized reason to help the early Methodists find their way through conflicts. In the mid-twentieth century, Wesleyan scholar Albert Outler, developing John Wesley's own emphasis on practical holiness, added "experience" to scripture, tradition, and reason, and called this four-fold collation the "Quadrilateral."[32] Though the specific use of a Quadrilateral wasn't part of historic Wesleyan practice, nor are all four elements mentioned together in John Wesley's writing, this creative method offers a way of discerning God's work in our lives. Here is my summary of the Quadrilateral based on the work of several scholars and resources (see the notes for references):

1. **Scripture:** When participants read scripture for discernment, they engage in a living conversation with the writings in all their diversity, interpreting them for their community's context.
2. **Tradition**: John Wesley drew ecumenically from the resources of the early church, the Church of England, Lutheran and Anglican pietism, Catholic monasticism, and Orthodox theology. Tradition for Wesley and for contemporary Methodists is not just church history but also a dynamic and lived practice of faith. Tradition incorporates all the theology and history handed down to us from a long line of communion of saints, and which we enact daily in our Christian lives. These examples, stories, or theological teachings can provide the group with insight and wisdom to discern God's will for issues before them.
3. **Reason:** Reason is the artful practice of reflecting on theology, scripture, history, and experience to more faithfully discern God's ways. Reason enabled Wesley and the people called Methodists to live thoughtful and faithful lives—and it continues to support discernment of Christian faith today. In discernment processes, reason means gathering the wisdom of the group and distilling together a consensus position through the guidance of the Holy Spirit.
4. **Experience:** For John Wesley, experience meant a kind of practical wisdom, learning through trial and error and observation.[33] Wesley's "Aldersgate Experience" in which he felt his "heart strangely warmed" as he sensed assurance of God's forgiveness of his sins exemplifies the significance of personal encounters with God.[34] Experience encompasses our emotions and relationship with God—how we live and embrace our Christian faith.

Through the practice of the Quadrilateral, communal practices of discernment become Christian conferencing, or holy conferencing. People receive a means of grace as they experience God's presence, create deeper friendships with one another, and discern a real consensus. Through reading scripture together, sharing stories (the church's and their own), reasoning through discernment practices, and offering their honest experiences, people move from conflict into joyous belonging. In John Wesley's words, they experience peace and spiritual fruit.[35]

A Way Forward

Group spiritual direction provides a way forward through communal discernment—*something* to practice so that conflict doesn't rip our communities apart. We see this way throughout our Christian story. Generations of Christians from all different traditions—Catholic, Eastern Orthodox, Anabaptist, and Protestant—have discerned together how God was leading them. We can join this great cloud of witnesses in this practice that leads us out of turmoil and toward possibilities of belonging, friendship, and unity. In and through our differences, God at work in communal discernment can make us into a community of friends that extend God's love out into the world.[36]

Rather than vote taking and side-taking, group spiritual direction offers a way to share our stories on an issue before us. Through a structured spiritual practice of communal discernment from the Christian tradition, we listen to one another's perspectives and experiences. We drop our own defensiveness and rigidity about our own "rightness." As we offer our stories on a particular issue before the congregation and develop empathy and insight, the practice of group spiritual direction for communal discernment makes consensus possible. The whole community sees the way God might be calling them on a question or issue, and they walk in it. People may begin with different opinions, but by participation in this contemplative prayer practice, they listen their way into unity in the Spirit, leaving the practice saying things like, "I feel centered and at peace; this has been holy ground." It sounds miraculous, but when we trust in the Holy Spirit in our discernment together, wonders can happen.

NOTES

1. Elizabeth Liebert, *The Way of Discernment: Spiritual Practices for Decision-Making* (Louisville: Westminster John Knox, 2008) 9.
2. Luke Timothy Johnson, *Scripture and Discernment: Decision Making in the Church* (Nashville: Abingdon, 1996), 109–10.

3. Elizabeth Liebert, *The Soul of Discernment: A Spiritual Practice for Communities and Institutions* (Louisville: Westminster John Knox Press, 2015), 1.
4. Rose Mary Dougherty, *Group Spiritual Direction: Community for Discernment* (New York: Paulist Press, 1995), 27–28.
5. Johnson, *Scripture and Discernment,* 109. This is, in effect, Johnson's argument in this book—that discernment is a practice of the church—and that scripture is essential in that discernment.
6. Ruth Haley Barton, *Pursuing God's Will Together: A Discernment Practice for Leadership Groups* (Downers Grove, IL: Intervarsity Press, 2012), 20.
7. Spiritual Formation Program of the Grace Institute, "Communal Discernment Leaders Guide," August 2013.
8. Johnson, *Scripture and Discernment,* 109.
9. Susan Beaumont, *How to Lead When You Don't Know Where You are Going: Leading in a Liminal Season,* (Lanham, MD: Rowman and Littlefield, 2019), 88. I'll note that some people and organizations call communal discernment a consensus process. For clarity, I name the process communal discernment and the end goal "consensus."
10. Larry Dressler, *Consensus through Conversation: How to Achieve High-Commitment Decisions* (San Francisco: Berrett-Koehler, 2006), 4.
11. Dressler, *Consensus through Conversation,* 3–4.
12. World Council of Churches, "Introduction to the General Assembly"(lecture at the WCC General Assembly, Stuttgart, Germany, August 31, 2022) The World Council of Churches uses a discernment process to consensus make decisions with over three hundred different church bodies, denominations, and traditions. Of course, individual lives and each person's own vocational discernment is impacted by communal discernment.
13. Amy Oden, "Discernment" (lecture in the Spiritual Direction Certification Program, Lutheran Theological Southern Seminary of Lenoir-Rhyne University, January 13, 2023).
14. Informed by Beaumont, *How to Lead When You Don't Know Where You are Going,* 75. Oden, "Discernment" lecture. For Methodists, this is more of an Arminian understanding of free will.
15. Oden, "Discernment" lecture.
16. For more on the idea of congruence and the work of the Holy Spirit see Liebert, *The Way of Discernment,* 15.
17. Liebert, 15.
18. Liebert, 11.
19. Metropolitan Vasilios and Kristina Mantasasvilla. "Approaching Moral Questions from the Conscience of the Church." In *Churches and Moral Discernment,* edited by Myriam Wijlens and Vladimir Shmaliy, vol. 1, *Learning from Tradition,* 5. Faith and Order Paper no. 228. Geneva: World Council of Churches Publications, 2021. This essay describes the communal nature of Orthodox discernment based upon scripture, tradition, canons, and the conscience of the church.
20. Liebert, *The Soul of Discernment,* 22.

21. Ignatius, *Spiritual Exercises of St. Ignatius,* ed. Louis Puhl, (Westminster, MD: Newman, 1951), 142.
22. Gervais Dumeige, 'Communal Discernment of Spirits And The Ignatian Method Of Deliberation in a General Congregation, Way Supplement, 20, 1973 (Bedfordshire, England: Turpin Distribution Services Ltd), 57. They utilized this practice of communal discernment no less than thirteen times between August 1534 and March 1539.
23. Dominic Maruca, Johannes Codurius, and Petrus Faber, *The Deliberation of Our First Fathers: Woodstock Letters* (Jersey City, NJ: Program to Adapt the Spiritual Exercises, 1966).
24. Rachel Muers, "Peace at the Heart of Ecclesial Moral Discernment" *Churches and Moral Discernment,* vol. 1: Learning from Tradition, Faith and Order paper no. 228, ed. Myriam Wijlens and Vladimir Shmaliy (Geneva: World Council of Churches Publications, 2021), 91–92.
25. Elton Trueblood, "The Quaker Method of Reaching Decisions," *Beyond Dilemmas: Quakers Look at Life,* ed. Sceva Bright Laughlin (Port Washington, NY: Kennikat Press, 1937), 123–24 as cited in Merrie Schoenman Carson, "Stewardship, Discernment, and Congregational Decision-Making," *The Covenant Quarterly* 71, no. 3–4 (November 2013): 88.
26. John Carroll Futrell, "Communal Discernment: Reflections on Experience," *Studies in the Spirituality of Jesuits* 4, no. 5 (November 1972): 159–92.
27. Dumeige, "Communal Discernment of Spirits and the Ignatian Method of Deliberation in a General Congregation," 66.
28. William Barry, "Toward Communal Discernment: Some Practical Suggestions" *The Way.* Supplement 58 (Spring 1987): 108.
29. Barry, "Toward Communal Discernment," 111. Barry offers an example in which a group that was in conflict was, after use of the first week of the Spiritual Exercises in a communal discernment process, able to dream and hope again together.
30. Dumeige, "Communal Discernment of Spirits and the Ignatian Method of Deliberation in a General Congregation," 71.
31. W. Stephen Gunter, "The Quadrilateral and the "Middle Way" in *Wesley and the Quadrilateral: Renewing the Conversation* (Nashville: Abingdon, 1997), 18, 332–35. Archbishop Thomas Cranmer provided the foundation for a theology of a "middle way" between Catholic and Reformed theology through his development of the Book of Common Prayer (1549, 1552, 1553), Thirty-nine Articles (1552, 1571). Hooker's book was called the *Laws of Ecclesiastical Polity,* published in 1594.
32. Albert C. Outler, *John Wesley* (Oxford: Oxford University Press, 1964). Outler makes an argument in this book for the role of experience in Wesley's thought, which helped to formulate what is called the Quadrilateral. Outler described the use of the Quadrilateral as part of a common Wesleyan theological method for the *Book of Discipline* for the newly formed United Methodist Church in 1968. See *Book of Discipline,* "Our Theological Method." It has come under considerable critique from some scholars; however, it remains a part of the *Discipline* and ministerial formation and thus maintains significant use among United Methodists.

33. Randy Maddox, "The Enriching Role of Experience," in *Wesley and the Quadrilateral: Renewing the Conversation* (Nashville: Abingdon], 1997), 108–12.
34. Morag Logan, "The Role of Authority in Moral Discernment," in *Churches and Moral Discernment,* ed. Myriam Wijlens and Vladimir Shmaliy, vol.1: Learning from Tradition, Faith and Order paper no. 228 (Geneva: World Council of Churches Publications, 2021), 118.
35. Richard Heitzenrater, *Wesley and the People Called Methodists,* 2nd edition (Nashville: Abingdon, 2013), 169. Heitzenrater cites Wesley's reading of Edward Stillingfleet's *Irenicum*, which argues that the focus should not be on decisions of church polity but on spiritual fruit.
36. Stanley Hauerwas and Charles Pinches, *Christians Among the Virtues: Theological Conversations with Ancient and Modern Ethics* (Notre Dame: University of Notre Dame Press, 1997), 15. This model of friendship, which includes diversity, resembles Jesus's kenotic life, death, and resurrection, and offers that love out into the world. See also James McClendon Jr. "Three Strands of Christian Ethics," in *The Collected Works of James Wm. McClendon, Jr., Volume 2,* ed. Ryan Andrew Newson and Andrew C. Wright (Waco, TX: Baylor University Press, 2014), 22. Ryan Andrew Newson, *Radical Friendship: The Politics of Communal Discernment* (Minneapolis: Fortress, 2017), 171–72.

7.

Holy Conferencing Leads to Harmony (The Why)

A young adult stood at a microphone at a major legislative session of a denominational gathering, juggling a couple of large manuals. "I'm sorry. I'm still trying to figure out this *Robert Rules of Order*. Y'all are going to have to help me out. I think I want to discuss this motion according to this paragraph in the rules. Is that correct?" The young person takes a deep breath, feet shifting back and forth, waits for the presiding bishop's confirmation of the correct process, and then launches into three minutes of debate on the motion.

The process goes forward, and the motion eventually receives a vote. In subsequent legislative action, delegates get tangled up in all the rules of Robert's Rules as they revise motions, make substitutions, or decide to refer motions to legislative committees. The presiding bishop consults with the professional parliamentarian seated to the right, and with others, to untangle complicated processes. All in attendance become exhausted by the details of making decisions by parliamentary processes and constant voting. Some occasionally insert spoken prayers, but mostly the people make decisions by a secular rule book.

Though the governing processes differs according to church tradition, every church body seems to be facing a common challenge today: it has become increasingly difficult for the church to make decisions. In some churches the word "discernment" has been corrupted to mean just church politics before a vote. It doesn't have to be this way. We need something other than voting and parliamentary processes to find our way into God's future for us in turbulent times. Church votes have split congregations and left us estranged from one another. We need *something else*.

The good news is that we have something else—communal practices of discernment. In order to understand why we need communal discernment, we first need to understand why we've forgotten our own traditions of communal discernment and how parliamentary processes and voting came to dominate church life, often leaving us dissatisfied and sometimes estranged from each other. Because many of us are either unaccustomed to practices of discernment and used to parliamentary processes that lead to voting, which erroneously have been called discernment, it's important for us to differentiate between communal discernment and processes of decision-making or voting. In this chapter we will tackle these matters, as well as consider when we need communal discernment—and when it's better not to choose it.

When communal discernment is needed, it can transform hard problems or conflict into a means of grace and create belonging to one another as a form of "holy conferencing." Though that may sound miraculous, when we trust the Holy Spirit in our discernment together, we can receive gifts of belonging, consensus, and renewal.

Why We Need to Reclaim Communal Discernment

As we saw in the previous chapter, practices of prayer and discernment for making collective decisions have been a part of our history and tradition throughout church history. Yet sadly we've lost the form of the monastic chapterhouse meeting, or group spiritual direction, or the Ignatian Deliberation, or real holy conferencing. In the focus on rationality and "thinking" of the Enlightenment, many Christians abandoned spiritual practices, particularly those that included contemplation, deep listening, and silence.

This loss applied to Catholics and Protestants alike. For example, the Ignatian Deliberation practice was lost over time due to an emphasis on constitutional processes within the Jesuit order. However, the Roman Catholic Church in its Second Ecumenical Council of the Vatican (Vatican II) in the 1960s issued an invitation to reclaim practices of communal discernment among laity and clergy to find solutions to problems. Jesuits, with their history and charism (gift) for discernment, played a key role in in this reclamation work by translating Ignatius's writings, such as the *Spiritual Exercises,* into modern languages. This work of reclamation resulted in a renewal movement of Catholics who practiced forms of spiritual direction and four-week directed retreats on the *Spiritual Exercises*.[1] Jesuit priests such as Jules Toner and John Carroll Futrell then published works on communal discernment in the Ignatian tradition, which created a revival of such practices among Catholics.[2]

Among Methodists in the early United States, the practices of discernment as seen in the early class meetings, conferences, and quarterly meetings were lost. Sunday schools, which focused on teaching and information, replaced class meetings, which had an emphasis on mutual sharing and encouragement. American governmental processes of voting, parliamentary procedure, legislation, and business practices shaped church practices of decision-making more than scripture or more "traditioned" forms of discernment. Now, after a couple of centuries of legislative operations of church boards and assemblies, Christians of every variety are disgruntled with these processes and the institutionalism of their churches. With the resurgent interest in spiritual practices sparked by Vatican II and a postmodern quest for meaningful experiences, many church folk have a renewed interest in reclaiming communal discernment practices toward consensus.[3]

Let's consider a few reasons why we need to reclaim communal discernment for consensus.

1. Parliamentary Process and Roberts Rules of Order Aren't Christian Practices

Churches have forgotten or jettisoned the spiritual practices of discernment toward consensus in favor of the supposed efficiency and limitation of conflict through parliamentary process.⁴ In particular, procedures for church assemblies became standardized into Robert's Rules of Order, rather than from Christian life and practice. It's illuminating to understand how this happened.

Robert's Rules were developed in the 1860s and published in 1876 by a general in the US Army named Henry Martyn Robert. Born into a family of enslavers on a plantation in South Carolina, Robert's father emancipated people whom he owned, moved away from the South, became an American Baptist pastor and, eventually, the first president of Morehouse College (a historically Black college). Robert's mother's sympathies, however, stayed with the Confederacy and her family members, who remained enslavers. Indelibly shaped by the extreme tensions caused by slavery and the American Civil War in his family and life, Robert sought a way to prevent social catastrophe; people were literally throwing chairs at each other in church meetings. Frustrated by contentious and ineptly run meetings at his American Baptist Church, Robert drafted a legislative rule of order based upon Thomas Jefferson's rules for the US Congress. As Kent Puckett indicates in his article on Robert's Rules and race, the Rules provided his response to the real complications of the American violence of white supremacy and segregated democracy; his formal process and abstract language offered a method to displace the racial tensions raging in post-Civil War American life.⁵

However, these seemingly standardized and consistent rules didn't create a neutral process. Robert's Rules still gave cover to abuses of power and to those most adept at manipulating the rules to their advantage. His own daughter-in-law, Sarah Corbin Robert, utilized Robert's Rules of Order to justify the exclusion of a black singer, Marian Anderson, through a "whites only clause" for a performance in Washington DC, in 1939.⁶ The dry and complicated language and process of this parliamentary process privileges those with power to best decipher and use it.

What's more, these parliamentary rules offer no space for prayer or discernment on issues that really matter to a congregation. In church settings, the rules often feel dissatisfactory and clunky; most people don't fully know the Robert's Rules but know them enough to get confused on when something gets seconded and when it is time to call for a vote. Robert's Rules orient to the end of a vote and produce winning and losing factions. It's worth asking why churches, for their significant discernments, continue to use a cumbersome, complicated, and biased instrument from post-Civil War America that isn't based in Christian practices. Christians need to be experts in practices of prayer, not practices of parliament.

2. Voting and Compromise Create More Conflict Than Consensus

Another reason we need communal discernment practices is that the voting-based model of decision-making using parliamentary processes often leads to further division rather than cultivating consensus. The results of voting can unfold in several ways, which Larry Dressler describes in his book *Consensus through Conversation*. There could be a unanimous vote, in which everyone gets their "first choice" because they all agree. Everybody leaves happy, and the effort was minimal. This isn't discernment; it's a vote of people who were already on the same page. It doesn't really foster community or deepen relationship with God.

Majority voting, in which most people get their way but some do not, also does not create the harmony of consensus. The minority in this case might feel silenced and can start ripples of discontent and resistance. Parking lot meetings ensue. The minority can continue to cause conflicts in meetings and prevent the church from engaging proactively in mission and ministry.

Compromise, in which everyone gives up something important to them to arrive at a decision agreed upon by the whole, also does not engender consensus. Though sometimes efficient, compromise can result in a generalized feeling of dissatisfaction, low commitment to the decision, and passivity. Since nobody really likes or feels called to the decision or vote, often it is not implemented. People can feel irritated or frustrated and blame each other when no one fully gets their way, and no one wants to do the work.[7]

In the end, the tools of Robert's Rules of Order and other parliamentary processes haven't served congregations or denominational bodies well. The practice of taking votes by congregations often ends in people choosing sides and no one winning—least of all, God. We only wind up griping in the parking lot afterward. Consensus, in which we all commit to supporting a decision together through the guidance of the Holy Spirit, doesn't happen.

3. Voting Leads to Estrangement from One Another

A third reason we need to reclaim communal discernment is that voting leads to division and estrangement. We have lost sight of each other's humanity and the dignity in each person's story. Instead of upholding and telling our common story in the scripture and the history of the church (Tradition), and then interpreting our own lives through it, many of us have succumbed to telling only our version of the story in our churches. We've divided into separate camps based on who tells the Christian story or reads the Bible in the same way we do, and we've stopped listening to the diversity of ways in which God might be moving among us.

As a result, many of our churches remain mired in conflict. Sometimes the conflict festers within one congregation; sometimes it manifests between churches in the same neighborhood or region. Sometimes, as in the case of human sexuality, it ranges throughout a denomination. Many of us are tired and weary of being estranged from God, from each other, and from ourselves. Clergy are worn out and exhausted by voting processes that leave only more conflict in their wake. Lay and congregational leaders are disheartened and frustrated. Leaders are also disillusioned from so-called discernment processes that really are political maneuverings, full of disinformation and manipulation rather than the prayerful listening of true discernment.

4. We Need Movement Toward God's Desires, Not Our Desires

Another convincing reason we need to reclaim communal discernment toward consensus as a practice of faith is, as Luke Timothy Johnson observes in *Scripture and Discernment*, that it holds a greater capacity to nudge people toward God's desires, rather than our personal ones.[8] Votes generally represent people's personal desires. Using Robert's Rules of Order might restrain violence and chair throwing, but it doesn't soften people's defense mechanisms.

Discernment toward consensus through group spiritual direction can do this, helping people to relinquish personal vendettas or agendas. Most important, discernment as "faith seeking understanding" draws people closer to God and one another as they arrive at a decision they mutually support.

5. Communal Discernment Is a Means of Grace

A final reason we need to reclaim communal discernment for consensus is that it serves as a means of grace. John Wesley understood "holy conferencing"—or Christian gatherings for discernment, prayer, and worship—as an instituted (given by Jesus Christ) means of grace and urged his early Methodists to practice them regularly. Christians, particularly those in the Wesleyan tradition, need to reclaim practices of communal discernment because they lead us into the fullness of life with God. Communal discernment as "holy conferencing" holds the real potential for orienting congregations on the path God desires—and God's desires for us always hold love and grace. Through this practice a congregation taps into the movement of the Holy Spirit. The energy in the room shifts; a sense of God's presence fills the space, or a communal sense of peace or joy or freedom or wholeness dwells collectively in people's hearts. People leave after a communal discernment practice saying things like, "I feel centered and at peace. This has been holy ground." By so doing, they experience "holy conferencing"—a real means of grace.[9]

Through holy conferencing, people become true friends of one another. As a prudential means of grace, people practice holy conferencing through the spiritual discipline of loving each other as friends.[10] They enter into each other's stories on a particular problem, respect one another's perspectives and insights, and mutually pursue the common good. They might disagree and struggle with each other's opinions, but in the end they come to experience each other as a necessary part of the body of Christ and essential to one another's flourishing. It's common both during and after a communal discernment process for people to hug, cry, and linger in conversation. The beauty of something conflictual or problematic serving to bring us closer together as friends names the work of holy conferencing as a means of grace.

Communal Discernment Versus Decision Making/Voting

Now that we've considered why we need to reclaim communal discernment, let's bring even more clarity to the difference between communal discernment and decision-making or voting.

Decision-making by voting represents a school of thought and practice known as conflict resolution. "Conflict" describes the relational tension and "heat" that results from people's different approaches to a problem, or inequitable experience of a process, or challenge with people involved in a decision. Conflict resolution seeks to solve the conflict, whether its causation is the problem, the process, or the people.[11] Most church folk are familiar with this way of running meetings and addressing collective issues—running the church like a "business." In conflict resolution, people focus on the conflict as a problem that needs "fixing," and on how to do so in the most efficient way. Conflict resolution is a transactional practice in which the needs of both parties in the conflict are addressed. The conflict resolution process is time limited and focused upon negotiation. Ambiguity at the end of the process is deemed failure, and usually one side "wins" while the other "loses." The spirit of the process can be anxious and tense. While a problem might be solved, people aren't usually happy with the final resolution—or with one another.[12]

Conflict resolution uses Robert's Rules or other meeting management tools like it to resolve differences, conserve resources, maintain order, and produce an outcome. These decision-making processes use reason, logical thinking, and a strict process to efficiently arrive at a solution, often through a vote. For example, in a meeting agenda, the problem is named, solutions offered, pros and cons argued, a vote is called, the outcome is recorded.[13] In truth, Robert's Rules add extra work when something isn't that consequential, and the use of Robert's Rules often stimulates frustration and more conflict when it is.

By contrast, the process of conflict transformation views conflict as natural, normal, and necessary, instead of as a problem; conflict presents opportunity and disagreement invites engagement.[14] The focus in conflict transformation is on the people rather than the problem, and on healing relationships and structures while building creative solutions. Often, the problem is an injustice in which people were harmed, and the conflict exists because of this wounding. The most pressing matter isn't to resolve the "problem" but to identify the causes of distrust, understand one another, and begin building or rebuilding trust. The emotional dynamic of the process includes anxiety and fear, because talking through and naming these difficult feelings is the only path to healing.

Conflict transformation helps people to live into being with one another not as enemies but as friends. The other person is seen as a sibling and someone with whom the other party is called to cultivate healthier ways of interaction. Conflict transformation acknowledges that ambiguity is part of life and doesn't need to be "solved." In the process, space is made for all voices; but when a voice engages in racism, sexism, or other forms of harmful speech, it will be named as unsustainable. Success within conflict transformation is a renewed relationship and a collaborative plan that everyone fully supports.

As Jes Stolzfus Buller explains in *Peaceful Practices*, Christian communal

> **Other Forms of Conflict Transformation**
>
> Other forms of conflict transformation could include Native American circles where each person passes a "listening stick," or Truth and Reconciliation Commission, such as the one South Africa held after apartheid.

discernment could be classified as a spiritual discipline or practice within the discipline of conflict transformation.[15] Communal discernment, like other practices of conflict transformation, promotes understanding rather than persuasion or defense. The use of group spiritual direction for seeking God's path for a community gives space for each voice, fosters active listening, and shifts power dynamics to inclusion rather than exclusion. Buller observes, "If we intentionally invite God into our disputes and acknowledge God's presence in our conflicts, healthy dialogue becomes a spiritual practice . . . to draw near to God."[16] People let go of defenses and whatever they are holding onto, and learn to be patient, staying in a liminal space long enough for God's grace and strength to work through them. This is how conflict is transformed.

To help clarify the differences between deciding (forms of conflict resolution) and discerning (forms of conflict transformation), I've created the following chart, with inspiration from Susan Beaumont's work.[17] Both practices can serve the ordering of the life of the church and most churches will use a blend of the two, depending on the purpose and goals of the process. Working with your church leadership, you can select which approach best suits your needs and timelines.

Element	Decision-Making/Voting (Conflict Resolution)	Communal Discernment (Conflict Transformation)
Focus	The problem or issue	God's will or mission, relationships
Purpose	Solve the problem/restore order/produce outcome	Discern God's will through the Holy Spirit in our community
Process	Robert's Rules, management processes: define problem, look for causes, research alternatives/options, evaluate options, select/vote on options	Group spiritual direction for communal discernment: frame the issue, ground it in core principles, shed ego/biases, listen for Spirit, explore options, weigh options, test the decision
Time Frame	Limited, in accordance with meeting agenda or organizational calendar or deadline	Spacious, in the fullness of God's time—while also respecting organizational deadlines
Tools	Parliamentary procedures, majority rule/voting, decision models, use of reason/logic	Prayer/silence, listening, Scripture, storytelling, clearness committees, consolation/desolation
Human dynamics	Winners/losers, dissatisfaction with a compromise, low commitment to result, sometimes hierarchical leadership	Consensus, unity, high commitment, mutuality, leadership is shared

When to Choose Group Spiritual Direction for Communal Discernment

Not every decision in a church deserves the time, effort, and commitment that a communal discernment process toward consensus requires. Sometimes a church administrator needs to decide quickly who to call to fix a leaking pipe, or a new television screen needs to be purchased based on a short, fact-filled discussion. So, when is communal discernment a good option? Here are a few key elements to look for, adapted from lists provided by Ruth Haley Barton and Larry Dressler:

1. This is a high stakes decision. If the decision is made poorly and without congregational input, fragmentation and dissent could occur.
2. This decision concerns a community's identity, mission, policies, values, and direction.
3. Significant resources, whether money, human labor, energy, or time, need to be allocated for this decision.
4. Strong congregational support is needed for the implementation and support of the decision.
5. No single individual in the congregation has the authority or knowledge necessary to make the decision.
6. Different perspectives on the decision exist in the congregation, which need to be brought together.
7. A creative solution is needed that is not yet clear to the leadership team or congregation.
8. A congregation is longing for a means of grace and the gifts of group spiritual direction (see pages 277–79).
9. The congregation needs discernment on a decision or issue and holds mutual respect and trust for one another.[18]

For example, the church council of the church I assisted with communal discernment knew that tensions were running high. They had a high stakes decision to make regarding the church's stance on human sexuality, and they knew that a "quick" congregational vote would only lead to more dissension and division. They wanted broad congregational input and strong congregational support of the end decision; they clearly knew that no one individual, or even themselves as a leadership team, had the authority to make this decision without congregational affirmation and voice. The council clearly had experienced different perspectives on this issue and wanted to bring them together in a space of mutual conversation, reflection, and prayer. The church council longed for a creative, communal process to hear God's voice.

The council believed that the congregation could practice mutual respect and trust. Members of the LGBTQIA2S+ community had participated in the life and leadership of the congregation for decades; they served on committees, led Sunday school classes, and served on the church council. The church already had a couple of small groups that were intentionally affirming of the queer community. While people had felt hurt in the immediate aftermath of a denominational conference, the queer leaders at the church felt open to trust a communal discernment process. If trust had not been present, those emotions and issues would have needed to be acknowledged and aired at the beginning. In the case of this church, if the distrust had been too high, the congregation might have needed to back up and do practices of forgiveness and reconciliation before beginning a discernment about their stance on human sexuality.

When *Not* to Choose Group Spiritual Direction for Communal Discernment

There are times when group spiritual direction for communal discernment is *not* the best path to take. Larry Dressler says that consensus processes don't work when:

1. The decision is already determined. People know when their input matters, and when it is just a formality.
2. The decision isn't important enough to justify the time and energy necessary for a process.
3. The decision must be made quickly and under time pressure.
4. Individuals/groups important to the process refuse to participate.

5. Distrust is too high.
6. The congregation needs to practice forms of contemplative prayer and group spiritual direction first to learn how to prayerfully listen.

For the church I worked with on communal discernment, the decision wasn't predetermined and everyone on the church council felt strongly that the issue deserved copious offerings of time and energy for a communal discernment process. Leaders gifted with practices of contemplative prayer as well as some spiritual directors already were a part of the congregation and felt called to lead in the discernment process. If that hadn't been the case, a leadership team might have chosen to engage in group spiritual direction for friendship (part 1 of this book) first so that people could learn how to sit in silence, listen, and be open to the movement of the Holy Spirit. Those spiritual direction skills then would support the congregation in the work of communal discernment.

Of course, the process of communal discernment isn't perfect. Without a clear and strong framework, communal discernment can get hijacked by someone commandeering the process for their own opinions. People can baptize their position as "God's will" and "biblical" by splashing a Bible text into the conversation. Cliques also can dominate the process. Good leadership and a clear process and framework are necessary to enable a congregation to better attend to the Holy and avoid human dysfunction. Yet despite the imperfections in the process, the likelihood of continued dissension and dispute is far less in a discernment-to-consensus process rather than in a vote.

If the above reasons *not* to try communal discernment aren't present, then it's worth trying this spiritual practice and trusting in the Holy Spirit's work among you. The effort is worth it because you and your congregation just might be surprised by the gifts you will experience.

Three Gifts of Communal Discernment

There are many gifts of communal discernment, but for our purposes, let's consider three significant ones.

1. Belonging

The huge gift that can come out of practices of communal discernment is belonging. Rather than vote taking and side-taking, group spiritual direction for communal discernment offers a way to share our stories together on an issue before us. We listen to one another's perspectives and experiences. We drop our own defensiveness and rigidity about our own "rightness." As we seek the common story that the Holy Spirit is weaving for our life together, we emotionally and spiritually bond to each other such that we can overcome division and conflict between us.

The power of belonging through mutual storytelling is interwoven in our God-created humanity and increasingly supported through medical science. Out of his own medical practice and research, U.S. Surgeon Gen. Dr. Vivek Murthy asserts, "We are wired to associate belonging with the sharing of stories, feelings, memories, and concerns. The stories give meaning to our struggles, comfort us in times of suffering, and bond us. That's why our bodies relax, and our spirits lift when we connect in genuine friendship and love."[19] These strong emotional connections add joy and meaning to our lives and enable us to hear each other through any conflict. Group spiritual direction fosters belonging, which in turn fosters our ability to cooperate with each other and seek consensus.

2. Consensus and Unity

In a world of conflict and division, the church needs communal discernment practices that lead to consensus—to group solidarity and mutual commitment on a common issue or problem. As Susan Beaumont affirms, by using the ancient tools of communal discernment within Christian scripture and tradition, church communities can rediscover ways to make high-stake decisions that lead to consensus and promote an experience of unity in the Holy Spirit.[20]

Like belonging, we need consensus because it is wired into our survival as human beings. God created us to seek emotional consensus. Humans developed stories to record and cultivate such consensus so that, as Surgeon Gen. Murthy documents, "others can share our emotional reaction."[21] Psychologist Bill von Hippel's work argues that early humans lived together in small communities for mutual aid. Our ability to connect in social groups aided our survival as we shared information and coordinated goals for protection and for hunting food.[22] We sought emotional consensus with each other to develop trust. This trust not only enabled us to bring down a lion for food by cooperation, but also gave the security and relational networks to raise children together and to teach one another. Von Hippel writes, "We're the only animal on the planet that goes out of its way to share the contents of our minds with others, even when there is no immediate gain."[23] He explains that this learning enables us to get on the same page, understand each other, and cooperate better.

This human need for consensus and trust for learning remains vital for congregations seeking not only to survive but also to thrive in raising children, teaching the faith, and doing God's work. As we offer our stories on a particular issue before the congregation and develop empathy and insight, consensus becomes possible. The whole community sees the way God might be calling us on a question or issue, and we walk in it. We may begin with different opinions, but by participation in communal discernment, we listen our way into unity in the Spirit.

3. Renewal and Mission

The communal discernments we make inform our mission and ministry in our congregations and communities. Since God always desires more love, justice, and peace among people, God's desires for us will lead us into ministry with those who both reflect and need God's love. We come to see together how God is calling us to be faithful.

Conflict can be transformed into God's heart and mission for a community. A church fighting about what to do with its parking lot, for example, can discern a calling to become a site for a farmer's market that revitalizes the congregation. Conflict transformation becomes a means of grace—a way the Holy Spirit works to change a problem into missional possibilities. Instead of young adults fumbling to understand the arcane Robert's Rules of Order, they can become a part of renewed mission in the world. As I've said before, it may sound miraculous, but when we trust the Holy Spirit in our discernment together, wonders can happen.

NOTES

1. William Barry, "Toward Communal Discernment: Some Practical Suggestions" *The Way.* Supplement 58 (Spring 1987), 107.
2. Barry, "Toward Communal Discernment," 105.
3. Danny E. Morris and Charles M. Olsen, *Discerning God's Will Together: A Spiritual Practice for the Church*, 29. World Council of Churches, *Facilitating Dialogue to Build Koinonia in Churches and Moral Discernment* volume 3, Faith and Order Paper No. 235 (Geneva: WCC Publications, 2021). This publication offers a tool for dialogue for processes of moral discernment on p. 51. The WCC's extensive study of communal discernment indicates the global Christian desire for rediscovering ways to dialogue and make decisions on issues of moral concern.
4. Morris and Olsen, *Discerning God's Will Together,* 27–28.
5. Kent Puckett, "B-sides: Reading, Race, and Robert's Rules of Order," on Public Books: a magazine of ideas, arts, and scholarship. Accessed May 15, 2024 https://www.publicbooks.org/reading-race-and-roberts-rules-of-order/#:~:text=Henry%20Martyn%20Robert%20was%20born,bathos%2C%20%E2%80%9Cthe%20war%20came%20%E2%80%A6.
6. Allan Keiler, *Marian Anderson: A Singer's Journey* (Champaign: University of Illinois Press, 2002), 188.
7. Larry Dressler, *Consensus through Conversation,* (Oakland, CA: Berrett-Koehler Publishers, 2006), 7–9.
8. Luke Timothy Johnson, *Scripture and Discernment: Decision Making in the Church*, (Nashville: Abingdon, 1996), 23). Johnson argues that "Reaching decision in the church should be an articulation of faith." Since faith involves both intellectual commitments and active response, decisions about a congregation's life involves an active practice of discernment, or "faith seeking understanding," p. 26
9. John Wesley understood the instituted means of grace as those described and given by Jesus Christ, including prayer, worship, Communion, fasting, and holy conferencing. See chapter 2 for more description.
10. Ryan Andrew Newson, *Radical Friendship: The Politics of Communal Discernment* (Minneapolis: Fortress, 2017), 179–85. Newson argues that communal discernment allows friendship to develop from the practice of common judgment. He goes on to offer the friendship of Ann Atwater (a black female civil rights activist) and C. P. Ellis (a white male member of the Ku Klux Klan).
11. Lombard Mennonite Peace Center, "Conflict Transformation Skills for Churches," workshop manual, p. A1–3. Attended workshop May 14, 2024. The workbook describes conflict as caused by people, process, or problems.
12. Dr. Nina Balmaceda and Dr. Yvette Pressley, "Conflict Transformation" (lecture given at Lutheran Theological Southern Seminary in MIN 540 Leadership in God's Mission class, October 31, 2022).
13. Susan Beaumont, *How to Lead When You Don't Know Where You're Going* (Lanham, MD: Rowland and Littlefield, 2019), 71–72.
14. Lombard Mennonite Peace Center, "Conflict Transformation Skills for Churches," workshop manual, p. D1. Attended workshop May 14, 2024.

15. Jes Stoltzfus Buller, *Peaceful Practices: A Guide to Healthy Communication in Conflict*, ed. Kirstin De Mello and Ed Nyce, (Mennonite Central Committee, 2021), 7.
16. Buller, *Peaceful Practices*, 7.
17. Beaumont, *How to Lead When You Don't Know Where You are Going*, 73. Her chart on a "Deciding Approach versus a Discerning Approach really informed my own chart.
18. Larry Dressler, *Consensus through Conversation*, 6–7. Ruth Haley Barton, *Pursuing God's Will Together: A Discernment Practice for Leadership Groups* (Downers Grove, IL: Intervarsity Press, 2012), 174–75.
19. Vivek Murthy, *Together: The Healing Power of Human Connection in a Sometimes Lonely World* (New York: Harper Collins, 2020), 32. Murthy goes on to detail the hormones and neurotransmitters in the body such as oxytocin, dopamine, and endorphins that release when we feel connection, or promote us to seek connection when we feel lonely, p. 33
20. Beaumont, *How to Lead When You Don't Know Where You're Going*, 71.
21. Murthy, *Together*, 31.
22. Murthy, 29–30. Murthy references a conversation he had with psychologist Dr. Bill von Hippel, who wrote *The Social Leap*. Murthy also cites and calls upon John Cacioppo's work on loneliness.
23. Murthy, 31. Murthy is quoting from an apparent conversation that he had with von Hippel.

8.

Understanding the Process of Communal Discernment

> As the congregation I was leading through communal discernment gathered in their fellowship hall on a summer afternoon, they knew that they were meeting to reflect together on the question of whether to affiliate with Reconciling Ministries Network (an organization seeking the inclusion of people of all sexual orientations and gender identities in both the policy and practices of the denomination) and become a "Reconciling Church." Through a comprehensive communications, education, and information process, they understood that this wasn't a congregational vote. Instead, the church members knew four discernment sessions would occur that summer that would be based on learning, listening, and discernment. As they took cookies and lemonade and settled in circles of blue chairs, a couple of members commented that they didn't know exactly "how" this gathering would function but they were eager to participate and contribute their voice.

Many of us are unfamiliar with the "how" of communal discernment because we've never experienced it. "Discernment" has sometimes been used to name more political processes of rhetoric, campaigning, and voting rather than sacred listening. As Ruth Haley Barton has observed, many church folk have little experience with discernment as a Christian practice of distinguishing what is God's will and desire for our lives. Many of us don't know how to listen for the One true voice of God with and for a community.[1]

This chapter is meant to teach you the "how" of communal discernment so that you can be led by the Holy Spirit closer to one another and closer to who God is calling you to be as a beloved community while prayerfully seeking God's leading on a particular issue, question, or problem.

There are twelve steps in this practice of communal discernment to consensus, ordered here like a worship service in four parts (see pages 273–76 in the appendix for a handout on these steps: Guide to the Process of Communal Discernment for Consensus). The pattern of the four-fold worship practice (Entrance, Proclamation and Response, Communion, Sending Forth) reminds people of God's abiding presence in the work, affirms the Christian ethics involved in discernment, and provides a familiar ordering to the process—though the discernment isn't itself a worship service. The story of the church I assisted in the practice of communal discernment to consensus (which I have referenced elsewhere in this book) serves as an example throughout the chapter (see also Sample Outline of One Church's Communal Discernment Process Using Group Spiritual Direction, pages 286–88 in the appendix).

At the end of the chapter, I discuss a shorter, more succinct practice of discernment for a church council or committee meeting. Discernment can occur in a one-hour meeting or in a multi-month congregation-wide process. Your process may vary as appropriate to your context, community, and the issue for discernment. Whatever the process may look like for your community, remember that God is with you as you do this holy work of discerning God's will.

I. Entrance: Preparing for Discernment

Step 1: Prayerful Preparation (prayer, framing the question, communication)

Practices of prayer make such a difference in preparing hearts and spirits for the work of communal discernment. Participants can be encouraged to pray over their community's upcoming practice of discernment, asking God to guide their minds and help them to confess anything that might keep them from openness to the Holy Spirit—grudges against the leadership or other participants; feelings of anger, fear, or worry; or their own sense of the "rightness" of their opinion or position. People engaged in discernment must also be engaged in prayer as a foundational discipline so they may have the capacity to hear and know God's voice and be transformed by it.

Practices of Prayer

Christian tradition abounds with different kinds of prayer that can be utilized—reading the Psalms or other scriptures, using a devotional book, or practicing fixed-hour prayer (Morning, Midday, or Evening prayer, often found in hymnals or prayer books such as the *Book of Common Prayer*). Practices such as centering prayer, in which we listen for God in silence, are extremely helpful. Other practices of silent listening, such as journaling, mindful walking, or repetitive reading of a short passage of scripture, can deepen our capacity to hear the leading of the Holy Spirit's voice (see the handout Contemplative Spiritual Practices to Support Listening to God, pages 252–58 in the appendix). Your leadership team might provide practices such as a prayer walk around the campus or an intentional prayer service/time before the process begins. You also might invite participants to practice fasting—from food or from media—to prepare physically and mentally for the discernment process. Those who have practiced group spiritual direction before this time of discernment will have excellent preparation for a process of community discernment.

Framing the Question

Usually, the leadership team offers a clear statement of the question or issue for discernment before the process begins. This framing of the subject for discernment gives focus and boundaries on the key "gist" of the issue. What is this work together about and what is it not? The real question for discernment (not the most strategic, easy, or obvious question) will always include the heart of God or the mind of Christ as essential to the discernment. A framing question might be, "What is God's will for the future of the worship service at our church?" You might invite participants to better frame the question or issue for discernment as an early part of the process. Then pray over the framed question for discernment together, refraining from developing individual answers or solutions and staying open to the presence of God.

Informational Sessions/Communication

Your faith community may hold informational sessions or distribute communication on the discernment process before it begins. You might offer the framed question for discernment in this communication so that the congregation is clearly aware of the specific work of discernment before them. Make it clear that attendance in any of these sessions—or attention to emails, newsletters, or announcements—will greatly aid in prayerful participation. Encourage participants to pay attention so that they do not miss out on these educational and communication efforts.

> A person on the discernment team who was gifted in prayer led several congregational prayer walks around the church building in the month leading up to the start of the discernment process. Everyone could participate in this prayer. The process was prayed over in church meetings and in the worship services prior to its commencement. The clergy and church leadership encouraged each person to be in prayer as well.
>
> The framing question for the discernment process, which the church council formulated in advance was the discernment of whether or not to become a Reconciling Church. The framing of the question came out of the congregation's long affiliation with Reconciling Ministries Network (RNM) through adult Sunday school classes and small groups; deciding whether or not to affiliate as a whole congregation seemed like the next right step. The church council and communications staff extensively communicated the framing question and the process to the congregation six weeks prior to the start of the discernment sessions through email, church newsletters, pulpit announcements, social media, and in person by small group/Sunday school leaders.
>
> The prayerful preparation also included two informational sessions staffed by a retired clergyperson and a respected member of the

church council. These sessions communicated about the church's process and what Reconciling Ministries Network is, allowing time and space for questions and answers. A handout on frequently asked questions was available as well. People also could use a designated email address and phone line for communication of any questions and concerns in advance.

Step 2: Gathering

Your congregation's practice of communal discernment could be in a retreat setting, or a "day apart" at the church, or a series of meetings over a period of time. As participants arrive, have them turn off any distracting devices such as phones and commit to be fully present, coming into the space in a spirit of prayer. Encourage everyone to practice openheartedness to the people who are there and to the practice of discernment before the group. Invite them to look for the face of God in the faces of those around them—especially in the faces of those they think might hold a different position.

Determine in advance who will serve in a role in the process. Some possible roles include:

- Prayer intercessor—someone gifted and called to uphold the group in prayer as they proceed. (A prayer intercessor may be in the room or off-site and may or may not participate in the process.)
- Sage—a wise elder or saint who is trustworthy and holds great experience or expertise in the area being discerned.
- Facilitator/spiritual director/discernamentarian—the person supporting and leading the process. This person may or may not be a member of the faith community and holds great experience in listening and in the facilitation of groups.
- Scribe/secretary—the person who can keep good notes and record the significant conversations and agreements in the process. (This written documentation ensures greater accuracy and confirmation of the discernment process—and records how God has been active.)

- Teacher/expert—a person with expertise or knowledge on the issue being discussed, who provides content and experience for discernment.
- Staff/key volunteers—those who may carry out the course of the discernment and its action items.
- Leadership team—those who have constructed the discernment process and done the work of preparation.
- Circle leaders—a person within each small group who helps to guide and support the process of communal discernment within this circle.[2]

If the gathering is large, there may be several circles of chairs for the small groups in the space. Alternatively, you might begin in a large space (the worship space), move to smaller rooms for discernment, and then come back again into the large space. The facilitator may invite participants to sit with different people and even do "sorting" games (by assigning numbers or inviting longtime members to sit with new members), encouraging them to be open to whoever sits with them in the circle of discernment and whatever movements to different spaces they might be asked to make.

The gathering might include a short time of worship with singing and prayer, a fixed-hour prayer (morning or evening prayer), a practice of *lectio divina*, or the simple lighting of a candle and a time of silence. The gathering should be in a sacred space that feels safe and invitational.

The facilitator invites everyone to take a breath and open themselves to God's presence as they enter the task of discernment ahead.

> The gathering took place in the fellowship hall. Eight chairs were arranged in each of ten circles, with no tables. Circle leaders arranged themselves so that one person was already in each circle. As the facilitator, I greeted people as they came in and welcomed the guest speaker. At the beginning, I invited the people who were fans of the local college team to stand and disperse among the circles, and then those of the state college rival to stand and disperse themselves. This mixed people up and brought some laughter. Once everyone settled into their seats, I invited them to briefly introduce themselves and share why they had joined this church community.

Step 3: Covenant Making

According to Ruth Haley Barton, covenant-making in a discernment process includes creating a structure of public accountability for the process and sets expectations for participants' and leaders' behavior to one another and with God.[3] Like a monastic rule and John Wesley's General Rules, a written covenant establishes a "rule of life" for your community—guidelines and accountability for how you will live your life together. By agreeing to the covenant, people commit publicly to these expectations and promise to be held accountable to them. It's not a foolproof way to prevent egregious or harmful behavior, but it provides a significant practice to create safety, build trust, and engender mutuality in the work. In communal discernment, three to four covenant guidelines tend to be sufficient—people can't remember and hold more than that. Here are some possible guidelines culled from my own experience and several other sources:

1. Practice presence
    - Be open to God's transforming presence and grace
    - Honor the image of God in each other.
    - Be here now (and turn off electronic devices)

2. Listen Well
    - Listen in a compassionate and empathetic way.
    - Listen to the inner heart of speech.
    - Listen without trying to fix, save, analyze, advise, or correct others. Don't interrupt.
    - Listen to the group as a whole; hold your desires and opinions lightly
    - Listen in any silences—silence is God's first language.

3. Be Attentive
    - Uphold the discernment process and these guidelines/covenant.
    - Refrain from side conversations or references.

- Be aware of sharing—let all speak a first time before speaking a second time.
- Attend to your experience and speak for yourself only. Use "I" statements.

4. Practice Wonder
- If your inner life becomes turbulent because of conflict, turn to wonder. Ask questions of yourself such as, "I wonder what my reaction teaches me about my own life. I wonder what in the other person's life shaped them to hold this belief. I wonder what the other person could be feeling right now?"
- Offer open-ended questions that invite further exploration and reflection. For example, "I wonder where God is in this for you?"

The covenant might be displayed on a screen or handout and should be written and visible throughout the process. The facilitator might ask participants to initial or sign a printed form of the guidelines or offer their verbal consent and commit to upholding the covenant, emphasizing that it matters for the health and success of the process.

In my work as the facilitator in the discernment process for the church I was assisting, I developed the following five covenant guidelines in consultation with the leadership team.

- The circles are representative of the ongoing circle of the Holy Spirit's work among and through participants.
- The circles are a place of holy listening.
- What is said in the circle is a gift.
- There is no cross talk and no questions as someone is sharing.
- The highest confidentiality is honored within the circles.

The guidelines established that this is a discernment process in which we receive the other persons and their sharing in the circle as gift, not as opinions to be challenged. I gave the large group time for any questions and feedback. Everyone assented with raised hands to uphold the agreed-upon covenant. I reiterated the covenant at each subsequent discernment session.

Step 4: Guiding Principle(s)

A clear guiding principle, according to Barton, sets the boundaries for the process and affirms a core value or belief of the faith community in connection to the issue or question for discernment.[4] As Morris and Olsen clarify, it is shaped by the ethics, beliefs, and purpose of the discerning community.[5] A small group doing discernment (such as a church council or ministry team) could establish their own principles; for a large group or congregational-wide discernment, it's best if the leadership team establishes the guiding principle and then communicates it in the beginning of the process.

> The guiding principle of the church where I was serving as communal discernment facilitator expressed qualities of inclusive love and grace for all people, which were qualities that the church council wanted the discernment process to embody. During a high stakes conflict, the council's commitment to a guiding principle of inclusivity helped the church to discern how God might be moving them toward healing and reconciliation in their church community.

II. Word and Response: Discerning God's Will Together

Step 5: Prayer of "Shedding" (or Prayer for Indifference)

The group now moves into more of the active work of discernment, which starts with the work of letting go of anything that separates us from God. As Susan Beaumont explains, in a practice of "shedding," people "name and lay aside anything that might prevent the group from focusing on God's will as the ultimate outcome."[6] This might include any biases and expectations for the outcome to go "your" way. It involves both an individual and a communal "letting go" of the process. Shedding invites us to ask, "What needs to die in us individually and collectively so that we can discern God's gifts and leading?"[7]

This time of shedding could be called the prayer for indifference, which has roots in both Ignatian and Quaker spirituality. Rather than meaning "not caring" or "not interested," the principle of indifference means 'I am indifferent to my own ego, desire for prestige, power or control, need for approval, or pride.' It means that a person and the group value the doing of God's will more than their own personal agendas. In a prayer for indifference, a person or group asks, "What will I shed so that I will be open to new gifts of grace or unexpected forms of ministry?' The practice of indifference isn't easy or natural; it's hard to let go of cherished opinions or interests for the sake of the collective whole.

Having a clear process of naming, talking out, praying over, and shedding any impediments to indifference can help a group to be ready to practice discernment to consensus. Then, the facilitator can lead a "check-in" to determine if anyone is still attached to a certain outcome. Quakers call this "testing for indifference." The facilitator may ask, "How many are indifferent to all but God's will?"[8] They may give a space for verbal sharing on obstacles to openness to God's direction. Participants might confess that they are still holding onto their own opinion, or that they've invested lots of "sweat equity" already in an issue and are struggling to let that go. The rest of the group receives this honest sharing with grace and trust and commits to ongoing prayer for those still struggling with indifference.

> *Indifference*—valuing God's will more than your own personal agenda

Several concrete practices can help with the act of shedding. People can be invited to write down what they need to shed on index cards. After folding them, the cards are collected in a basket or offering plate in which they remain visible until after the discernment process is complete. Participants also might shape clay or draw art that represents the baggage they need to discard. The shedding could include a prayer of confession as a way of collectively naming what needs to be let go so that the group may be open to the leading of God.

These practices may not bring all in the group to a perfect state of relinquishment; letting go of ego and our own baggage comes from God's grace. We pray for indifference so that God might give us beyond our own limited expectations. Once group members have done their best effort at shedding their own biases, the process moves on with trust in the grace of the Holy Spirit for our own imperfect human practice. As Ruth Haley Barton suggests, this step of the process might conclude with a prayer for wisdom in the spirit of James 1:5—"If any of you is lacking in wisdom, ask God, who gives to all generously and ungrudgingly, and it will be given you" (James 1:5-8).[9]

> The church I was facilitating in the discernment process didn't do an intentional process of shedding, confession, or indifference, but that would have been helpful. As Dietrich Bonhoeffer indicates, "The community of Christ can only be formed when individual 'wish dreams' have been shattered" for the larger sake of life together.[10] Thankfully, the people were able to let go of personal agendas without an intentional practice of indifference.

Step 6: Prompt and Centering Silence

The prompt serves as "something" to center everyone at the beginning of the discernment work. The prompt chosen by your congregation's leadership team might be a selection from scripture, a reading from church tradition, an image/artwork/photograph, a selection of music, or a prayer. It also might be a short time of teaching or information sharing on the topic on which your church is practicing discernment or a restatement of the framing question for discernment. The lead team or facilitator might share the history of the circumstances that have brought this issue or question of discernment to the fore and any thought or research they've expended on this issue already.

The prompt offers something that can collectively gather people's hearts, minds, and spirits. This "third thing" between the people and the Holy Spirit, as Parker Palmer would call it, serves to center people, gives a common source for reflection, and focuses the discernment process.[11] As Morris and Olsen note, this step of "rooting" in the biblical, theological, historical, or musical tradition of the church undergirds the discernment work with a unifying language and story.[12]

The facilitator might offer a period of silence after the sharing of the prompt for you to reflect on God's direction of your community. This could involve sending you from the main meeting space for a time of solitude and prayer, or it might simply be a few moments of silence in your seat. The facilitator might offer suggestions on how to enter the silence. Some possibilities for reflection include:

- Pay attention to a word, phrase, lyric, aspect of the image, or part of the teaching that speaks to you for the question of discernment and pray with that gift in the silence.
- Pay attention to what is rising up as significant for you from the prompt. Perhaps it brings forth a memory or resonates for you in some way. Be aware of what brings joy and peace (consolation) or if you are feeling stress or concerned (desolation). Take a moment to dedicate these insights and feelings to the direction of the Holy Spirit.

Silence plays a significant role throughout a discernment process to aid a group in hearing God's calling in the issue. Silence helps us to hear the inner promptings of the Holy Spirit. Silence sharpens our awareness of our sense of joy, peace, gentleness, wonder, and goodness—which are signs of God's movement. Silence readies us to hear God, in whatever forms God might communicate to us. It may feel strange and awkward to sit and be in silence, but trust that God is at work among you in the quiet.

> The "prompt" portion of the discernment process was quite substantive and rooted in scripture and tradition. As the facilitator, I described the biblical model of discernment in Acts 15 of the Jerusalem Council and read a short portion of that scripture. I then shared quotes from John Wesley's "Catholic Spirit" sermon and shared of Wesley's own practice of being of "one heart though we are not of one opinion" in issues of theological disagreement.[13] I also lifted up Wesley's exhortation to practice love of God and love of neighbor, which he repeated consistently

throughout his sermons and writings. I then invited them to listen for a word or phrase that stood out to them in the forthcoming teaching time with the speaker. In effect, I was using the so-called Quadrilateral, which includes Scripture, tradition, reason, and experience.

Step 7: Holy Listening and Exploring

This step is the heart of group spiritual direction as a practice of communal discernment. We practice holy listening both to God and to other human beings to hear the direction the Holy Spirit is leading us together. This form of listening is very different from common forms of communication in meetings or gatherings. Ruth Haley Barton offers these guidelines for holy listening:

- Listen with your whole self (senses, feelings, imagination, reasoning).
- Stay fully focused on what each person says, without formulating a mental response.
- Don't challenge or question what others say. Don't interrupt or offer rebuttals.
- Reflect prayerfully on what a speaker has said, allowing silence before the next speaker.
- Hold your desires and opinions gently. Be open to receiving what others say.[14]

There are many different ways that your congregation or community might practice holy listening. You might start with one practice and shift to another. Keep an open heart and mind, continually listening to God and trusting that the Holy Spirit is guiding you through the practice of discernment, even if things alter or change. Listening might extend beyond the people in each gathering to include surveys, interviews, and focus groups prior to or during the discernment process. Asking "Whose voices do we need to hear for this discernment?" might encourage the faith community to reach out to people who are on the margins or "edge" to bring their voices more to the center. (For handouts about different forms of holy listening from the Christian tradition that your community might use in your communal discernment process—group spiritual direction (monastic tradition), Ignatian Deliberation, the Quaker "Sense of the Meeting," and the Wesleyan Quadrilateral—see chapter 6 and pages 277–85 in the appendix.)

After the "prompt" of the twenty-minute teaching period, the group reflected on a set of questions in a kind of *lectio divina* practice. The questions were:

1. When the speaker was speaking, what one word or phrase captured your attention? (After a minute of silence, the circle members shared just their word or phrase.)
2. What in your past or present life made that word or phrase speak to you? What in your life caused that word to captivate your attention? (After a short time of silence, members had two minutes to share, with the facilitator keeping time. This was a strict listening practice with no feedback given by the circle.)
3. If Jesus is sitting beside you right now, what would you say to Jesus about that phrase or word? What do you think Jesus would say back? (After a short time of silence, members had two minutes to share, with the facilitator keeping time. This was a listening practice, with no feedback given by the circle)

People shared on each question in their circles, with the circle leader facilitating the process. The short time of sharing still allowed for significant and substantive storytelling and profound listening to other people's experiences by the circle members.

In addition to these discernment practices, holy listening might include any necessary learning on the issue or question at hand. This learning or exploring could be guided by the question "What are the possible options within our guiding principles, and what more do we need to know about those options?" The leadership team or designated participants could research whatever learning might be needed—identifying possibilities, evaluating options, and discarding those that don't uphold the guiding principles.[15] Possibilities for exploration might include:

- Pertinent data on the question—demographic analysis, financial reports, government reports/data, statistics, surveys, expert advice as appropriate to the issue.
- Voices from the community—interviews, focus groups, wise ones with experience in the issue, those who will be impacted by the discernment.
- Scripture—Are there scriptures that offer guidance on the options we are considering? Is there a theme from scripture that supports our work of discernment on this option?
- Tradition—Are there resources from the larger church tradition or history, or from our own denominational or congregational/community history, that might provide insight or guidance on the options before us?[16]
- Experience—Are there any stories from the church's history that might inform the current discernment? Could mission or vision statements shape the discernment?

After the data is gathered, the lead team can summarize, distill, or interpret the data for presentation of the best options to the larger group. It's easy to be "captured" by the data and allow discernment gatherings to devolve into decision-making based upon the data. If that happens, the facilitator can draw the gathering back into silence, holy listening, and discernment—and away from trying to find answers in the data.[17] The goal in the time of exploring is to remain focused on learning about the best options without getting captured too soon by the desire for an outcome.

> The leadership team performed the first part of exploration prior to the discernment sessions. The leaders decided that the best option for a response was to decide whether to affiliate as a congregation with Reconciling Ministry Network. Other possible options of response—including disaffiliation from the denomination (not popular), or doing

nothing, or continuing to support small groups/classes joining RMN—weren't satisfactory to the church council. The lead team presented research and information on joining RMN through the information sessions before the actual discernment began.

The second part of "exploring" occurred during the discernment sessions as experts, teachers, and experienced church members taught on different topics related to the discernment for about twenty minutes. The learning on issues of scripture, tradition, and the church helped guide and inform the discernment.

Step 8: Life-giving Responses

Participants now have an opportunity to respond in various ways to all they have heard and shared—from sharing responses, to improving, to weighing, and finally to silent listening. Let's consider each one briefly.

Responding

The facilitator might offer open-ended questions that explore how God might be at work in this issue of discernment. The facilitator could offer guiding questions such as:

- What is your prayer now in this (issue of discernment/from the prompt)?
- What is your soul's longing in this issue? How would you like for God to satisfy that soul's longing?
- How might the Spirit be whispering to you in this situation or issue of discernment?

These questions are offered without an expectation of an answer from everyone. Rather, the questions guide the group further into hearing how God is at work in the issue before them.

In a large gathering, the responses to the question on preferential options might be gathered in small groups, distilled by circle leaders, and then shared by the facilitator. The facilitator listens for a sense of best options that are arising and then take those options down as a "minute," or as the choice with the most affirmation. These affirmed options even could be taken down on newsprint or on a screen/board.

Improving

As the group listens together, they may discern an option that is good but needs improvement. The facilitator could lead the group with questions such as, *Is the Spirit inviting any improvements to that path or option? Might the Spirit be inviting us to combine the best out of two options to create a new "best" third option?*

This work of "improving" could involve inviting individual silent prayer and then moving to holy listening together around what the Spirit has given as improvements. Small groups also could listen together, taking notes on the improvements that come to them and then sharing them with the larger group. The larger group then could listen for what improvements the Holy Spirit is leading them to adopt. The facilitator then summarizes the improvements and offers the altered options, asking questions such as, *Does the option with improvements capture both the discussion and the way the Spirit is leading us? Are we comfortable with moving to the next step?* If anyone is uncomfortable, the group listens to that person's concerns and adjusts as needed.

Weighing

This next step, called "weighing," requires a trust in the indwelling Spirit of God as actively engaged, as well as the employment of all the wisdom possible in human judgment. The discernment group now moves toward affirming a path or option that has been identified and improved. A question the facilitator might ask is: *Upon which option or path will the Spirit rest?*[18] This is called "placing a path near the heart" to see if it brings joy and peace (consolation)—even if the work seems challenging or difficult.[19]

If the group needs more help to reach clarity, the facilitator or lead team can utilize a variety of different discernment tools to weigh the best option in discernment. Some of those "weigh options" could include:

- *Fruits of the Spirit*—What option brings love, joy, peace, patience, kindness, goodness, faithfulness, gentleness, self-control (Galatians 5:22-23)?

- *Good upon Good*—No weaknesses are found in the options under consideration. Victoria Curtiss, in her *Guidelines for Communal Discernment writes that* each person prays over the good in each and asks the Spirit which one has the "weightier good." Participants pray in silence for where the Holy Spirit rests and which one draws them closer to God. The group gathers and names the good in each option. "Good is added to good," until the one option with the weightier good becomes clear.[20]
- *Ignatian Deliberation*—Basically testing the cons and pros of each option. (See the handout Ignatian Deliberation in Communal Discernment to Consensus, pages 280–81 in the appendix).
- *Ignatian Examen*—Each person prays over each option and lists which one brings consolation (joy, peace, God's presence) or Desolation (drained, negativity, God's absence). They may gather and share their lists, and a collective list could be tabulated. Then, each person prays again silently over what they have heard. They reconvene, working until all receive consolation. (See handout Ignatian Deliberation in Communal Discernment to Consensus on pages 280–81 in the appendix.)
- *Biblical Theological Exploration*—explore how an option resembles a Bible story and what insight the story, a character, or the teaching in the story might offer. Alternatively, the group could be led to use their imagination to place themselves in the story (Ignatian imagination).
- *Guided Imagery*—1) Select a symbol or a picture (could use Google images or other online sites to find pictures/symbols) to represent the best options or paths. Sit with the picture, praying yourself into it. What does God say to you about the option that the picture represents as you sit with it? When you have rested with the picture long enough, say goodbye to it, receiving what you need from God to take back to the larger

group. 2) Envision a favorite space or place. Imagine a wise and holy person coming to meet you in that space as a spiritual director. Share with them about the option or path before you. What guidance does the sage offer to you about the options? Listen and sit with what you receive. When the time is ready, say goodbye to the sage and come back into the space with the rest of the group.[21]

Any of these tools assist in giving "weight" to the option that lies best within God's will. This step of weighing requires spiritual and emotional maturity from the group and a real trust that the Holy Spirit is present and at work in this process. It always amazes me that the Spirit does indeed work when we give space for the Spirit to do so; clarity on the best option(s) will emerge.

Silence to Hear God (Intercessory Prayer)

After "weighing" the options, the facilitator may guide you into a time of silent listening. In this silence, you are listening for how God is speaking into the issue of discernment. Possible questions in this time might be:

- God, what is your prayer for this process of discernment?
- What do you want my prayer to be?
- Is there anything I need to surrender to you to join your prayer for this congregation? What in me stands in the way (my judgment, my curiosity, my need to solve the problem or to try to make someone happy?)
- What invitation might you (God) be offering me through my fellow circle member's stories?
- Upon what option are you resting?
- Where do I feel energy, inspiration, or God's presence?
- Where do I feel negative, tired, frustrated, isolated, or alone (God's absence)?

Ask God to help you hear how God is guiding you individually and the church collectively.

> As the facilitator, I guided the group gently from the "holy listening" step in the circles to a time of collective silence. I indicated that this was a time to listen for God, including how God was directing our community on the question of affiliating with RMN. "What is God's prayer for us in this decision?" We listened in silence for a minute or so.

III. Communion: Communal Discernment to Consensus

Step 9: Reflection on Consensus

After the holy listening and the time of life-giving responses, with active improvement and weighing of options, the time comes to test for consensus on an option or path before the gathering.

Stating the "Minute"

The facilitator, in consultation with the leadership team as needed, could state the best, refined option for the congregation. This step is called "stating the minute" in Quaker tradition. As Victoria Curtiss describes, it's also called "floating a trial balloon," in which the facilitator makes a summary statement that expresses where the Holy Spirit is leading the congregation.[22]

Sense of the Meeting

Then, the facilitator could call for a testing of consensus, checking for what Quakers call "the sense of the meeting." In the Quaker tradition, unity at this point means that the community has discerned God's will, because unity indicates Christ's being and work.[23] Indeed, for Christians, consensus comes by arriving together at the common ground of God's will or heart—often by weaving together a stronger idea or solution than anyone could have come up with on their own.[24]

The facilitator can then ask if this articulated decision, or "minute," seems to reflect God's will to the best of each person's ability to discern it. Danny Morris and Charles Olsen offer these statements that can help people determine where they are on the path to consensus:

- I agree fully without reservation with the discernment as stated. (consensus)
- I agree but with some reservation. However, I can go forward in peace and fully support the decision as stated. (consensus)
- I don't agree, but I feel comfortable deferring to those who have greater wisdom on this and to the consensus of the body. I will support the decision as stated. (consensus)
- I don't agree and cannot go forward. I need further time for prayer and discernment. (non-consensus)[25]

Another method of testing consensus is the five finger method. In this method, participants hold up the number of fingers to convey their level of support for the trial balloon, or "minute." Virgina Curtiss narrates the method this way:

- "Five fingers = I am fully supportive.
- Four fingers = I am mostly in agreement and am willing to support the majority.
- Three fingers = I have concerns or reservations; I'm not persuaded and need to hear more from the supporters.
- Two fingers = I am somewhat opposed and have concerns.
- One finger = I cannot support this at this time."[26]

Generally, if all participants are at five or four, the group is at consensus. If people indicate three or below, more discernment needs to happen.

Using colored cards throughout the discernment is another way to assess consensus. For example, a green card can indicate support while a red card signifies opposition. The World Council of Churches uses colored cards in their global Assemblies to gauge support for proposals, avoid repetitious speeches/actions, and assist the movement to consensus.

If anyone raises concerns or offers reservations, welcome them. The person offering the concern might be offering a word of truth that the whole group needs to hear. These concerns indicate that the Spirit is still at work and that the stated option might need some refinement, or a new option or decision might be the right direction. The facilitator or another clerk records any concerns. If consensus doesn't seem possible and the group remains divided, Susan Beaumont suggests several options for continuing group discernment:

- Repeat the discernment process. Shed any concern for outcome. Restate the guiding principle(s). Offer a prompt, which could be a restated option or "minute" raised out of the concerns. Participate in life-giving responses. Improve and weigh the options.
- Make space for silent prayer and individual discernment. The group might need a break, a chance to refresh and go on a walk, or time for individual silent prayer. This break might be for minutes or days or a month between gatherings.
- Decide by majority. Although not full consensus, this may be the best option if a decision is pressing and needs to be made to meet a deadline.
- Drop the discernment. If there is no clear leading and the decision can wait, the group might decide that they will stop discernment on the matter. They may celebrate the process and what they have learned. The gathering might take up the process again at another time or simply let it rest.[27] This isn't failure, this is faithfulness.

The facilitator might lead a consensus check to make a choice on these options, or discern with the leadership team the way the gathering is being led. Deliberate care and affirmation of every voice in the process will confer credibility to whatever the outcome might be.

If the group reaches consensus, there will be a sense of connection, unity, and purpose in the space; people will feel bonded to one another and to the decision they've discerned together. They will feel energy for the work of implementation before them. The belonging, friendship, and unity experienced in the Holy Spirit will give common purpose and even joy.

> I stated the "minute"—or really the three possible options all together—and explained that they were to close their eyes and silently raise their hands for their choice. In this way, I was gathering the "sense of the meeting."

- "Are you comfortable with the church becoming a part of Reconciling Ministries Network? If so, silently raise your hand." (silence as hands were raised and circle facilitators counted them)
- "Are you NOT comfortable with becoming a part of RMN?" (silence as hands were raised and circle facilitators counted them)
- "Are you unsure about becoming a part of RMN?" (silence as hands were raised and circle facilitators counted them).

This time of response was silent and quiet. However, it also clearly showed people's leadings to the lead team. By the time of the fourth discernment session, I felt moved by the Spirit to invite everyone to open their eyes and keep their hands raised. As everyone looked up and saw all their hands raised, the sense of wonder at the spirit of unity rippled throughout the room. People audibly took deep breaths, offered sighs of relief/amazement, and visibly smiled. Clearly, the congregation was at a place of consensus on affiliating with RMN. By listening together to the Spirit in circles of group spiritual direction, we could see the unfolding of God's work in each other's hearts and thus determine more clearly how God was calling us to go.

Step 10: Resting the Decision

The next stage in the communal discernment process consists of resting the decision. This time of resting could be for a short time during the actual meeting, in which people are given time to go pray in silence. It could be an overnight if the discernment is held as a retreat, or it could be a week or month. The time interval of resting is determined by what makes sense in the church's process and timeline.

Holding the Decision to the Heart

In this time of resting, participants hold the decision near their hearts and check in to see if it brings consolation or desolation. As they pray over the decision, they seek mutual confirmation from God of peace and unity, rather than distress and division. The group might pray with the question "Is our decision God's will: nothing more, nothing less, nothing else?"[28] The participants will know that the decision has come to "rest" when each person experiences an inner peace, which is confirmed by the whole body.

Testing the Discernment

The gathering may come back together to test the time of resting. Participants share about the results of their time of resting the decision. Has everyone felt the sense of deep inner peace with the decision? If not, perhaps one aspect of the decision needs to be tweaked, or a larger change might need to be made. Rather than feeling frustration or irritation if everyone hasn't discerned similarly, trust that God is at work in the process. If the gathering needs to go back through the discerning process again with a change, it's okay. The outcome will be better if the process is done again until there is consensus. If there is harmony, though, then the decision is affirmed and celebrated. Hallelujah!

> The church rested the decision for close to a month, with a scheduled church council vote at that time. The lead team crafted a report summarizing the results of the entire process. Though no one knew during the month of resting how the church council would ultimately vote, there was a feeling of consolation and unity among the congregation.

Step 11: Prayer of Thanksgiving and Offering of Commitment

Directly after the testing of the discernment and the determination of consensus, the facilitator or clerk writes it down so that it is recorded; this statement could be read aloud to the assembly. Then, the facilitator, pastor, or other lead team member can offer a prayer of thanksgiving. What a joy to thank the God who brought the community through this process and led it to unity! Depending upon the setting, the community might celebrate Communion together as a sign of God's work of grace among them and of the unity at God's banquet table. Forms of commitment or offerings for participation in the result of the discernment (serve on a committee, offer financial resources, commit to a volunteer day, etc.) could be distributed to participants, and they could bring them forward to an altar.

IV. Sending Forth

Step 12: Celebration

Celebration is important! Particularly after an arduous or time-involved discernment process, people need to celebrate the gift of the discernment. Sing songs or celebrate the lead team in some way. The joy and unity that comes out of communal discernment to consensus deserves a party!

A Shorter Discernment Process for Meetings

At times you may need a more succinct and abridged process of discernment for an issue, problem, or possibility that is before a church council or committee. Though not as in-depth or time-consuming as the process for congregational-wide discernments, a shortened process still can open a group to God's leading in an issue or problem. The committee or team will need to be open to maintaining prayerful listening, reflection, deliberation, and discussion as guidelines. See the handout Abbreviated Communal Discernment Practice for a One-Hour Meeting on page 289 in the appendix for an outline of the steps).

A team or committee can move through this process in an hour or less, particularly if they've already trained on communal discernment practices. Consider this example:

> Grace Church's church council names a desire to be more open and welcoming to their community. They've previously done their "exploring" and research work and have narrowed this desire down to concrete options—offer their parking lot for a community farmer's

market once a week or renovate the aging Sunday school class building and use it for affordable housing or for a childcare program. Their time of "holy listening" includes a presentation on the costs and the pros and cons of each option by a subcommittee. They pray in silence and then share their responses to the presentations, pausing between each person's sharing. A preference begins to emerge for the farmer's market option, and the chairperson states this as a "minute." She tests for consensus by asking members to raise fingers (1–5) indicating the strength of their support. After a concern for liability for the church is addressed by a trustee, the chair tests the discernment again. The council clearly supports hosting a farmer's market and celebrates this discernment—then distributes jobs for the work to different members. People leave feeling excited and united—after an hour-long church meeting.

Yes, Communal Discernment Works!

You can do this practice! Feel free to shorten steps, leave out something, circle back and do something twice—make this process your own. There's no "right" or "wrong" way; there is only practice. It's so much better than the alternatives of divisive votes, arguments over who seconded something in Robert's Rules of Order, or meetings after the meeting in the parking lot.

As the theologian Henri Nouwen's work affirms, the practice of discernment lifts us into God's dwelling place and we experience deep renewal.[29] It *can* happen. As the people of the church I assisted in communal discernment listened together in those circles of chairs, they held one another in "loving Presence." The energy of the large fellowship hall softened and calmed. In the words of Nouwen, they "shared in the knowledge of God's heart, a deeper wisdom, a new way of living and loving."[30] People shared afterward that they felt an inner quiet, refreshed, and a greater connection to God and one another.

As did the early Methodists, we experienced what John Wesley described as a deeper caring for one another and a "bearing of one another's burdens" (see Galatians 6:2). Our four discernment sessions were a kind of "labor of love" that allowed us to be knit more closely together as the body of Christ through grace.[31] This sense of unity and connection is a clear sign that the discernment has arrived at a place of consensus—and that we had experienced the means of grace in actual "holy conferencing." Such is the power of communal discernment. God can work miracles of consensus among us amid conflict; all we must do is listen—to each other and to God.

NOTES

1. Ruth Haley Barton, *Pursing God's Will Together: A Discernment Practice for Leadership Groups* (Downers Grove, IL: Intervarsity Press, 2012), 10, 39.
2. Danny Morris and Charles Olsen, *Discerning God's Will Together: A Spiritual Practice for the Church* (Lanham, MD: Rowman & Littlefield, 2012), 60–61.Barton, *Pursuing God's Will Together: A Discernment Practice for Leadership Groups*, 178–84. This section includes an in-depth exploration of different roles in a discernment process.
3. Barton, *Pursuing God's Will Together*, 154–55.
4. Barton, 184.
5. Morris and Olsen, *Discerning God's Will Together*, 60.
6. Susan Beaumont, *How to Lead When You Don't Know Where You are Going: Leading in a Liminal Season*, (Lanham, MD: Rowman & Littlefield, 2019), 85.
7. Morris and Olsen, *Discerning God's Will Together*, 109.
8. Barton, *Pursuing God's Will Together*, 191.
9. Barton, 193.
10. In Morris and Olsen, *Discerning God's Will Together*, 71
11. Parker Palmer calls the use of a prompt of content in a small group the "third thing." I learned this in a training on his Circles of Trust practice.
12. In Morris and Olsen, *Discerning God's Will Together*, 109–110.
13. John Wesley, "Catholic Spirit," in *John Wesley's Sermons: An Anthology*, ed. Albert Outler and Richard Heitzenrater (Abingdon: Nashville, 1991), 301.
14. Barton, *Pursuing God's Will Together*, 207.
15. Beaumont, *How to Lead When You Don't Know Where You're Going*, 87.
16. Barton, *Pursuing God's Will Together*, 208–209.
17. Beaumont, *How to Lead When You Don't Know Where You're Going*, 86–87.
18. Morris and Olsen, *Discerning God's Will Together*, 78.
19. Barton, *Pursuing God's Will Together*, 217
20. Victoria G. Curtiss, "Guidelines for Communal Discernment" (Louisville: Presbyterian Peacemaking Program, 2007), 8.
21. Olson and Morris, *Discerning God's Will Together*, 79, 80.
22. Curtiss, "Guidelines for Communal Discernment," 8.
23. Barton, *Pursuing God's Will Together*, 185.
24. Garrie Stevens, Pamela Lardear, and Sharon Duger, *Seeking and Doing God's Will: Discernment for the Community of Faith* (Nashville: Discipleship Resources, 1998), 29.

25. Morris and Olsen, *Discerning God's Will Together,* 82–83.
26. Curtiss, "Guidelines for Communal Discernment," 9.
27. Beaumont, *How to Lead When You Don't Know Where You Are Going,* 89. Morris and Olsen, *Discerning God's Will Together,* 81–84
28. Morris and Olsen, 85.
29. This is informed by Henri Nouwen's thought.
30. Henri Nouwen, *Discernment,* ed. Michael Christensen and Rebecca Laird (Harper Collins: New York, 2013), 17. The holding together by Loving Presence is described in Lois Lindbloom, *Prayerful Listening: Cultivating Discernment in Community* (Northfield, MN: Ashmore Ink, 2007), 11.
31. The language of "labor of love" comes from Wesley's description of a class meeting. Wesley, "A Plain Account of the People called Methodists," in *Works,* 9:262. Lois Lindbloom, *Prayerful Listening,* 20. Lindbloom notes that group spiritual direction brings an "interconnectedness with one another and with God, something no easier to describe than were not our hearts burning within us? (Luke 24:32)."

9.

Leading a Congregational Discernment Process

The journey of congregational discernment I shared in the previous chapter began one spring. As azaleas bloomed all around us, I answered the phone call from the church that was contacting me regarding facilitating the process. One of the church's beloved leaders said, "I'm calling on behalf of the church council. We've decided we must respond to the turmoil in our church right now. The council decided to focus on the question of joining the Reconciling Ministries Network as a church. We've set up two information sessions and four discernment sessions over the course of the summer months. We think you are the right person to help lead us through this discernment process. Are you available, and would you consider serving as the facilitator?"

After taking a deep breath, my first thoughts were, "What exactly am I being asked to do here? It seems like I'm being asked to lead the congregation through its tumultuous conflict. Lord, have mercy." What I said to her was, "Wow. I'm so glad you opted for a discernment process instead of immediately taking a potentially divisive vote. Can you say more about how the church council has decided about the process? What am I being asked to do within it?"

> She responded, "We are aware of the 'high stakes' nature of the decision and want to give each person in the church a chance to have a voice in the matter. We've determined the topics and guest speakers for the four discernment sessions. We'd like you to facilitate those sessions as you see fit."
>
> I looked quickly at my calendar app. "I can actually make those dates work," I said.
>
> I thought to myself, "So I have no external reason to say no."
>
> "I will think and pray on this," I told her. "I'll let you know my decision in a few days. Thanks for considering me for this significant work."
>
> When I ended the phone call, I had a sense that I would say yes—yes to facilitating a discernment process for a congregation in conflict about a significant issue. This is what I was being asked to do.

If you or your church team is considering or being asked to lead a congregational discernment process, this chapter is designed to equip you for this leadership work. In the first part, we will cover the steps for preparing a leadership team to facilitate a communal discernment process. In the second part, we will explore how to create a communal discernment process for *your* church (see the handout for Creating a Communal Discernment Process in Your Church on pages 299–300 in the appendix). From preparation to implementation, remember that step-by-step, God is with you in this important work.

Preparing a Leadership Team for Communal Discernment

A lead team must be recruited that holds the gifts and skills for discernment, and then taught and formed in the contemplative practices of prayer that sustain communal listening to God. Then the team, along with a facilitator, designs a group discernment process that meets their congregation's needs. This preparation will involve time and commitment, but the results of harmonious consensus about something that really matters to the community are worth it.[1] Here's how to do the work of preparation:

Name the Courage and Gifts Necessary for the Work

Doing this work isn't easy. Leading a discernment process toward consensus in a church in turmoil requires commitment and spiritual maturity. It requires leaders who themselves have the capacity to listen to God while also hearing people's pain. Holding such a stance requires true courage. As twelfth-century theologian and profoundly influential "doctor of the church" Thomas Aquinas described it, courage names the capacity to do what is necessary for the sake of what is loved.[2] What is loved within communal discernment is the community and its ability to live into God's calling for its life together. Courageous leaders put the communal good ahead of their own individual desires, often making personal sacrifices of time, effort, and opinion to do so. At the same time, leaders are human. They may feel reactive and the urge to respond quickly to "put out fires"—which can sometimes ignite new ones. Staying centered in God's peace amid conflict requires a kind of lion-heart disposition (courage) that stays soft in God's grace while strong on boundaries that prevent harm to others or self.

In addition to courage, the leadership team requires all kinds of gifts. As Susan Beaumont states, "We need both organizational savvy and spiritual maturity within the leadership body. We need organizationally strong leaders with deep spiritual rootedness who are open to what might emerge from the practice of discernment."[3] Your team needs people who can craft the form of the discernment process and people who can pray over it. You need people who can hold the congregation to a covenant and people who can facilitate their practice of it.

Another way of thinking about gifts comes through reflection on the virtues needed on a team. The four classic virtues of wisdom, justice, courage, and temperance are good gifts to hold within the members of a team.

Wisdom. Often called prudence, this gift describes the virtuous ability to make right judgments, which also describes discernment. Wise ones listen, hear the inner truth of what people are sharing, demonstrate caring, and admit readily to mistakes. They can discern between truth and error and exercise good judgment. Those gifted with prudence understand their own limitations and boundaries. They are widely respected and admired by others in the community.

Justice. This virtue means to render to every human and creature what is their due, with fairness and consistency, so that relationships flourish. People who practice justice care deeply about others and can apply knowledge in a situation in a judicious way. They make meaningful connections between ideas and the people with fairness.

Courage. This is the strength to do what is right, in and through fear, for the sake of what is loved. Those with courage orient always to what will ultimately keep the community aiming toward the love of God. They can hold to the right course amid great pressure and fear otherwise.

Temperance. This is the ability to not be swayed too easily from one extreme to the other. This virtue enables the team to hold the middle in the space of competing ends or opinions.[4] Temperate people can make clear choices amid muddled waters and can distinguish the middle way (*via media*) when it seems lost.

A team that holds all four of these virtues within its members contains the greatest potential for implementing a healthy discernment process.

Create a Team

This work of communal discernment requires a team for leadership. No one person can nor should be responsible for a discernment process. That person too easily becomes blamed or shamed, targeted for everyone's anxiety and fear, or rendered a failure. For a communal process of discernment to consensus to work, it must begin with communal leadership.

There might naturally be a church leadership body, such as a church council, that can lead the discernment process. Or, the church council could create a subcommittee, such as a Discernment Team, that takes the lead on the process. If there isn't a functioning and healthy leadership body in the church, you can create a leadership team with the church's clergy and supportive lay leadership. Pray for insight about who has rich spiritual life and emotional maturity. Whom might God be leading you to within the church who brings gifts for listening or who holds respect within the community? Who holds the virtues of wisdom, courage, justice, or prudence? As faces and names of people come to you, pray over them, and then personally invite them to consider serving on this team. As your team comes together, let it be prayerful and as Spirit-led as possible.

Call a Leader/Facilitator

The leadership team will need to call a leader to shepherd the process of discernment with the congregation and with the team itself. Dividing up parts of the process to different members of the leadership team can make the flow feel disjointed and bumpy. As Susan Beaumont suggests, having one, or at most two, people designated as the leaders keeps the process on track, supports better group dynamics, and aids in the movement toward consensus.[5]

This leader, as Danny Morris and Charles Olsen in their book, *Discerning God's Will Together"* indicate, might be called the "discernamentarian"—a group spiritual guide who supports the process and remains attuned to the work of the Holy Spirit in gatherings. Other names for the leader could be facilitator or spiritual director. Whatever the name the team decides to use, the leader is someone well practiced in spiritual direction and disciplines who also is gifted in listening and leading groups. This person should hold trust by the leadership team and be patient and capable to see a discernment process through to the end.[6]

A spiritual director or facilitator may be on the leadership team already; however, this person must have no personal agenda to protect. If the decision is high stakes, it might be best if the discernmentarian/facilitator isn't also the clergy leader. Clergy can easily become lightning rods for blame or accusations of partiality. So, having pastors simply be "pray-ers" can be liberating for them. Someone from outside the congregation might be a great choice, especially since this person would be free from any attachment to outcomes or relationships with participants.

Prayerful Preparation: Cultivate Contemplative Practices

With a team and a facilitator in place, leaders need to learn and practice contemplative forms of prayer. Contemplative prayer practices prepare leaders in discernment processes by centering them in God's presence, rooting them in their true selves, lessening anxiety, and forming them in habits of holy listening to God and others. By developing a comfort level with silence, stillness, and listening to God, leaders gain the spiritual maturity necessary to support communal discernment. Through learning to calm the flurry within their own minds, leaders can meet with equanimity and wisdom whatever flurry might come at them from the congregation. As Susan Beaumont indicates, "The discerning leader must be able to access stillness and encourage it in others . . . our ability to discern is dependent upon the quality of our attention, on our capacity for stillness, our ability to quiet our minds and disassociate from the constant chatter in our brains."[7] Practices such as centering prayer, the Ignatian Examen, practicing the presence, and gentle awareness are all excellent ways to cultivate the capacity to listen to God in stillness (see the handout Contemplative Spiritual Practices to Support Listening to God on pages 252–58 in the appendix). As Jesus withdrew to deserted places to pray and listen to God (Luke 5:16), so too we can use silence and solitude to give space to hear God's still voice in our souls.

The leadership team also could commit to regular contemplative practices together. They could engage in group spiritual direction for friendship to build trust, purpose, and relationship with one another (see chapters 2–4). Other practices might be a *lectio divina* group or centering prayer group. These contemplative prayer practices open our hearts, minds, and spirits so that we can let go of our analytical, logical, and opinionated responses and enter instead into the mystery and movement of the Holy Spirit—together.

Name the Fears

At the same time, acknowledging the fears and anxieties that members of the leadership team have can be healing, both personally and for the team. In a meeting at the beginning of the planning process, you might give people a way to name their fears, worries, and anxieties about the process. Lead team members could write these fears on a piece of paper, or on a posterboard, or simply name them aloud in the space. The team could pray for God's strength, peace, and wisdom amid their fear. (See also the naming of fears in chapter 5.) Susan Beaumont says that in naming fears and offering them to

God, leaders move from a sense of "knowing" to a spirit of "unknowing"—of trusting that God's grace meets them in their preparation and will guide them in ways the team can't anticipate.[8]

Prepare for Conflict and Challenges

Many lead team members may fear the conflict itself, and the possibility for further division, conflict, and destruction of relationships. What people really fear in conflict is loss—the loss of friends or their community as they've known it. When we're stirred at such an emotional level, we move into our embedded ways of coping with conflict. Understanding our own conflict style, and those of others on the team, can help us to grow, support each other, and maybe even have a little humor about our responses. Encourage team members to name themselves as one of the styles described in chapter 5: accommodators, avoiders, competitors, compromisers, or collaborators, and discuss your styles together. As peace educator Jes Stoltzfus Buller indicates, the combination of self-awareness and group awareness in recognizing, evaluating, and valuing our different ways of engaging conflict can help our team to encourage the best in ourselves and others so that we might be a Spirit-filled body, engaging in the holy work of conflict transformation.[9] Understanding and appreciating our style and that of others supports a healthy process of communal discernment.

God's "more excellent way" (1 Corinthians 12:31) of communal discernment includes the courage and the fears, the gifts, and the conflict styles of the interdependent body of Christ. Of course, even with this naming and claiming of virtues, gifts, and conflict styles—conflict can and will happen. The team can embrace it as an opportunity for conflict transformation. If the team senses that they or the congregation will need more work to understand conflict in healthier ways, excellent resources exist, such as the *Peaceful Practices* curriculum or the book *Crucial Conversations*.[10] The leadership team may want to work through one of these resources as part of their preparation or teach the congregation on conflict transformation. (See chapter 7 for more on conflict transformation.)

Anticipate that there will be challenges in your process—which is a sign that this work matters to the community. Study and reflect on these challenges as a leadership team. You could do role-plays as a way of anticipating and preparing for these challenges. Conflict can be a positive engine for transformative change; these challenges aren't "bad" but rather opportunities to grow in our practice together. As we did in chapter 5, let's review some common group challenges followed by individual ones, this time focusing specifically on the challenges for the communal discernment leadership team.

Group Challenges

Lack of leadership. Lack of strong leadership can torpedo a discernment process. When the stakes feel high and people are emotionally taut about an issue or decision before the congregation, it's essential that the leaders—both the facilitator, the leadership team, and any other leaders (circle leaders, hospitality team, sages, prayer team)—are fully committed to the discernment process, versus "taking a vote." As previously mentioned, all leaders need to be grounded in their own prayer practices and strong trust in the Holy Spirit's guidance. When conflict arises, the leadership then moves together from a place of centeredness that can meet the conflict with equanimity and peace. The leaders need to be committed to showing up as spiritual guides for this process.

Lack of prayerfulness. Lack of prayerfulness could occur in the overall process, or in smaller listening circles, or among the leadership team. In each case, the leadership guides the group back into an openness to the Holy Spirit. If the facilitator loses it, they remain open to being nudged by others on the leadership team. If a circle loses prayerfulness, the leader could ask, "Have we lost our spirit of prayerfulness? Let's pause for a moment of silence and ask God to guide us back into God's presence." Any breaches of prayerfulness are to be immediately recognized, named, and addressed. Ignoring the loss of prayerfulness can lead to a loss of how the Spirit might be moving the group to consensus.

Superficiality. Superficiality can take place in the listening circles, especially if there is lack of trust in the circle. The facilitator models appropriate levels of disclosure and invites deeper reflection if necessary. For example, "Mary, thanks for sharing. Is there anything more that you might have on your heart about this that would be important for the group to hear?" The facilitator encourages honest and true sharing, but also acknowledges that vulnerability isn't comfortable. Superficiality is often a false peace as well. For a listening circle to really do its work of discernment and movement toward consensus, people need to take gentle steps into telling their story courageously, knowing that they are held in a circle of trust and confidentiality.

Simmering or Open Conflict. Conflict can simmer under the surface or "boil" out in the open. The reason the church is engaging in the discernment process is that most likely there are diverse viewpoints on the question at hand. Acknowledge the reality of conflict, affirm each person's humanity and the different identities (in race/ethnicity/gender/sexuality/religion/class/ability) and life experiences that have shaped different viewpoints. In truth, disagreement can lead to a stronger decision through consensus. Larry Dressler, an expert in consensus-group-based process, says, "We use the tension created by our differences to move toward creative solutions—not toward compromise or mediocrity."[11] If leaders can embrace disagreement as a positive force that the Spirit can use to strengthen the discernment process, their comfort with conflict communicates to the rest of their group that they all can exhale (maybe to the count of eight!) and stay open to the work of God among them.

When conflict simmers between two or more people, the facilitator or a circle leader needs first to acknowledge and name the issue. For example, the leader might say, "We are encountering differing perspectives. This is normal and healthy in a discernment process. We acknowledge that these differences about . . . (name it)."

Then, the facilitator acknowledges that based on our conflict styles and identity, this difference of opinion or perspective stirs lots of different feelings and emotions in us. The facilitator can say, "Let's take a moment of silence to name for ourselves our emotions and feelings. What is moving in you right now? (anger, frustration, anxiety) . . . Now that we have named our feelings to ourselves, let us turn to wonder and get curious. Where is this emotion coming from? Why is it getting stirred? Let go of any attempt to control others' feelings. Now, reflect on the people's feelings differing from yours. Open to God's presence and love for those persons. Why might they feel and see this issue differently?" Then, the facilitator could invite the people on either side of the conflict to share their feelings and emotions with each other, either one-on-one, in a small group, or perhaps in the large group. Instruct them to use "I feel" language, such as, "I wonder why we see this differently," or "Help me understand your concerns." The facilitator or circle leader can moderate this discussion as needed. [12]

If there is still an impasse after sharing about their feelings, the facilitator might invite people to reflect on their identity. What are their three greatest strengths? What are the three opposites of those strengths? Perhaps invite people to write them down. The place of the "opposite" will often be where people get sparked the most. This might be a good place to pause for prayer, take a break, and give people some time apart to be in silence or time for one-on-one conversations to understand each other better. People will feel seen, validated, and heard through this clear address of their conflict. They might even learn something about themselves!

Individual Challenges

The Dominator. In any group process, there can be a dominator; they have much to say or feel the need to control out of their own insecurity or fear. The best way to curb this behavior is to follow the discernment process, including the timing structure, as well as the covenant guidelines. Group leaders can affirm that the person is being heard in the space and time given in the process, which each member has agreed to abide by through the covenant. If the dominator is trying to coerce or conform others to their way of thinking, the leader can remind them that this is a Spirit-led process; any efforts to conform or pressure others leads away from the Spirit and hinders the practice of discernment.

The Oversharer. This person, often due to intense current personal experiences (grief/loss/illness/etc.), shares too much. Excessive vulnerability or oversharing also can overwhelm the process and turn the focus to the individual's issues. If a person demonstrates a need to be heard about personal challenges, the facilitator or circle leader should step in with compassion and guidance simultaneously. It could look like, "Sally, our hearts go to you. The grief over your recent husband's death is so real and hard. We love you and are with you. Thank you for sharing your story and your pain with us (maybe ask if Sally would like a gesture of support such as a hug or gentle touch). We've come to the end of your time for sharing. We do want to keep the focus on the communal discernment at hand. Let's turn gently back to the question before us . . . " The leader could then follow up with Sally afterward, one-on-one.

The Reluctant. For those who are reluctant or silent, the facilitator/discernamentarian can affirm that this is an invitational process, and no one will be forced to share. However, the person might have the insight or story that everyone needs to hear and simply needs a little encouragement to share. The group leader might come back to them at the end to see if they might have been prompted through the process to feel comfort in sharing. If there is a break in the session, the leader also might check in with the quiet one. The leader also needs to give space to accept that the reluctant or quiet one might be genuinely wanting to pass and not pressure them. Their listening presence might be the role needed to fulfill in the group.

The Absent. The last individual challenge is absence. In a discernment process, it's important for people to be present, and for this requirement to be communicated well in advance. When people are well-informed and understand the importance of their presence and participation, they'll be more likely to prioritize the discernment process in their schedule. Absence breaks the quality of the person's participation in the communal discernment.

Whew! You made it through the challenge section, and the Spirit will guide you through whatever challenges come in your own discernment process. Challenges and conflict present opportunities for growth and greater clarity in the discernment.

Creating a Communal Discernment Process for *Your* Church

Communal spiritual discernment involves a prayerful process with different movements (chapter 8 describes these movements). Your team can creatively adapt these movements for your context and situation. You may move through them linearly, but you may also skip over one, or come back and revisit a step again—moving more cyclically than in a line.[13] Make this process yours—just be sure to have a clear structure and process. As Susan Beaumont states, "We need a process that attends to the mystery of the Holy while minimizing the foibles of human bias and self-interest."[14] The time and attention given to the creation of a discernment process is well worth it and will foster an experience of seeking God's will together. At first, this work might feel cumbersome and effortful, but as your leadership team and congregation practice communal discernment, it will feel more easeful, grace-filled, and life-giving. Eventually, discernment becomes a part of your church's DNA, and you'll be able to use it in church council meetings and other settings without as much effort and planning.

Framing the Question

The first step of creating a discernment process for your church is to create the boundary around what the decision, problem, or issue really *is*. The task of framing the question takes intention, conversation, and prayer by the leadership team. The issue may be somewhat murky or unclear, or too "big" or problematic. The team might ask, "God, what are you guiding us to do in our issue/problem/question?" and focus on this question in prayer and discussion. Then the group converses until a clear consensus emerges on the framing subject. The team might need to test out various frames of the problem and narrow down to the most pertinent framing question.

Covenant Making

In a high-stakes discernment, a covenant upholds clear expectations and boundaries so that the process doesn't get derailed or sidetracked by personal animosities or agendas. Though important, covenant guidelines don't have to be difficult or arduous to create (for sample covenant guidelines, see pages 167–69 in chapter 8 or Covenant Guidelines for Group Spiritual Direction on pages 239–40 in the appendix) Some guidelines specific to communal discernment are: be intentional about developing relationships with one another to build and maintain Christian community, use "I" messages to speak openly and transparently regarding one's intentions, concerns, values, and interests, and focus on ideas rather than questioning people's motives, intelligence, or integrity.

You might consider selecting some of these guidelines as your covenant and then seek participant input and approval in the first session. The covenant should be written down and displayed during the discernment and verbally read or stated out loud before each session. The discernment process should offer regular covenant "check-ins" throughout to ensure that people know they will be held accountable, and so that the leadership team can readily address any issues or conflict as they arise. The covenant provides an invaluable boundary that supports the framed question and the guiding principle—and a healthy discernment process.

Determining a Guiding Principle(s)

After framing a question for discernment and creating the covenant, a leadership team can move to grounding their work of discernment in a "guiding principle." A guiding principle should be relevant to the issue being discerned and support the boundaries created by the framing question. The principle could come from scripture, a previous mission or vision statement, core values of the community, or its larger religious tradition. The principle should be important to the leadership team, while also avoiding personal agendas and biases or contradictions.[15] The facilitator/spiritual director of the process, along with a couple of other leaders, could prepare some tentative guiding principles in advance, which then can be refined and adapted by the larger leadership body. If the team has a difficult time settling on a guiding principle for the work, they can continue in prayer and discernment together. If there is still an impasse, the facilitator might suggest something broad, such as "to follow the Holy Spirit's guidance" or "to attend to God's will," so that the process can continue moving while still holding to a principle that all can hold.

Choosing the Discernment Process

The leadership team will need to determine what kind of practices they want to implement in their discernment process. I'll offer guidance below for when to do the kinds of holy listening from the Christian tradition discussed in chapter 6. In the appendix, I've included additional Listening Practices for Communal Discernment (pages 292–96) you might consider. In your own community's practice, you might combine different aspects of these types to create your own "recipe" of communal discernment that works for your community, context, and the kind of discernment you are doing.

1. Group Spiritual Direction (Monastic Tradition)

This form of holy listening and responses works for when the options for discernment aren't clear, or when its vital that everyone's voice, perspective, and feelings are heard. It also works well with the integration of spiritual practices, such as *lectio divina,* as part of the prompt. The discernment process of the church I worked with used a form of group spiritual direction in which people were asked a series of the same questions each time and given space to respond without interruption. The style of sharing was modeled on the practice of *lectio divina,* adapted to questions on the teaching material of the session. The sharing in the group spiritual direction circles fostered relationships and enabled participants to hear and recognize one another's humanity and perspective.

2. Ignatian Deliberation

This kind of discernment works particularly well when there are clear options for discernment. For example, let's say that a church is discerning the future of their Sunday morning worship services, in which they currently have one service in the sanctuary with hymns, use of an organ, and a formal liturgy and a second service in the fellowship hall with praise songs, use of a band, and a more informal liturgy displayed on screens. They no longer have enough participants or financial resources to sustain the labor and expense for two services. They are discerning between four options, which the lead team determined in advance:

1. Keep the formal service in the sanctuary as is and end the fellowship hall service.
2. Keep the fellowship hall service and end the service in the sanctuary.

3. Incorporate elements of the praise and worship service into the sanctuary service.
4. Incorporate elements of the sanctuary service into the praise and worship service.

The Deliberation model would help them to clearly come up with pros and cons for each option while keeping them open to how the Holy Spirit might work to shape an option in an unknown way. Through the Deliberation practice of prayer, sharing pros and cons, evaluation, and discovery, they'll come to the option that God is guiding them to for their future worship life.

4. Quaker "Sense of the Meeting"

The Quaker model is helpful for a discernment in which a problem or issue can be framed but options or proposals aren't clear yet. The community needs the movement of the Holy Spirit to help them hear possibilities that are yet unclear or unknown. For example, one church has framed the problem "How are we called to engage in ministry with our neighborhood?" but has no clear sense what that looks like or with whom they are to partner. The Quaker model allows for leadings of the Holy Spirit to rise and to be tested until a "sense of the meeting" is arrived at for an answer to this question. Perhaps through silence, waiting, and prayer the community discerns that the Spirit is leading them to partner with the elementary school across the street as tutors and to provide support and encouragement for teachers.[16]

4. The Wesleyan Quadrilateral

The Wesleyan Quadrilateral, which we explored in chapter 6, offers a concrete theological method for discernment that integrates the communal and the individual experience of faith and use of reason, while grounding it in scripture and tradition.[17] If the congregation needs to understand church history or its denominational tradition, study scripture as a part of the discernment, or learn more on an issue, the Quadrilateral model provides space for that learning. A congregation's lead team could employ the Quadrilateral in these ways.

Scripture. Choose relevant scripture passages for reflection and study on the issue before the congregation. Consider reading the scripture together in a prayerful practice like *lectio divina,* in which the group focuses on one passage together (see Prompts for Leading Group Spiritual Direction on pages 259–63 in the appendix for directions). You also could have conversations on a passage in small groups and then lift up your insights for the larger group. In the process at the church where I facilitated discernment, I read the story of the Council of Jerusalem's discernment in Acts 15 at each of the discernment sessions. I simply invited people to let the story rest deeply in their soul and mind after reading, without further discussion. The story served as a powerful example of Christian discernment and a steady biblical reminder that unity was possible. For one session, a seminary professor of New Testament taught on human sexuality and the Bible, providing thoughtful scholarship on significant verses.

Tradition. The leadership team discerns what stories might be most supportive for their discernment—whether from the congregation's own history or the denominational history or faithful Christians throughout the church's history, such as Augustine, Martin Luther, Teresa of Ávila, John Wesley, Richard Allen, or many others. In the discernment process I facilitated, I used John Wesley's sermon *Catholic Spirit* to teach about his way of seeking another person's hand in unity, even though they might differ significantly on the theological question of predestination. We also had a session in which someone taught on the United Methodist *Book of Discipline* to understand our denomination's story. The church's development of its identity statement was shared in a different teaching session, reminding the congregation of its own history and story.

Reason. Reason really supports the creative process of group spiritual direction and discernment to consensus. "Mutual understanding, helping to improve each other's ideas, bringing together differing ideas into a new proposal, and summarizing the conversation of the group are all functions of reason in the discernment process."[18] In the process of the church I worked with, the reasoning occurred as people processed the material from scripture and the teaching sessions (tradition) in combination with hearing each other's stories (experience).

Experience. Spiritual disciplines of prayer and silence through the communal discernment practice offer people an experience of God's presence and greater clarity of God's will. Participants' sharing of their own stories and life experiences not only connects people to each other, but also serves to help them see collectively how God is at work in the community. In the discernment practice I facilitated, people shared how they saw or heard God in the teaching session; this sharing bonded people and helped them to hear how God was calling the community on the focus question.

Structuring the Process

After determining the kind of discernment, the team can more easily discern the structure of their process. The structure answers the question of "how" the discernment process will be carried out. If it is a practice of Ignatian Deliberation, perhaps the structure will be a Saturday congregational retreat with a day-long retreat schedule. If it is the Quaker model, perhaps they schedule a two-hour time of discernment on a Sunday afternoon, with openness to the possibility of more. With a group spiritual direction model, the team may discern that several sessions over the course of weeks or months are needed to build trust and relationships.

Logistics

The kind of discernment and the structure determine in large part the logistics—the "where" (place) and "when" (dates/duration) of the discernment process. For example, if the kind of discernment is an Ignatian Deliberation and the structure is to practice in a one-time weekend retreat, then the team needs to determine the best weekend for the retreat for their community, secure a retreat location for that weekend, and create a schedule for how the weekend will flow—most likely in partnership with the facilitator/spiritual director. If the process is to be a form of group spiritual direction, then the team will need to schedule a series of meetings over a course of weeks and/or months—perhaps at the church facility. Logistics can feel like "nuts and bolts" but deserve prayer and intentionality to accrue the optimal participation of the most members of the community.

Logistical discernment also includes the physical set up of the space used for discernment. Will there be one large circle of chairs? Several circles of chairs in small groups? Will you use additional break-out rooms? Will you use tables? How will the space be made to feel peaceful, welcoming, and worshipful? The discernment leadership team I worked with decided to use listening circles, with no more than nine chairs set up in each circle with no table;[19] the team decided that a table would be more distancing.

Recruiting and Training Additional Leaders

Based upon the kind of discernment and the logistics, the lead team might need to recruit more leaders for their process. For example, the lead team might need "sages" or "wise ones" who observe the process, offer insights, and discern any sense of the movement of the Spirit. The leadership team might recruit those in the congregation with gifts or virtues not yet represented in the process. Because leadership roles for people in the congregation give them more "buy-in," it generally benefits the discernment to include more people in roles of leadership that utilize their gifts.

The leadership team might create a training session for the new leaders. Here are some elements you might include in your training:

- Give space for them to introduce themselves.
- Review the covenant guidelines established for your process.
- Offer a clear definition of communal discernment and consensus and how it is different from decision-based processes (see chapter 7 for help with this).
- Teach them through an outline of the process your congregation will use the section Using Group Spiritual Direction (see Sample Outline of One Church's Communal Discernment Process, pages 286–88 in the appendix, for an example process).
- Indicate any timing structure you might be using.
- Offer guidance on listening well and offering open-ended responses (see the handout Guidelines for Holy Listening and Life-giving Responses on pages 265–68 in the appendix for suggestions).

- Name what their role and job description will be during the process.
- If you have time, do a sample practice of the process.
- Close with silent or spoken prayer for each leader and bless them and the discernment process before you.

As Susan Beaumont remarks, your team of leaders will be "strengthened by their shared experience of having been led by the Holy Spirit."[20]

30-Minute Training Process Outline

- Opening prayer and a "thank you" for their service (1 minute)
- Introductions (3 minutes)
- Review of covenant guidelines (1 minute)
- Teaching on group spiritual direction structure (5 minutes)
- Guidance for holy listening and offering life-giving responses (5 minutes)
- Gathering the "sense of the meeting" (5 minutes)
- Questions? (5 minutes)
- Closing prayer (5 minutes)

Exploring

The leadership team might want to explore all potential options or possibilities within the framing question. This exploration could include research from surveys, listening sessions, neighborhood asset-based mapping, or questionnaires. As Morris and Olsen in their book, *Discerning God's Will Together* indicate, the team may do brainstorming for the best options, identifying all possibilities and paths and then refining them.[21] They may then eliminate the ones that don't hold promise or that don't fit the framing question. The team could whittle the options down to three or four "best" possibilities. In the Quaker tradition, these "best" options could be stated as a "minute" for further discernment by the congregation.

For example, in the case of the church discerning how to be more involved in their community, a leadership team could do an asset map of their neighborhood.[22] They could engage in conversations with neighbors, organizations, and businesses in their immediate vicinity, as well as nonprofits or community organizations already at work in their area. Through this research, the team then could discern the most viable options for their involvement and educate the congregation on those possibilities as part of the discernment.

Through the work of exploring, the church leadership team discerned these three best options for community involvement:

- Elementary school across the street—Through conversations with the school principal and teachers, the team learned that this Title 1 school really needed reading tutors for their students and donations of snacks and cleaning supplies for the teachers.
- Community garden organization—A plot of land near the church had been developed by the city for the community; a lack of participation and volunteers resulted in an untended, weedy, and neglected garden space.
- Use of the church's commercial kitchen—Several local food entrepreneurs wanted to start micro-businesses of a bakery and fresh juices but needed a commercial-grade and USDA certified kitchen. With some renovations and updates, the church could offer its kitchen to these entrepreneurs.

By their research and winnowing of options to these three instead of limitless and unknown possibilities, the leadership team helped the congregation's work of discernment to be much more focused and specific. They homed in on the elementary school as the best option for them, due to its proximity, the number of church folk who felt called to be tutors, and the ease with which this church organizes donation drives.

Prayerful Preparation with the Community

By this stage, the leadership team has done most of the work of preparing its leaders and creating the process of discernment. It begins to invite the congregation or participants to join in, which starts at the first step of prayerful preparation (see chapter 8). The leaders have been engaged in prayer practices all along until this point. The process is ready to be launched!

Communication Plan and Implementation

Now, the team can collaborate with the church's communications/social media/clergy team or staff to develop a communication plan for the congregation. The communication of the discernment process shares valuable information and educates the congregation to prepare them for participation. Consider developing a short description about what communal discernment is, what your framing question is, your guiding principle, and your process. Clearly share the dates/times/places of any meetings or retreats as far in advance as possible. Use multiple channels of communication so that everyone is informed—email, bulletin, pulpit announcements, church newsletter, text messaging, and social media. Communication and education help tremendously in preparing congregation members not for a "vote-taking" but for a prayerful and Spirit-led discernment process.

Formation/Teaching

The facilitator/spiritual director of the process, in combination with members of the leadership team, could educate the congregation on what discernment is, the kind of discernment you are using, and offer contemplative spiritual practices to help the congregation learn how to listen for the Holy Spirit. This formation could be as simple as one teaching session, or the team could implement a whole series on spiritual practices over the course of weeks or months. If the congregation is in high conflict and needs to learn to see one another as human, the team might begin with the practice of group spiritual direction for friendship (see chapters 2–5). For example, the church could hold group spiritual direction for friendship during Lent and begin the actual discernment process in the spring or summer.

Gathering

Setting of the Physical Space

Give attention to the setting and set-up of your discernment location. You might consider creating a hospitality team, perhaps composed of participants and/or members of the leadership team, with the intentional focus on setting, welcome, and greeting. The space should be warm and inviting; refreshments and candles always help! Consider circle(s) of chairs instead of rows or tables. If you are using break-out rooms for small circles of discernment, equip each room with a candle. If the covenant has been determined in advance, have paper copies or displays (on a screen or even large poster paper) of the covenant, along with the framing question and guiding principles. Consider also having an outline of your discernment process with the timing structure as a handout or on display in the room. The more informed and equipped people are, the better they can relax into the process. If people will be writing down whatever they need to "shed" to fully participate, have cards and pens ready.

Welcome

Intentionally welcome each person as they come into the space. Designated greeters or members of the hospitality team can meet people at the door and help them with nametags, if you are using those. You might even have a set greeting worked out in advance, such as: "Thank you so much for coming. How wonderful that you are here. We have been anticipating you. We invite you into this practice of discernment. God is with you!"[23]

Opening Worship

You might choose to begin with an opening prayer to help center people. You also might choose an opening hymn or song that your community sings well and loves. Suggestions include "This is a Day of New Beginnings," "Open My Eyes," "Spirit of the Living God, Fall Afresh on Us," "Breathe on Me, Breath of God," or "I'm Gonna Live So God Can Use Me." After the music, you could offer a prayer, or simply invite a couple of minutes of silence. You also could read a scripture verse, particularly one that might serve as a theme for the discernment process.

At this point you might have a celebration of Communion—or save that until the end of the process. Coming to the Lord's Table to receive God's grace can be a powerful way to begin a process of discernment. This also offers a way for the pastor to be involved in leadership—even if not directly leading the discernment process.

You may decide not to have any opening worship, and that's fine too. The discernment process itself holds space for silence and prayer. You could simply begin with a short verbal welcome and move into the "covenant-making" stage—offering the framing question, guiding principle, and covenant rules. The opening centering silence and whatever "prompt" you use (scripture, story from the church tradition, theological teaching, quote, etc.) can also serve as a form of worship.

As you begin your preparation and training for communal discernment, know that I am praying for you. May you and your leaders and facilitators trust in the Spirit's guidance and walk together in the path of belonging. Remember that in your leadership team, in your covenant, and in your group discernment, God is with you, guiding you in grace as you seek God's will together.

NOTES

1. Susan Beaumont, *How to Lead When You Don't Know Where You are Going: Leading in a Liminal Season* (Lanham, MD: Rowman & Littlefield, 2019), 74–75.
2. Thomas Aquinas, *Summa Theologica* II-II 123.4. https://ccel.org/ccel/aquinas/summa/summa.SS_Q123_A4.html.
3. Beaumont, *How to Lead When You Don't Know Where You are Going*, 78.
4. These virtues come originally from Plato and Aristotle and were developed in Christian thought as the "cardinal virtues," particularly through significant theologians such as Augustine of Hippo and Thomas Aquinas. Aquinas, *ST* I-II 57.4 (prudence) https://ccel.org/ccel/aquinas/summa/summa.FS_Q57_A4.html, Aquinas, *ST* II-II 58 (justice) https://ccel.org/ccel/aquinas/summa/summa.SS_Q58.html, Aquinas, *ST* II-II 123 (courage) https://ccel.org/ccel/aquinas/summa/summa.SS_Q123.html , Aquinas, *ST* II-II (temperance) https://ccel.org/ccel/aquinas/summa/summa.SS_Q141.html. I'm translating Aquinas's language into my own on the cardinal virtues.
5. Beaumont, *How to Lead When You Don't Know Where You are Going*, 82.
6. Danny Morris and Charles M. Olsen, *Discerning God's Will Together: A Spiritual Practice for the Church* (Lanham, MD: Rowman & Littlefield, 2012), 54–55.
7. Beaumont, *How to Lead When You Don't Know Where You are Going*, 79.
8. Beaumont, 37. Also, Karen Scheib, *Pastoral Care: Telling the Stories of our Lives*, (Nashville: Abingdon, 2016), 63–64.
9. Jes Stoltzfus Buller, *Peaceful Practices: A Guide to Healthy Communication in Conflict*, ed. Kirstin De Mello and Ed Nyce (Mennonite Central Committee, 2021), 32–33.
10. Buller, *Peaceful Practices*, 1. Joseph Grenny et al., *Crucial Conversations: Tools for Talking When Stakes are High* 3rd edition (New York: McGraw Hill, 2022. John

Paul Lederach, *The Little Book of Conflict Transformation: Clear Articulation of the Guiding Principles by A Pioneer in the Field* (New York: Good Books, 2003). John Paul Lederach, *Reconcile: Conflict Transformation for Ordinary Christians* (Harrisonburg, VA: Herald Press, 2014).
11. Larry Dressler, *Consensus Through Conversation* (Oakland, CA: Berrett-Koehler Publishers, 2006), 8.
12. These practices of giving space for feelings, asking wondering questions, and exploring a person's identity, come from the book by Douglas Stone, Bruce Patton, and Sheila Heen, *Difficult Conversations: How to Discuss What Matters Most* (New York: Penguin Books, 2010). This could be a good resource for members of the leadership team to look at if more resources are needed. These authors note that the reason conversations are difficult is because of feelings and identity.
13. Morris and Olsen, *Discerning God's Will Together*, 61–63. Morris and Olsen offer helpful pictures of the process as a reflection pool of steppingstones, as a spiral around the magnetic core of God's will, and use the agricultural metaphor of the planting, maturing, and harvesting of seed.
14. Beaumont, *How to Lead When You Don't Know Where You are Going*, 81.
15. Morris and Olsen, *Discerning God's Will Together*, 67–68.
16. Parker Palmer, *A Hidden Wholeness: The Journey toward an Undivided Life* (San Francisco: Jossey-Bass, 2008), 27. Out of his Quaker background and tradition of the meeting, theologian Parker Palmer developed a form of group spiritual direction he calls a "circle of trust." As he describes it, "circle of trust holds us in a space where we can make our own discernments, in our own way and time, in the encouraging and challenging presence of other people." Palmer encourages a practice of silence, deep listening, and open-ended responses and questions.

    Through the founding of Palmer's organization, the Center for Courage and Renewal, this practice of communal discernment with its use of open-ended questions, is used to transform organizations and institutions. For more see Center for Courage and Renewal, https://couragerenewal.org/partner-with-center-for-courage-renewal/. Accessed May 29, 2023.
17. Garrie Stevens, Pamela Lardear, and Sharon Duger, *Seeking & Doing God's Will: Discernment for the Community of Faith* (Nashville: Discipleship Resources, 1998), 20–26. This workbook offers a clear and helpful description of a discernment process based upon the Quadrilateral, and details chapter by chapter how to enact this process. Though not group spiritual direction necessarily, this resource offers practical stories, guidelines, and checklists to lead a discernment process.
18. Stevens, Lardear, Duger, *Seeking and Doing God's Will*, 67.
19. The insight on using circles of chairs came from Rev. Jim Dent and their process at First Baptist Greenville, along with the practice of Circles of Trust in Parker Palmer's Center for Courage and Renewal, which doesn't use tables in between people.
20. Beaumont, *How to Lead When You Don't Know Where You are Going*, 91.
21. Morris and Olsen, *Discerning God's Will Together*, 76–77.
22. For information on asset-based community development and asset mapping of neighborhoods, check out the resources available here: https://resources.depaul.edu/abcd-institute/resources/Pages/Faith-based-Resources.aspx.

23. See Gregory C. Ellison II, *Fearless Dialogues: A New Movement for Justice* (Louisville: Westminister John Knox Press, 2017). Ellison gives great attention to the practice of hospitality in his program. The space is set up with art or interactive exhibits. Leaders in the program intentionally welcome each person with the greeting, "I am so glad to see you. Welcome."

EPILOGUE

The Miracle of Belonging

On a sticky, humid summer evening, the church council and interested church members gathered in the chapel. After a summer of discernment sessions and a month of "resting" the discernment, the time had come for the church council members to vote on whether to affiliate with the Reconciling Ministries Network. People milled about in the pews, chatting animatedly as those of us on the discernment leadership team hurriedly confirmed last details for the meeting. Attendees flipped through the pages of our final report on the discernment process, which the team had assembled over the past couple of weeks through a multitudinous set of emails and hard work.

The pastor called us to order. We prayed. Leaders in the discernment team, including myself, presented about the discernment process. After I described the content and experience of the discernment sessions, I said,

"It was clear that consensus was at work. The Spirit seemed to be at work each time the straw poll vote was called, and hands went up all over the room affirming affiliation with RMN. In the silence of raised hands, we saw the courage and conviction of a church ready to stand for justice."

The church council chairperson shared his own story and experience. We prayed again. Finally, the church council voted, writing their vote on slips of paper. Ushers collected the slips in offering plates and delivered them to the chancel area. Several designees began counting the vote, with multiple practices to ensure accuracy. The rest of us chatted in nervous, hushed tones or sat in silent prayer.

After what seemed like forever but was probably just a few minutes, the church council chairperson came to the lectern. He took a deep breath, and we all instinctively joined him. "The vote to join Reconciling Ministries Network is . . . unanimous!" Shouts and whoops resounded from the pews. A boisterous round of applause reverberated off the stone walls of the chapel for several minutes. It felt like the inbreaking wind of the Holy Spirit. People stood up and hugged each other. A few wept. After calming us down, the council chairperson informed us of next steps, and the pastor closed us in prayer. We filed out of the chapel, jubilant—not only because of the decision but also because of its unanimity. The unity of the vote pointed to the power of communal discernment for consensus. Afterward, one council member said to the pastor, "Even if I wasn't personally comfortable with affiliating with RMN, I could not deny the consensus of the church and the integrity of the process. I put my full support behind it."

The outcome of unanimity for the discernment process wasn't foreseen or predicted. For many of us involved in leadership, the unity in the decision felt like a miracle of the Holy Spirit—joined with our full participation and work. The process of communal discernment with practices of group spiritual direction had indeed shaped us to be a beloved community to one another. We felt a deeper sense of belonging to each other and had developed stronger friendships among those of us involved in the leadership team. The congregational participants also remarked on how they learned more about each other and grew in compassion and empathy for one another. Though it looked like they were just sitting in circles of blue chairs, they were in fact walking in each other's shoes—and empathizing with what that path felt like. Our hearts grew tender to each other, and we felt buoyed by being loved and understood while sharing our stories of life with God.

Just as group spiritual direction helped the earliest Methodists to "labor in love" and grow into the body of Christ, so it helped us belong to one another in and through our differences.[1] We experienced true oneness in the Spirit and unity in the body of Christ. Our gatherings for discernment and decision-making became true "holy conferences" in which we experienced God's grace moving among us. Belonging through shared life together in a communal discernment process healed our divisions and fractiousness. Miracles *can* happen.

The Holy Spirit can and will work miracles of belonging in *your* community too. For Christians worn out by church and unable to drag themselves to worship, much less to a church committee meeting, group spiritual direction for friendship provides spiritual invigoration and a touch with the Holy in community with others. For our young people—many of whom feel alone, isolated, depressed, and anxious—this way of being with others provides healing in a circle of friends. For clergy who are exhausted, burned out, and considering leaving ministry altogether, small circles of listening might offer a miraculous means of grace.

If you or your congregation are weary of conflict and strife, communal discernment might provide the harmony you need. If your leadership team yearns for a practice other than divisive voting for congregational decision-making, communal discernment can move you to consensus on God's will for the issue before you. Belonging, as cultivated through group spiritual direction and communal discernment, can work a miracle—a miracle that sounds like applause reverberating for several jubilant minutes off stone walls. The miracle of Pentecost, when God made one body out of disparate peoples—who couldn't hear each other, didn't speak the same language, and didn't agree about theology—can still catch flame in our midst.

The Hope of Belonging

If anything can bring hope, if anything can offer the possibility of seeing the image of God in each other, and if anything can mend us together—the Holy Spirit can through our participation in circles of holy listening. For those in the Wesleyan tradition and beyond, we've been at our most faithful when we've gathered in small groups that integrate all of God's diversity and extend care into the world as practiced by the earliest Methodists. Perhaps we are invited to become a small "holy club" in our time—a band of disciples offering love and care to each other in friendship and practicing a love that radiates out into the world in acts of mercy and justice.

As Dwight Zscheile, a scholar of mission, indicates, the church of the now and the future is no longer one of voluntary association with lots of programs and committees but one of trusting relationships (friendship) and belonging—of being edified in love in a broken world.[2] Group spiritual direction and other small group practices like it offer a circle of trust in which people can experience the kind of profound welcome, friendship, and belonging for which their souls long. This gathering represents a "micro community"[3] that provides a space of friendship connection, healing, and difference-making. We don't need burdensome physical plants; we simply need small sanctuaries of belonging—places into which the sunlight of empathy, care, and love shines. A circle of blue plastic chairs will work. Perhaps in these holy and small circles of group spiritual direction, Jesus might show up to our people and say, "Your faith has made you well. Go in peace." (Mark 5:34). Perhaps the miracle of Pentecost will ignite among us and unify us into the body of Christ.

A Blessing Upon Your Practice

As you embark on this hard, beautiful, holy, life-giving work, I offer this blessing upon your practice of group spiritual direction for friendship and/or for communal discernment. I hold you in heart and in prayer:

> God who has created us to be your one body,
> May you be with us as we begin.
> We are unsure and uncertain.
> We don't really know what we are doing.
> We don't know where this will end.
> We are worried, anxious, and afraid.
> We feel separate apart from each other.

May you pour your grace into our midst.
May you direct us as we form a practice of group spiritual direction.
May you help us to hear you at work in each other's lives and stories.
May you form us into your body of Christ.

When we lose our way, and our love fails
May you help us to see your image in each other again.
May you guide us in our discernment
That we might know your will for our lives and for our community.
May you give us prudence, courage, justice, and temperance
That we might cultivate lives of flourishing together,
That we might be your one body
In which we all belong
And call each other friends.

Amen.

NOTES

1. John Wesley, *The Works of John Wesley*, vol. 9, "Plain Account of the Methodists," ed. Rupert E. Davies (Nashville: Abingdon, 1989), 262.
2. Dwight Zscheile, "From the Age of Association to Authenticity: What the End of the Age of Association Means for the Church" Faith and Leader e-news, Luther Seminary, August 11, 2021. https://faithlead.luthersem.edu/from-the-age-of-association-to-authenticity/?utm_medium=email&utm_source=sharpspring&sslid=Mzc0MrM0tzCyMDY1AQA&sseid=MzKyNDS2MDE2MgIA&jobid=56751a80-3ff5-423b-81c4-1d77bb96e0ae. Accessed Feb. 5, 2022.
3. Ted Smith, "No Longer Shall They Teach One Another: The End of Theological Education," Opening Sprunt Lecture, Union Presbyterian Seminary, May 3, 2023. https://youtu.be/i_9peSje2HQ.

APPENDIX

Downloadable Handouts

http://bit.ly/45Wp4Ah

Scan the QR code or access the web page to download and print handouts.

How to Find a Spiritual Director for One-with-One Spiritual Direction

- *Pray.* Pray over your search for a spiritual director, asking God to lead you to a life-giving relationship. (While prayer is appropriate at every step, this process highlights two times for concentrated prayer.)
- *Discern.* Discern what is most important to you in a spiritual director. Possible areas for discernment might include denominational affiliation, theological perspectives, personality, gender/sexuality identity, church experience, ability to meet in-person/online, and experience in spiritual disciplines.
- *Search.* Spiritual Directors International (SDI) has a search function on their website for spiritual directors (https://sdiworld.org). Retreat centers, monasteries, seminaries, and other programs that offer training, degrees, or certifications in spiritual direction often keep directories of their graduates or local spiritual directors. Some denominations or their local judicatories keep lists of spiritual directors. For example, Hearts on Fire is a fellowship of United Methodist spiritual directors that maintains a directory on their website (https://fumsdrl.org/).
- *Meet.* Set up meetings with up to three spiritual directors who fit your discerned criteria. As you meet with them, pay

From *Belong: Group Spiritual Direction for Christian Friendship and Communal Discernment.*
Copyright © 2025 Abingdon Press. Permission granted to reproduce for personal or local church use.

attention to how you feel. Do you sense that you are in God's presence when you are with them? Do you have a feeling of warmth, of respect, and of being heard, seen, and understood? Do you feel belonging to God and to them? Ask questions about their rate (what they charge per session), how frequently you would meet (usually once a month), what a typical session would be like, what their theological background is, how/where they trained in spiritual direction, and what their expectations would be of you as a directee.

- *Pray.* Pray over your potential director. With whom do you sense God is leading you to as a spiritual director? Confirm your prayerful discernment with the chosen director.
- *Practice.* Establish a consistent practice of meeting with your spiritual director (usually once a month). Grow together with God! Flourish in this space of belonging.

From *Belong: Group Spiritual Direction for Christian Friendship and Communal Discernment.* Copyright © 2025 Abingdon Press. Permission granted to reproduce for personal or local church use.

Models of Group Spiritual Direction

Model	Preparation	Timing	Practice	Facilitator	Directee	Group Members
GSD for friendship	Prayer by all group members on what the Holy Spirit is nudging them to bring for discernment.	Depends upon the timing structure utilized and the number of people in the group. All members receive the same amount of time as a directee.	All group members receive and give spiritual direction to each other.	Usually, there is a facilitator in this practice, who upholds the covenant and timing structure. Sometimes the group will rotate the facilitator role. The facilitator may choose to not receive time as a directee if they are teaching the group the practice, or if time is running short.	Usually, every group member has a turn as the directee. During their turn, the directee shares what is most present in their life with God for the prescribed time amount (3 minutes, 4 minutes, 10 minutes, etc.)	Group members serve as spiritual directors for the person sharing as the directee. During the group response time, they offer open-ended questions or statements. They pray for the directee during the intercessory prayer time.

From *Belong: Group Spiritual Direction for Christian Friendship and Communal Discernment*.
Copyright © 2025 Abingdon Press. Permission granted to reproduce for personal or local church use.

Model	Preparation	Timing	Practice	Facilitator	Directee	Group Members
GSD with a focus person(s)	Those who will be directees pray about what the Holy Spirit is nudging them to bring for discernment.	Each focus person receives about 30 minutes of time; the total time commitment depends upon the number of focus people. For example, a meeting with two focus people will last about an hour; with four focus people, two hours, etc.	Group members offer group spiritual direction to the focus person(s).	There can be a facilitator who supports the group covenant and the timing structure, or the role might be shared among group members.	The directee(s) receives substantive spiritual direction from their fellow group members on whatever they bring for discernment.	Group members serve as spiritual directors for the person sharing as the directee. During the group response time, they offer open-ended questions or statements. They pray for the directee during the intercessory prayer time.

From *Belong: Group Spiritual Direction for Christian Friendship and Communal Discernment*. Copyright © 2025 Abingdon Press. Permission granted to reproduce for personal or local church use.

Model	Preparation	Timing	Practice	Facilitator	Directee	Group Members
Clearness Committee (Quaker tradition)	Focus person provides a written synopsis of their question for discernment to the group in advance of the meeting. Generally, the focus person calls together the group.	2 hours	The focus person presents their question for discernment. The committee then offers open-ended questions for the focus person, with space for silence. Toward the end, the committee might mirror back what they have heard. The time ends with the committee offering the strengths and gifts they saw in the focus person.	Often called a "clerk," the facilitator takes notes during the practice for the focus person to have. This person may keep the committee to a covenant and guide the process.	Only the one focus person serves in the directee role. The person must be prepared for this degree of attention and discernment for the life question they bring.	The group members, or committee, provide spiritual direction to the directee, or focus person. They will not share about any of their own personal life's discernment or receive direction.

From *Belong: Group Spiritual Direction for Christian Friendship and Communal Discernment.*
Copyright © 2025 Abingdon Press. Permission granted to reproduce for personal or local church use.

Appendix

Model	Preparation	Timing	Practice	Facilitator	Directee	Group Members
GSD for Communal Discernment	Preparation may include the formation and training of a leadership team. GSD for friendship may be practiced to build trust and relationships. Contemplative spiritual practices may be offered. Information sessions and/or communication through various forms of media may occur. Research on the issue and the formulation of the question for discernment and guiding principles may take place.	There can be a wide variety of timing structures, from a weekend retreat to monthly or weekly sessions. The amount of time for each gathering will also vary depending upon the kind of practice used.	The Christian tradition offers a wide variety of communal discernment practices, from the Ignatian Deliberation to Quaker Meetings for Business to forms of Wesleyan discernment based upon the Quadrilateral. Different listening practices may also be utilized, including fish bowls, interviews, open forums, and posting of ideas.	A facilitator is essential to the practice. This person, in consultation with the leadership team, may create the type of discernment, lead the process, and mediate through experiences of conflict.	The issue or question for discernment is the focus, rather than a directee. The community is working through practices of discernment to come to a consensus on the Holy Spirit's guidance on that issue or question.	All the members of the community participate in the communal discernment practice. Group members may uphold different roles, such as lead team member, prayer, hospitality team member, facilitator in a small group, etc.

From *Belong: Group Spiritual Direction for Christian Friendship and Communal Discernment.*
Copyright © 2025 Abingdon Press. Permission granted to reproduce for personal or local church use.

The Steps of Group Spiritual Direction for Friendship

Step/Movement	Facilitator	Directee/Storyteller	Group Member
Gathering/ Beginning	• prays • arrives early • prepares/sets up any food/drinks • sets out copies of group covenant/timing structures • sets out candle/lighter • exhibits hospitable spirit		• prays • arrives punctually or in accordance with group culture • maintains openness of heart and spirit to other group members and process
Group Covenant/ Guidelines	• lifts up group covenant, checks in on agreement • lifts up/reiterates timing structures for the group's process		• participates in amending/affirming group covenant • gives attention to timing structures

From *Belong: Group Spiritual Direction for Christian Friendship and Communal Discernment.*
Copyright © 2025 Abingdon Press. Permission granted to reproduce for personal or local church use.

Appendix

Step/Movement	Facilitator	Directee/Storyteller	Group Member
Timing Structure	• presents to the group the timing structure they will use for the group (3-1-3-1, 4-4-4, etc.) • explains the pattern of silence, sharing, listening/responding, prayer that correlates to the timing structure • solicits group feedback and may amend the timing structure as the group gains experience • may only briefly reference the timing structure as the group progresses in their practice	• will uphold the amount of time given for their sharing when serving in the role of directee	• will uphold the time structure, particularly for the time given for their responses.
Prompt and Centering Silence	• prays and prepares in advance of prompt • offers prompt (reading, scripture, music, poem, etc.) • repeats reading as is helpful • guides group members into silence, perhaps with use of a bell, chimes, or singing bowl • keeps time of silence		

From *Belong: Group Spiritual Direction for Christian Friendship and Communal Discernment.* Copyright © 2025 Abingdon Press. Permission granted to reproduce for personal or local church use.

The Steps of Group Spiritual Direction for Friendship

Step/Movement	Facilitator	Directee/Storyteller	Group Member
Holy Listening	• invites someone to volunteer to share first (could establish the order of who will go second, third, etc.) • models listening without interruption • upholds time boundaries for directee • could give a space for clarifying questions by the group after the person has shared, if that is the group's practice (to understand the situation or to clarify specific information that might be confusing)	• shares as honestly and authentically as possible the story of their life with God • focuses on what is most important and significant to share for discernment • abide by the time limits for their sharing (could be 3 to 15 minutes)	• listens prayerfully without interruption • seeks to be present to God's presence in oneself and in the directee • pays attention to what they notice, appreciate, and wonder about the directee's storytelling • abides by the time limits for their sharing

From *Belong: Group Spiritual Direction for Christian Friendship and Communal Discernment.*
Copyright © 2025 Abingdon Press. Permission granted to reproduce for personal or local church use.

Appendix

Step/Movement	Facilitator	Directee/Storyteller	Group Member
Silence to Hear God	<ul><li>invites the group into prayerful and discerning listening to God in a time of silence</li><li>keeps time for the silence</li><li>gently invites the group out of the silence</li></ul>	<ul><li>listens for any thoughts or words of comfort or insight from the Holy Spirit from their sharing</li><li>rests in the silence</li></ul>	<ul><li>listens for God's prayer for the directee</li><li>reflects on what they have heard</li><li>notices what is of God or what might "shimmer" from the sharing</li><li>listens for what their prayer for the directee might be</li><li>lets go of anything that gets in the way of listening</li><li>listens for anything to share with the directee on God's behalf</li></ul>
Life-giving Responses	<ul><li>invites the group into a prayerful time of sharing</li><li>keeps the time for response sharing</li><li>models the offering of Spirit-led responses and questions</li><li>suggests a pause for silence if the group gets off track or if the group needs it</li></ul>	<ul><li>receives the responses and questions from others with an open heart</li><li>engages in conversation with the questions that seem fruitful or spark reflection</li><li>allows group responses/questions to simply rest without an answer if that is best</li><li>pauses for silence when needed</li></ul>	<ul><li>is determined neither to speak nor not to speak</li><li>is willing to remain silent and prayerfully hold the person's story</li><li>if nudged by the Holy Spirit, offers any questions, wonderings, noticings, and appreciations</li><li>may use prompt: "I noticed, I appreciated, I wonder . . ."</li><li>refrains from giving advice, sharing own story, or attempting to fix or change</li><li>remains attentive to time structure and doesn't overshare . . . or dominate the response time</li></ul>

From *Belong: Group Spiritual Direction for Christian Friendship and Communal Discernment*. Copyright © 2025 Abingdon Press. Permission granted to reproduce for personal or local church use.

The Steps of Group Spiritual Direction for Friendship

Step/Movement	Facilitator	Directee/Storyteller	Group Member
Intercessory Silent Prayer	• invites the group into a time of silent intercessory prayer for the directee • keeps time on the silence • may invite or offer verbal prayers of intercession if that is the group's practice • after all group members for the day have shared, prays for any absent members	• receives the gift of being prayed for by others • remains open to being held in the love of God by others	• prays for the directee • in silence, offers the person to the love of God and desire of God for their life • if it is the group's practice, offers verbal intercessions as nudged by the Holy Spirit

Step/Movement	Facilitator	Directee/Storyteller	Group Member
Reflections on Time Together	• invites the group to reflect on the practice of prayerful listening • offers questions such as "Did anything interfere with our prayerfulness?" and "Did we get off track at any point?" • checks in on the practice of covenant guidelines • keeps time on this reflection		• honestly offers reflections on the group's prayerfulness • reflects on the upholding of the covenant guidelines and adherence to the group's timing structures
Closing Prayer/ Housekeeping	• leads the group in a silent or verbal prayer of closure • checks in on scheduling the next meeting or any other "housekeeping" items for the group		• participates in prayer • makes the group spiritual direction meetings a priority in their schedule

Group Spiritual Direction Process[1] for Friendship-Based Groups

A Quick Guide

Gathering (5 to 15 minutes, depending on the group)

- The group gathers in a host home, gathering place (church, café, community center, library room, etc.) or online and shares in welcoming one another
- Possible sharing of food and drink refreshments
- At the appointed time, the group assembles in a seated circle or gathers their attention to begin on an online platform (Zoom, etc.)

Group Covenant (15 to 20 minutes in 1st gathering, 1 minute reminder thereafter)

- For the first gathering, the leader facilitates the group in determining their covenant. The leader or a scribe records the key points of the covenant and places the agreement in a visible place before the group. The group also could tick off the key points for their covenant from the "Covenant" section below.
- In subsequent gatherings, the covenant is reiterated and spoken aloud at the beginning of the assembly.

From *Belong: Group Spiritual Direction for Christian Friendship and Communal Discernment.* Copyright © 2025 Abingdon Press. Permission granted to reproduce for personal or local church use.

Timing Structure (less than a minute reminder)

- The timing structure could be determined by the Belong leader or Belong leadership team in advance. Depending upon context, each group could offer insight into which structure they want to employ.
- The timing structure is reiterated as needed after the first meeting during the review of the group covenant at the beginning of the group time.

Prompt and Centering Silence (1 minute to up to 5 minutes)

- The Belong leader or a volunteer offers a prompt to help people to center their hearts, minds, and spirits. This could be a scripture, poem, reading, image, or piece of music.
- The group then enters a period of silence to offer their hearts to God and to dedicate the time to God's direction in everyone's life.

Holy Listening to 1st Directee/Storyteller (3 to 5 minutes)

Group commitments

- The group listens prayerfully, without interruption, to the directee.
- The group seeks to be attentive to God's presence in oneself and in the directee.
- Group members pay attention to what they **notice, appreciate, and wonder** about the storytelling.

Directee commitments

- The directee shares as honestly and authentically as possible the story of their life with God at the time. This sharing may

---

From *Belong: Group Spiritual Direction for Christian Friendship and Communal Discernment.*
Copyright © 2025 Abingdon Press. Permission granted to reproduce for personal or local church use.

be informed by the prompt or may be a story the directee discerned in advance to share.

Silence to Hear God (Intercessory Prayer) (1 to 3 minutes)

- The group members listen for God's prayer for that person, and for any prayer they might have for the storyteller. Each member prays for direction as to anything to say to the person on God's behalf.
- Intercessory prayer questions include:
  - God, what is your prayer for this person?
  - What do you want my prayer to be for this person?
  - Is there anything I need to surrender to you in order to join your prayer for this person? (Do I need to release the need to fix, correct, change, or advise? Do I need to let go of my desire to tell my similar story?)
  - Is there anything you would have me to offer to this person on your behalf?[2]

Life-Giving Responses and Questions (3 to 10 minutes)

- Members of the group offer questions, wonderings, noticings, and appreciations for what the directee has shared. These sharings may be in the form of images, questions, words, or music. They also may offer what they have received as God's prayer for this person.
- Group members may use the response prompt: **I noticed, I wondered, I appreciated . . .**

Silent Prayer for Presenter (1 to 3 minutes)

- The group prays silently for the storyteller.
- The directee/storyteller can rest in the silence, reflect on the offerings, or write down notes on what they have received. The

From *Belong: Group Spiritual Direction for Christian Friendship and Communal Discernment.*
Copyright © 2025 Abingdon Press. Permission granted to reproduce for personal or local church use.

process is then repeated for each member of the group, using the same time structure for each person.

Reflection on time together (1 to 10 minutes after all presenters have shared)

- The group reflects together on the quality of their prayerfulness within the group. This also can be a time for additional observations and questions about the process.
- Questions might include: Did anything interfere with our prayerfulness? Was anything especially supportive of the prayerfulness? What was the group experience like for you?
- The group checks in on their practice of their covenant guidelines.

Closing Prayer (1 to 5 minutes)

- The group may reflect in silence on what God might have for each of them to carry forth from the group meeting. What seed have they received that they are being invited to take and plant in the soil of their souls, to tend and water until the next time the group meets.

NOTES

1. This handout, unless otherwise indicated in a note, is adapted from Nan Weir, "Group Spiritual Direction Group Process" unpublished handout for Shalem Institute training in Group Spiritual Direction, February 2003, revised February 2012 and April 2020 as adapted from Rose Mary Dougherty, *Group Spiritual Direction: Community for Discernment* (New York: Paulist Press, 1995).
2. These intercessory prayer questions come directly from the handout by Nan Weir.

From Belong: Group Spiritual Direction for Christian Friendship and Communal Discernment.
Copyright © 2025 Abingdon Press. Permission granted to reproduce for personal or local church use.

Covenant Guidelines for Group Spiritual Direction

Confidentiality: Hold another's sharing of their journey with God with reverence.[1] Practice a holy respect that acknowledges that everyone's voice and story is to be held in confidence. All sharing stays inside the group's circle.

Presence: Be fully present now—with whatever emotions or stories you bring. As the directee, be present with what is real for you in the moment. As a group member, be prayerfully present for and with each other as each person shares their story. Meet each person where they are. Practice presence by turning off any distracting electronic devices and inner chatter.

Honor the Process: Uphold the timing structure of the group. Observe time limits in your sharing and responses. Refrain from side conversations with group members.

Prayerful Listening: As the directee, listen for God in your life before the meeting and as you share your story.[2] As a group member, pray for those sharing. Listen for God's presence and work in the directee's life. Listen for what shimmers with the Holy. Listen for the inner heart of speech. Listen in a compassionate and nonjudgmental way.[3] Listen without trying to fix, change, correct, or advise in your own mind. Listen to the silence.

From Belong: Group Spiritual Direction for Christian Friendship and Communal Discernment.
Copyright © 2025 Abingdon Press. Permission granted to reproduce for personal or local church use.

Truthful Speech: As the directee, speak honestly as you offer your journey. Speak for yourself in the first person (I think, I wonder, I felt . . .) as you relay your experience. Set your boundaries as needed.[4] Say "pass" if you would rather not share; all speech is invitational.[5] Speak directly to a group member if a clarification is needed. As a group member, speak honestly from the guidance of the Spirit. Refrain from speaking out of ego or a need to appear knowledgeable or wise. Refrain from speech when silence is needed.

Life-giving Responses: As the directee, prayerfully receive what is offered from the group with the freedom to respond or not to respond. As a group member, offer invitational responses that move the directee into "appreciation of the holy dimension of their life."[6] Offer open-ended questions (where is God in this, what is your prayer in this?) and limited response starters (I noticed, I appreciated, I wondered).

Turn to wonder when things get rough for you. If you become upset, judgmental, or defensive, ask yourself, "I wonder what my reaction might be inviting me to explore?" or "I wonder how this person (whose sharing is stirring my emotions) might be feeling?" Be open to how your own struggle in the sharing might be a nudge toward your growth.[7]

NOTES

1. Nan Weir, adapted from Patience Robbins et al, "Group Spiritual Direction: Guidelines for Groups," from The Shalem Institute for Spiritual Formation, Personal Spiritual Deepening Program, Guidelines for Groups, 2009, rev. February 2012.
2. Nan Weir, adapted from Patience Robbins et al, "Group Spiritual Direction: Guidelines for Groups."
3. Diane Millis, *Re-creating A Life: Learning How to Tell Our Most Life-Giving Story* (Bellevue, WA: SDI Press, 2019), 170.
4. Millis, *Re-creating A Life,* 170.
5. Circle of Trust Touchstones, developed by Parker Palmer and the Center for Courage and Renewal. One of the touchstones is that "what is offered in the circle is by invitation and not demand."
6. Nan Weir, adapted from Patience Robbins et al., "Group Spiritual Direction: Guidelines for Groups."
7. Circle of Trust Touchstones, developed by Parker Palmer and the Center for Courage and Renewal.

From *Belong: Group Spiritual Direction for Christian Friendship and Communal Discernment.*
Copyright © 2025 Abingdon Press. Permission granted to reproduce for personal or local church use.

3-1-3-1 Timing Structure for Group Spiritual Direction[1]

(8 minutes per directee/storyteller)

Benefits:

- A great timing structure for new groups or for beginners.
- The shorter periods of silence (1 minute) support beginners in contemplative practice.
- More (or all) people in the group can share with the expedited time structure.
- The leader/facilitator usually has time to share as a directee.

Limitations:

- Directees must compress their sharing.
- Limited time for discernment for each directee.
- Response time is compressed.

Summary of 3-1-3-1 Timing Structure (8 minutes per person)

- 3-Directee/Storyteller shares for 3 minutes.
- 1-Silence to hear God—participants practice holy listening.

From *Belong: Group Spiritual Direction for Christian Friendship and Communal Discernment.*
Copyright © 2025 Abingdon Press. Permission granted to reproduce for personal or local church use.

- 3-Response time for the group and directee/storyteller.
- 1-Minute of silent prayer for directee/storyteller. (Repeat for each group member.)

Outline of Group Session

Gathering (5–10 minutes)

Group Covenant and Timing Structure (1–3 minutes)
- Members read or review their covenant at beginning of the assembly.
- The facilitator reminds the group of the timing structure

Prompt and Centering Silence (1–5 minutes)

First Directee/Storyteller Shares (3 minutes)

Silence to Hear God (Intercessory Prayer) (1 minute)

Life-Giving Responses and Questions (3 minutes)

Silent Prayer for Presenter (1 minute)

(The process of the steps printed in bold is then repeated for each member of the group, using the same time structure for each person.)

From *Belong: Group Spiritual Direction for Christian Friendship and Communal Discernment.*
Copyright © 2025 Abingdon Press. Permission granted to reproduce for personal or local church use.

Reflection on Time Together (1 to 5 minutes after all members have shared)

Closing Prayer (1 to 5 minutes)

NOTES

1. Adapted from Nan Weir, "Group Spiritual Direction Group Process" unpublished handout for Shalem Institute training in Group Spiritual Direction, Feb. 2003, revised February 2012 and April 2020 as adapted from Rose Mary Dougherty, *Group Spiritual Direction: Community for Discernment* (New York: Paulist Press, 1995).

From *Belong: Group Spiritual Direction for Christian Friendship and Communal Discernment.*
Copyright © 2025 Abingdon Press. Permission granted to reproduce for personal or local church use.

4-4-4 Timing Structure for Group Spiritual Direction

"Hearing into Speech" Structure from Diane Millis[1]

Benefits:

- A good timing structure for beginners, with shorter periods of silence (1 minute).
- All people in the group can share for four minutes with this time structure.
- The directee can simply listen during the group response time and has their own time for response.

Limitations:

- Directees must compress their sharing.
- Limited time for discernment for each directee.
- The response time can feel one-sided with the separation of the group members/directee responses.
- The directee can feel some pressure to offer a solo response for up to four minutes.

From Belong: Group Spiritual Direction for Christian Friendship and Communal Discernment. Copyright © 2025 Abingdon Press. Permission granted to reproduce for personal or local church use.

Summary of 4-4-4 Timing Structure

4—Telling

The directee/storyteller shares their story of their life with God. There is no interruption from the group.

4—Responding

The first minute of this time can be given to silence for the group members to listen to what God might have them to offer to the directee. Then the group members can share with the directee using the prompts:

    I noticed . . .
    I appreciated . . .
    I wondered . . .

The directee simply listens and takes in what others are offering but does not offer a response at this time.

4—Retelling

The directee/storyteller reflects upon the noticings, appreciations, and wonderings received from the group. The directee can use the group's insights, responses, and questions for further reflection on the work of God in their life. They may choose to retell or narrate their story with the new insights they've received.

Pausing

The group shares in a minute of silence to honor what has been shared and to hold the directee in silent prayer.

*The process is repeated for every member of the group.

From *Belong: Group Spiritual Direction for Christian Friendship and Communal Discernment.*
Copyright © 2025 Abingdon Press. Permission granted to reproduce for personal or local church use.

Outline of Group Session

Gathering (5–10 minutes)

Group Covenant and Timing Structure (1–3 minutes)
- Members read or review their covenant at beginning of the assembly.
- The facilitator reminds the group of the timing structure

Prompt and Centering Silence (1–5 minutes)

First Directee/Storyteller Shares (4 minutes)

Life-Giving Responses and Questions by group (4 minutes)

Retelling by the directee/storyteller (4 minutes)

Pausing (1 minute)

(The process of the steps printed in bold is then repeated for each member of the group, using the same time structure for each person.)

Reflection on Time Together (1 to 5 minutes after all members have shared)

Closing Prayer (1 to 5 minutes)

NOTES

1. Diane Millis, *Re-creating a Life: Learning How to Tell our Most Life-Giving Story* (Bellevue, WA: SDI Press, 2019), 153.

From *Belong: Group Spiritual Direction for Christian Friendship and Communal Discernment.*
Copyright © 2025 Abingdon Press. Permission granted to reproduce for personal or local church use.

Two Extended Timing Structures for Group Spiritual Direction[1]

Benefits:

- Each directee receives substantial time for discernment.
- Great for more experienced practitioners.
- Longer periods of silence allow for deeper listening.
- More immersion into the contemplative aspect of spiritual direction.

Limitations:

- Requires more time commitment for each meeting.
- Groups are smaller in number (4 people) for each to receive time.

Summary of 5-2-10-2 Timing Structure (19 minutes per directee/storyteller)

5-Directee shares for 5 minutes.
2-Two minutes of silence for group members to listen.
10-Ten minutes of response time for both group members and directee.
2-Two minutes of silent prayer for directee.

From *Belong: Group Spiritual Direction for Christian Friendship and Communal Discernment.*
Copyright © 2025 Abingdon Press. Permission granted to reproduce for personal or local church use.

Summary of 10-5-10-5 Timing Structure (30 minutes per directee/storyteller)

10-Directee shares their story for 10 minutes.
5-Group listens in silence for five minutes.
10-Ten minutes for open-ended questions and reflections from group.
5-Silent prayer for storyteller for five minutes.

Outline of Group Session

Beginning (5–10 minutes)—Gathering, chatting, and joyful laughter. Refreshments encouraged!

Settling (1–2 minutes)—Group finds seating in a comfortable circle.

Reading (1–5 minutes)—The facilitator shares a brief reading from scripture or another text in order to bring the group together to a common focus. The reading can be repeated a couple of times in a form of *lectio divina*, with silence for reflection after each reading.

Silent gathering (15 minutes or less)—The group settles into silence. People may choose to focus on their breath. They might reflect on a word or a phrase from the reading that speaks to them. Practice stillness. Rest in God's loving presence.

Invitation (1 minute or less)—The facilitator invites someone to share first. Before that person begins, the group may or may not determine the order in which the group will go—second, third, fourth, etc.

Sharing by Directee (5 minutes in 5-2-10-2 structure or 10 minutes in the 10-5-10-5 structure)—(Note: This could extend to 10 minutes for the directee shares without any interruption from the group. The facilitator may signal the closure of the time to the directee.

From *Belong: Group Spiritual Direction for Christian Friendship and Communal Discernment.*
Copyright © 2025 Abingdon Press. Permission granted to reproduce for personal or local church use.

Clarifying Questions (1 minute)—Group members may ask specific questions to clarify the storytelling. This is not to offer spiritual direction but to get answers on anything unclear or confusing.[2]

Silence (2 minutes in 5-2-10-2 or 5 minutes in 10-5-10-5)—The group reflects on what they have heard. They listen on what is "of God" in the person's story. They pay attention to what God's desires or prayer might be.

Responses (10 minutes in 5-2-10-2 or 10 minutes in 10-5-10-5)—Group members share what came to them in the silence, refraining from giving advice or telling their own story.

Silence (2 minutes in 5-2-10-2 or 5 minutes in 10-5-10-5—The group prays silently for the directee and over what they have shared. The directee reflects on what has been offered.

Second presentation or sharing—the group repeats the steps above for the next person.

Break (5–10 minutes as decided by the group)

Third and fourth presentations . . . The group repeats the practice for each group member.

Prayer for absent member (5 minutes)—Share what the person might have offered about why they missed the meeting. Offer prayer over the reason for the absence and any other specific requests for prayer.

Reflection on time together (5 minutes)—Focus on the experience of prayerful listening. Did anything get in the way of it? Did anything support it? Did the group get off track at any point?

From *Belong: Group Spiritual Direction for Christian Friendship and Communal Discernment*.
Copyright © 2025 Abingdon Press. Permission granted to reproduce for personal or local church use.

Reminders (1 minute—Remind group of the next meeting time and of covenant guidelines (upholding confidentiality, etc.).

NOTES

1. This structure is adapted from Shalem group spiritual direction guidelines and Lois Lindbloom, *Prayerful Listening: Cultivating Discernment in Community* (Northfield, MN: Ashmore Ink, 2007), 12–13. Rose Mary Dougherty, *Group Spiritual Direction for Discernment* (New York: Paulist Press, 1995), 50–55.
2. I find that clarifying questions can be difficult for beginning groups. They launch immediately into spiritual direction or offer substantive responses or indulge in curiosity. Clarifying questions are short and can be answered very briefly by the directee.

From *Belong: Group Spiritual Direction for Christian Friendship and Communal Discernment*.
Copyright © 2025 Abingdon Press. Permission granted to reproduce for personal or local church use.

Summary of Timing Structures for Group Spiritual Direction

1. **3-1-3-1 (8 minutes per directee/storyteller)**
   3-Storyteller shares for 3 minutes.
   1-Participants listen for a minute of silence.
   3-Response time for the group and storyteller.
   1-Minute of silent prayer for storyteller.
   (Repeat for each storyteller)

2. **4-4-4 (12 minutes per directee/storyteller)**
   4-Storyteller shares their story.
   4-Group members only offer their responses and open-ended questions.
   4- Storyteller responds to what has been shared.

3. **5-2-10-2 (19 minutes per directee/storyteller)**
   5-Storyteller shares for 5 minutes.
   2-Silence for group members to listen.
   10-Response time for both group members and storyteller.
   2- Silent prayer for storyteller.

4. **10-5-10-5 (30 minutes per directee/storyteller)**
   10-Storyteller shares for 10 minutes.
   5-Silence for group members to listen.
   10-Response time for both group members and storyteller.
   5-Silent prayer for storyteller.

From Belong: Group Spiritual Direction for Christian Friendship and Communal Discernment.
Copyright © 2025 Abingdon Press. Permission granted to reproduce for personal or local church use.

Contemplative Spiritual Practices to Support Listening to God

1. Centering Prayer

History

This prayer of sitting in silence has roots in the ancient monastic practice of *lectio divina* and was practiced in some form by Christian mystics such as John Cassian, Francis de Sales, Teresa of Ávila, St. John of the Cross, Therese of Lisieux and others. The Second Vatican Council of the Roman Catholic Church in the 1960s called for the revival of spiritual practices of early Christianity. By the 1970s, Trappist monks such as William Meninger, Basil Pennington, and Thomas Keating at St. Joseph's Abbey in Massachusetts responded to this call and developed a simple method of silent prayer for contemporary people. The name "centering prayer" developed out of Trappist monk Thomas Merton's description of the prayer as "centered entirely on the presence of God."[1]

Description

The practice of centering prayer involves sitting for twenty minutes in silence in openness to the presence of God. It describes both a relationship with God and a spiritual discipline to support that relationship.[2] The source of centering prayer is the indwelling Trinity: Father, Son, and Holy Spirit. Jesus's wisdom saying in the Sermon on the Mount in Matthew 6:6 to "go to your room, close the door, and pray to your Father who is in secret" provides scriptural support of the practice. Through the guidance of the Holy Spirit, a centering prayer practitioner sits in silence and, as directed by Jesus, opens the inner room of their heart to commune with God. The fruits of centering prayer often don't come in the practice itself—sometimes the prayer time can feel like a thousand "thought monkeys" jumping around on your shoulders. However, the capacity to sit and listen and stay present in the twenty-minute prayer brings the fruit of stability, peace, and greater listening in other arenas of our lives, particularly in the practice of spiritual direction.

Method

Centering prayer involves four central guidelines:

1. First, you choose a "sacred word" as a symbol of the intention to consent to God's presence within. A "sacred word" consists of a simple one- or two-syllable word—such as joy, peace, Jesus, love, listen, mercy, faith, trust, or hope—and serves as a word to come back to in your thoughts when your mind begins to drift to other things.
2. In the second guideline, you take a comfortable seat in which you can sit well for twenty minutes and not fall asleep. You close your eyes as a symbol of letting go of all things around you. You introduce the sacred word as a symbol of your consent to God's presence and action within you—as gently as laying a feather on a pillow.
3. Third, when you lose focus or get engaged with your thoughts, you return gently to the sacred word. You simply come back to the word without judgment or recrimination, and then open your heart and mind back up to the presence of God. "Thoughts" in centering prayer teaching include any bodily sensations, feelings, images, memories, ideas, plans, commentaries, concepts—and

From *Belong: Group Spiritual Direction for Christian Friendship and Communal Discernment.*
Copyright © 2025 Abingdon Press. Permission granted to reproduce for personal or local church use.

they are inevitable! You will get distracted; the practice of centering prayer is to return to the sacred word, which is the only (but significant) effort involved in the prayer. Physical pains, twitches, itches, and sensations often result from the untying of emotional knots in the body and are normal.
4. In the fourth guideline, after the twenty minutes of sitting is up, you remain in silence for a couple of minutes with eyes closed. You may transition out of the centering prayer time by offering the Lord's Prayer and/or any prayers of intercession for others.

For more resources on centering prayer, see https://www.contemplativeoutreach.org/centering-prayer-method.

2. Adaptation of Ignatian Examen

History

This practice originates from sixteenth-century Basque Spaniard Iñigo López de Oñaz y Loyola, later Ignatius of Loyola. Ignatius had profound experiences of God's presence and absence, which he termed consolation and desolation. He penned what became the *Spiritual Exercises,* a book that guides a four-week retreat, and includes an examination of conscience—an exploration of how God is present or absent in our daily lives. Ignatius taught this practice to friends who gathered around him, as they were drawn to his disciplined and practical spiritual life. These friends would become a new order in the Roman Catholic Church called the Society of Jesus, known as the Jesuits. The Ignatian Examen became a staple practice of the Jesuits—a spiritual exercise that Ignatius would guide his friends in at the end of every day.

Description

The Ignatian Examen involves the exploration of our feelings and desires. Ignatius called the feelings that connect us to God, others, and ourselves "consolations" and the feelings that disconnect us from God, others, and ourselves "desolations." By acknowledging the whole range of human emotions

From *Belong: Group Spiritual Direction for Christian Friendship and Communal Discernment.*
Copyright © 2025 Abingdon Press. Permission granted to reproduce for personal or local church use.

and feelings, Ignatian spirituality offers a wholistic perspective on human life with God in which both the good, hard, and the seemingly insignificant moments of every day are all included. The practice helps us to be in touch with our experience with God, and to discern how God is at work in our lives. As Ignatius described it, the method of examination of conscience supports the practice "of seeking and finding the will of God in the disposition of our life for the salvation of our soul."[3]

Method

The practice of an Examen is good to do at the end of every day before you go to bed. In an Examen you review your day in all the mundane moments as a way of becoming aware of God's movement in your daily life. The practice generally involves five steps, which take about 10–15 minutes or so to complete. Over time through this practice, you'll begin to discern how God is at work in your life and to trust the actions, practices, and ways of being that lead you closer to God. This practice of discernment not only forms you in your own life; it shapes you to better hear and know how God might be at work in the lives of others as you practice group spiritual direction. Here are the five steps:

1. Become aware of God's presence: Open yourself to God's light and presence and invite God to guide you as you reflect over your day.
2. Give thanks: Offer gratitude for the gift of the day. Scan mentally through your day and offer thanks for any joy and delight in the day, from a good meal to a good interaction with a person. God is in the small details and pleasures of a day.
3. Review the day: Reflect back over the emotions of your day. When did you feel joy, peace, happiness, a sense of God's presence? Offer thanks for these consolations. When did you feel anger, emptiness, frustration, jealousy, boredom, exhaustion, or a sense of God's absence? Pay attention to these desolations.

From *Belong: Group Spiritual Direction for Christian Friendship and Communal Discernment.*
Copyright © 2025 Abingdon Press. Permission granted to reproduce for personal or local church use.

4. Acknowledge any shortcomings: Was there a time that you responded out of your own brokenness, rather than God's grace? Did you show up as less than your true, beloved self? Offer this time in confession to God. Turn to God and receive God's mercy and forgiveness. Reflect on how you might do differently the next time.
5. Look to tomorrow: Ask God to give you any strength, wisdom, or love for anything in your coming day. Ask for any help or understanding you might need. Offer your tomorrow into God's hands. Trust that you will be given what is needed for whatever is before you. Rest in God's love, grace, and mercy.[4]

3. Practicing the Presence

History

As narrated by Brother Lawrence, a seventeenth-century Carmelite monk, practicing the presence is simply a sensitivity to God at work in the dailiness of our lives. Brother Lawrence worked in the monastery's kitchen and would "practice the presence" as he cleaned out pans and washed dishes. "In the kitchen (a place to which I have a natural aversion), I have accustomed myself to doing everything there for the love of God. On all occasions, with prayer, I have found his grace to do my work well, and I have found it easy during the fifteen years in which I have been employed here. . . . My prayers are nothing other than a sense of the presence of God."[5] In the midst of tedious work and activity, Brother Lawerence wedded contemplation to tasks.

Description

The invitation is to become aware of God in the everyday moments of life, as we are going about our day. In the grind of daily chores, housework, and all the mundane tasks that fill our lives, we intentionally open to the love of God that suffuses all things—even the most tedious. This practice helps us to become attuned to the work of the Holy Spirit in the daily rhythms of our

---

From *Belong: Group Spiritual Direction for Christian Friendship and Communal Discernment.*
Copyright © 2025 Abingdon Press. Permission granted to reproduce for personal or local church use.

life, which then supports us in identifying the presence of God at work in the life of another in group spiritual direction.

Method

In the midst of tasks as you go through your day:

- "Ask God for grace. Offer God your whole heart. Over and again, in the midst of business, every moment if you can, just offer God your heart. This can be done without a single utterance escaping you."[6]
- "Do not get weighted down with a lot of rules, or forms, or ways; act with faith—just come. But come in an attitude of love and deep humility."[7]

4. Sacrament of the Present Moment or Gentle Awareness

History

Jean-Pierre de Caussade, a French Jesuit priest, wrote a text called *The Sacrament of the Present Moment*. In ways similar to Brother Lawrence, Caussade taught that God is in the mundane, the ordinary, and the insignificant moments of life. Yet, God's activity permeates all things, even the most trivial. The most ordinary experiences can have profound meaning if we pay attention. Caussade taught the nuns to whom he offered spiritual direction, "No moment is trivial, since each one contains a divine Kingdom, and heavenly sustenance."[8] The small corners of our life can be illuminated with the shimmer of holy.

Description

Another form of prayer in the same vein as Caussade's "sacrament of the present moment" is called "gentle awareness," which involves intentional awareness of God in life as it is. By taking a few minutes to stop and listen to the sounds around you (bird song, voices of family, traffic), or to notice in detail

From *Belong: Group Spiritual Direction for Christian Friendship and Communal Discernment*.
Copyright © 2025 Abingdon Press. Permission granted to reproduce for personal or local church use.

your surroundings (the color of a leaf, the design of a flower, the texture of a favorite blanket), you become aware of what is around you—without trying to fix, change, or alter it. You simply observe what comes to you through your senses, offer the time to God, and ask God to open your senses and self to all of life. This kind of awareness teaches us to be open to how other people are, appreciating them as they are, without trying to change or "fix" them, which is important for listening in spiritual direction.[9]

Method

- Pay attention to the present moment. Ask how God might be present amid the mundane and trivial.[10]
- Open up your senses to your surroundings in their detail. Become aware of what is around you and observe life.
- Be open to God's presence in your setting, appreciating what you receive there.

NOTES

1. "History of Centering Prayer," Contemplative Outreach, https://www.contemplativeoutreach.org/history-of-centering-prayer/. Accessed May 28, 2023.
2. Centering Prayer, Contemplative Outreach, https://www.contemplativeoutreach.org/centering-prayer-method/. Accessed October 25, 2024.
3. Ignatius of Loyola, *The Spiritual Exercises of St. Ignatius* trans. Louis Puhl, S.J. (Chicago: Loyola Press, 1951), 1.
4. Daniel Wolpert, *Creating a Life with God: The Call of Ancient Prayer Practices* (Nashville: Upper Room Books, 2003), 180–81.
5. Brother Lawrence and Frank Laubach, *Practicing His Presence* (Jacksonville, FL: The Seed Sowers, 1973), 47, 56.
6. Brother Lawrence and Frank Laubach, 73.
7. Brother Lawrence and Frank Laubach, 73.
8. Jean Pierre de Caussade, *Sacrament of the Present Moment* (San Francisco: Harper San Francisco, 2009), 53, 63.
9. Rose Mary Dougherty, *Group Spiritual Direction: Community for Discernment* (New York: Paulist Press, 1995), 78.
10. Caussade, *Sacrament of the Present Moment*, 53. This is the duty of the present moment.

From Belong: Group Spiritual Direction for Christian Friendship and Communal Discernment.
Copyright © 2025 Abingdon Press. Permission granted to reproduce for personal or local church use.

Prompts for Leading Group Spiritual Direction

Each of the spiritual practices described below offers a pathway to help people enter into group spiritual direction. This is called the "prompt" in the group spiritual direction process because it "prompts" us to pay attention to the movement of God in our lives. The prompt can come before or after the beginning centering silence. It helps people to go from "getting here" in the gathering to "being here"—being present to one another and to God. A prompt provides space for holy listening that many beginners—and those of us who have been practicing for years—need in order to listen well and hear the rustling of the Holy Spirit in the caverns of our own souls.

Choose one (or more) of these practices to serve as the prompt in group spiritual direction:

1. Silence

Inviting a group into a centering silence to listen to God is always "enough." The silence can settle people, soften the flurry of activity of the gathering, and tune people to the frequency of God. If you come to the group as a leader without any prompt prepared, trust that silence will always serve well to center a group.

From Belong: Group Spiritual Direction for Christian Friendship and Communal Discernment. *Copyright © 2025 Abingdon Press. Permission granted to reproduce for personal or local church use.*

2. Beginning Questions

Some groups might be helped by receiving an initial question for reflection, followed by a minute (or two or five, depending upon your timing structure) of silence to reflect and ponder what an answer to that question might be in their lives. Sample questions include:

- Can you think of a time in the past week (or month) in which you felt the most alive? The least alive? How did those times feel?
- Who or what in your life is bringing you a sense of God's love in these days/week/month?
- When or where were you most aware of God's presence in the past week/month?
- What is something you desire or are longing for in your life in these days? What do you think might be God's desire for you?[1]
- What is it like for you to be in the presence of God?
- What helps you to listen for and/or respond to God in your day-to-day life? What are the distractions?
- How have you been praying for yourself or for others? Is anything changing in your prayer life?
- What is drawing you to prayerful listening with others in group spiritual direction in this time?[2]

3. Scripture Reading (modified *lectio divina*)

A short reading of scripture is as a great way to center people in God's Word at the beginning of the practice. Just one to five verses serves as enough language for people to process. A lengthier passage, or a full pericope, can overwhelm people's capacity to hear a word or phrase of life for themselves. If desired, you can share the passage in advance of the meeting and invite group members to reflect on it before the gathering.

Scriptures to consider using include the Psalms, or whatever scripture might be the preaching text in worship on the past or coming Sunday. Many churches use the lectionary, which is a set of four scripture passages (Old Testament, Psalm, Gospel lesson, epistle lesson) for each Sunday that is set out in a three-year pattern.

Before you read the verses, invite the group members to listen for a word or phrase that stands out to them or speaks to them in some way. This listening question invites members into a way of engaging with scripture that is a shortened form of *lectio divina*, or sacred reading. Rather than reading scripture as a form of intellectual study, members are listening for how God might be speaking to them through it. Perhaps the word or phrase connects to an emotion or an experience they are currently having in their life with God. Perhaps it brings up a question, or a wondering, or an invitation. Instruct the group members that you will offer a short period of silence after the reading during which they can reflect on what the word or phrase means in their life.

They might feel led to bring this insight into their storytelling, or they might not. After the silence ends, read the passage of scripture again and/or offer a brief prayer, such as, "May the word of life we have received become a blessing to us and remain with us as we share our lives in God."

4. The Ignatian Examen Adaptation

Questions adapted from the Ignatian practice of examining the joys and the sorrows in life can also be a helpful way of beginning group spiritual direction. After settling into the circle, offer the questions of consolation and desolation below and then allow a short period of silence for personal reflection. The group member might bring this reflection into their time of sharing for direction—or not. Either way, the questions give a space for discerning how God is at work in a person's life.

Entry to the practice

- Become aware of God's presence: Open yourself to God's light and presence and invite God to guide you as you reflect over your week (or month, for a monthly gathering).
- Short silence.

From *Belong: Group Spiritual Direction for Christian Friendship and Communal Discernment.* Copyright © 2025 Abingdon Press. Permission granted to reproduce for personal or local church use.

Consolation

- When did you feel the most alive in the past week/month? When did you feel the most joy, peace, freedom, or love? Another way of asking this would be, when did you feel the strongest sense of God's presence? *Silence.*
- In silence, offer gratitude for the ways God has been present, loving, or alive to you.

Desolation

- When in the past week/month have you felt tired, bored, exhausted, frustrated, saddened? When did you feel the least loved or appreciated, or when did you feel you were the least loving? Another way of asking this would be, when did you feel God's absence or were least aware of the presence of God?[3] *Silence.*

5. Music

Another way to begin the centering might be through offering a piece of music. I often play music through my cell phone (or if I'm organized enough to remember a wireless speaker, I'll use that for better sound quality!). I'll choose a song, hymn, or musical piece that has spoken to me during the week of the gathering.

Music from monasteries, such as by Glenstal Abbey or Pluscarden Abbey, offer beautiful chants based on the liturgy of the hours. The music from the Taizé Community can offer a meditative, prayerful beginning. I also appreciate Christian artists such as Salt of the Sound, Luke Parker, One Hope Project, and Josh Garrells. The main point is to use a short clip of music that speaks to you and your group and provides a way of centering people in God's presence. Trust whatever musical offering you might be led to share and allow a space of silent reflection after playing it.

From *Belong: Group Spiritual Direction for Christian Friendship and Communal Discernment.*
Copyright © 2025 Abingdon Press. Permission granted to reproduce for personal or local church use.

6. *Visio Divina* (visual art or images)

Visio divina, or "sacred seeing," works similarly as *lectio divina* with scripture, except that images or artwork provide the source of reflection, rather than words. It's a form of Christian prayer in which we open our hearts and imaginations to reflect on an image, in silence, to see what God might have to offer us through it. *Visio divina* invites us to see at a "contemplative pace" what God might speak through an image or piece of art. Christian artwork throughout the ages can serve as helpful images, as well as art of creation or any other visual images that speak to you as a leader (images of sculptures can work too!).

Steps to the practice:

1. Open in prayer to God's presence. Ask God to speak to you through this image or artwork in a way that you can hear or see.
2. Look at the image. Rest your eyes on the characters, objects, or scenes depicted. Notice any feelings or reactions that come to you as your eyes absorb the picture.
3. Imagine that you are in this scene. What do you see from your vantage point? What do you hear? smell? sense? taste? What is God inviting you to experience through your senses? What might God be saying to you?
4. Continue in prayer. Ask the Holy Spirit to guide you. Does the image open a desire, longing, hope, or dream in your heart? How might God be calling you to respond? Gratitude? Wonder? Lament? Confession? Forgiveness? Praise? Silently make that offering.
5. Closure. What insight from this experience do you want to keep—perhaps for further reflection during your time of sharing in our group spiritual direction? Offer thanks to God for this time. Close your eyes, releasing the image from your vision. Open your heart, take a deep breath, open your eyes.[4]

From *Belong: Group Spiritual Direction for Christian Friendship and Communal Discernment*. Copyright © 2025 Abingdon Press. Permission granted to reproduce for personal or local church use.

NOTES

1. Alice Fryling, *Seeking God Together: an Introduction to Group Spiritual Direction* Downers Grove, IL: Intervarsity Press, 2009), 49–51.
2. Lois Lindbloom, *Prayerful Listening: Cultivating Discernment in Community,* Northfield, NM: Ashmore Ink, 2007), 16–17.
3. Fryling, 132–33. These questions are adapted from Fryling, which in turn is a revision of Ignatius's questions from the *Spiritual Exercises.*
4. These steps are adapted from "Visio Divina Workshop" Catholic Diocese of Biloxi. https://biloxidiocese.org/visio-divina#:~:text=Visio%20Divina%20%E2%80%94%20%E2%80%9Csacred%20seeing%E2%80%9D,have%20to%20say%20to%20us. Accessed on Dec. 7, 2022.

From *Belong: Group Spiritual Direction for Christian Friendship and Communal Discernment.*
Copyright © 2025 Abingdon Press. Permission granted to reproduce for personal or local church use.

Guidelines for Holy Listening and Life-giving Responses

Holy Listening During Directee's Sharing

- Listen with the Spirit. Listen to create an open space for a person to explore their story. Offer no verbal feedback, including interjections or questions.
- Listen with presence, focus, and attention. Lovingly hold the person sharing in prayer. Suspend any disbelief or judgment as it arises.
  - Notice—What body language, tone of voice, facial expressions, speech patterns, breathing patterns, repetition of words or phrases do you notice?
  - Appreciate—What aspects of the presenter's story inspire or draw you? What qualities of courage, perseverance, strength, or heartfulness in a person do you hear or observe? What "shimmers" for you? What stands out as holy, beautiful, or significant?
  - Wonder—What open-ended, life-giving questions arise for you as you listen?

From Belong: Group Spiritual Direction for Christian Friendship and Communal Discernment. Copyright © 2025 Abingdon Press. Permission granted to reproduce for personal or local church use.

Holy Listening During Silence/Intercessory Prayer (Directly after Directee's sharing)

Questions to ask God:

- God, what is your prayer for this person?
- What do you want my prayer to be?
- Is there anything I need to surrender to you in order to join your prayer for this person? What in me stands in the way (my judgment, my curiosity, my need to solve the problem or try to make someone happy)?
- Is there anything you want me to say to this person on your behalf?[1]

Life-giving Responses During Group Response Time

General Guidelines:

- Offer **contemplative** questions, which have a loving focus on the directee and decenter the questioner and their opinions, advice, or similar stories. Avoid questions that start with "why." Questions that start with "what" or "how" tend to be more contemplative. For example: What did you learn during that experience? How do you feel that in your body? What is giving you energy or life?
- Offer **open-ended** questions that invite the directee to explore their own spiritual journey and to reflect more deeply on their experience and convictions. Avoid questions that can be answered with a yes or a no. Ask questions in which you can't anticipate the answer. For example: What in your life is bringing you joy? What surprised you?
- **Stay or remain** with the person's language. For example: I heard you use the word "dry" several times. What does that mean to you?

From *Belong: Group Spiritual Direction for Christian Friendship and Communal Discernment.* Copyright © 2025 Abingdon Press. Permission granted to reproduce for personal or local church use.

- Give **silent, open space** after the question for the directee's reflection and discovery. Slow the pace of inquiry so that the directee isn't peppered with questions or responses but has time in silence to digest what is offered before another group member replies.

3-Fold Pattern: Notice, Appreciate, Wonder[2]

1. **I notice . . .** (offer reflection on any observed body language, tone of voice, facial expressions, speech patterns, breathing patterns, repetition of words or phrases, questions of noticing God in daily life)
2. **I appreciate . . .** (offer reflection on any aspects of the directee's story that inspire or draw you; qualities of courage, perseverance, strength, heartfulness in a person; what in the story "shimmers" for you)
3. **I wonder . . .** (open-ended, life-giving questions; can't predict an answer; refrain from "telling," advising, or fixing conventional questions)

Ignatian Questions (adapted)

- Consolation: What is bringing you energy, joy, or life? Where do you feel the presence of God?
- Desolation: What is drawing you away from God? What is taking energy?

Spiritual Life Questions

- What is your prayer in this? What is prayer like for you?
- What is your soul's longing for today? How would you like for God to satisfy that soul's longing?
- How would you describe your relationship with God now?
- How would you like God to help you in this?

From *Belong: Group Spiritual Direction for Christian Friendship and Communal Discernment*. Copyright © 2025 Abingdon Press. Permission granted to reproduce for personal or local church use.

- How are you being changed by what is happening in your life?
- How might the Spirit be whispering to you in this situation (see Elijah's listening to God's whisper in 1 Kings 19:11-13).[3]

NOTES

1. These four questions are quoted from Nan Weir, "Group Spiritual Direction: Group Process" handout, unpublished revised April 2020 from Rose Mary Doughterty, *Group Spiritual Direction: Community for Discernment* (New York: Paulist Press, 1995).
2. The 3-fold pattern of 'I notice, I appreciate, I wonder' is taken from Diane Millis, *Re-creating a Life: Learning How to Tell our Most Life-giving Story,* (Bellevue, WA: SDI Press, 2019), 148–51.
3. These are common questions in spiritual direction. See also Alice Fryling's questions in her chapter 5 "Asking Life Giving Questions" in her book: Alice Fryling, *Seeking God Together: An Introduction to Group Spiritual Direction* (Downers Grove, IL: IVP Books, 2009), 49–53.

From *Belong: Group Spiritual Direction for Christian Friendship and Communal Discernment.*
Copyright © 2025 Abingdon Press. Permission granted to reproduce for personal or local church use.

Belong Leader Training Session: Sample Agenda

(Approximately 2 hours)

2:45	Snacks and Gathering
3:00	Introductions, Worship Liturgy
3:15	Best Practices for Belong
	• Logistics (dates/time/duration)
	• Invitations to Belong: Recruiting members
	• Inclusion of children and youth
3:30	Teaching on Group Spiritual Direction
	• What is Belong? Define spiritual direction (introduction and chapter 1)
	• Ground group spiritual direction in the Christian tradition (chapter 1 & 2)
	• Group covenant suggestions and timing structures
	• Teaching on Holy Listening and Life-giving Responses
	• Addressing challenges
3:45	Stretch and snacks (may omit)

From *Belong: Group Spiritual Direction for Christian Friendship and Communal Discernment.*
Copyright © 2025 Abingdon Press. Permission granted to reproduce for personal or local church use.

3:50	Workshop—practice of group spiritual direction, ending with reflection/Q&A
4:45	Establish evaluation times (midway & at conclusion) with leaders
4:55	Blessing and Benediction

From *Belong: Group Spiritual Direction for Christian Friendship and Communal Discernment.*
Copyright © 2025 Abingdon Press. Permission granted to reproduce for personal or local church use.

Opening Worship for Use in Belong Groups and Belong Leader Training

(Bold italic type indicates a unison response.)

Gathering

Opening: Psalm 118

This is the day that the Lord has made
Let us rejoice and be glad in it

Prayers of Thanks

For Belong groups with children, each child may have their own candle to light and then share how they have experienced God in the week. Adults and teens may join in too!

Prayer of Intercession

Participants offer brief prayers for praises and concerns they carry on their hearts.

After each intercession:
Lord in your mercy
Hear our prayer

Lord's Prayer

Closing Prayer

Almighty God, we give you thanks for surrounding us with the brightness of your light; and we implore you of your great mercy that, as you enfold us with the radiance of this light, so you would shine into our hearts the brightness of your Holy Spirit; through Jesus Christ our Lord. **Amen.**

Circle of Blessing: Numbers 6:24-26

May the Lord bless you and keep you.
May the Lord make his face to shine upon you and be gracious unto you.
May the Lord lift up his countenance upon you and give you peace.

From *Belong: Group Spiritual Direction for Christian Friendship and Communal Discernment.*
Copyright © 2025 Abingdon Press. Permission granted to reproduce for personal or local church use.

Guide to the 12-Step Process of Communal Discernment for Consensus

I. Entrance: Prayerful Preparation

1. Prayerful preparation

- Practices of prayer: Preparing the community for a practice of discernment, offering contemplative spiritual practices (centering prayer, *lectio divina*, etc.), practicing group spiritual direction for a season before the discernment process to build trust (if needed).
- Framing the Question: The clear statement or question of the issue of discernment before the community.
- Info sessions/Communication: Clear use of all the community's media channels to inform the community. Info sessions and a FAQ sheet as needed.

2. Gathering

- Space arranged and prepared for discernment (circles of chairs, supplies, candles))

From Belong: Group Spiritual Direction for Christian Friendship and Communal Discernment.
Copyright © 2025 Abingdon Press. Permission granted to reproduce for personal or local church use.

- Hospitality: Intentional welcome as people physically gather to begin the practice.
- Opening worship: Song, prayer, scripture reading, silence.

3. Covenant Making

- Covenant: The covenantal rules that will guide people's behavior and interaction.

4. Guiding principle(s)

- A statement of the principles to the gathering to give boundaries to the process of discernment.

II. Word and Response: Discerning God's Will Together

5. Prayer of "Shedding" or Indifference

- Setting aside anything that prevents people from following God's will. It can include a "testing of indifference."

6. Prompt and Centering Silence

- Prompt: Content from the biblical, theological, or historical tradition of the church that helps to ground the community in a common context for discernment. This could be a scripture, hymn/song, a quote, or a text from the tradition—or any combination of those. This time of "prompt" also could include a short time of teaching on the issue.
- Silence to center in God's presence and intentionally listen to the guidance of the Spirit.

7. Holy Listening

- Sharing: Listening to how God is directing each member of the circle on the issue or question. Could use (each of these has a separate handout below):
    - Group spiritual direction

From *Belong: Group Spiritual Direction for Christian Friendship and Communal Discernment*. Copyright © 2025 Abingdon Press. Permission granted to reproduce for personal or local church use.

- Ignatian Deliberation
- Quaker Sense of the Meeting Practice
- Wesleyan Quadrilateral
- Other practices of listening
- Exploring: "What more do we need to know about those options?" Further research and exploration of the best options, if necessary.

8. Life-giving Responses

- Responses: Sharing of noticings, wonderings, appreciations for people's sharing—OR offering Spirit's leading upon the issue, question, or problem at hand. The facilitator could offer a question for responses such as: Have we come to a preference for a particular path or option?
- Improving: Making improvements or adjustments to the best option. Might utilize more time of silence and response-gathering.
- Weighing: Using tools of discernment to clarify the best option for the gathering.
- Silence to hear God.

III. Communion: Communal Discernment to Consensus

9. Reflection to Consensus

- Stating the minute: The best option as discerned by the community is stated by the facilitator.
- Sense of the meeting: A testing of the best option to determine consensus. This best option could be stated again afterward as the "final minute."

From *Belong: Group Spiritual Direction for Christian Friendship and Communal Discernment.* Copyright © 2025 Abingdon Press. Permission granted to reproduce for personal or local church use.

10. Resting the Decision

- Holding decision to the heart: This best option is prayed over by the members of the gathering to determine if it brings peace or needs further refinement. If further improvement is needed, the gathering moves back to no. 3.
- Testing the discernment: The gathering affirms the decision as the best way forward in God's will for the community.

11. Prayer of Thanksgiving and Offering of Commitment

- The final decision is recorded and stated before the assembly.
- Prayers of thanksgiving are offered for the discernment process.
- Communion can be celebrated.
- Forms of commitment or personal offering to the outcome of the discernment are given.

IV. Sending Forth

12. Celebration!

- The decision is celebrated by the community. There might be a worship service and/or a party. The story might be told in church and local media, as appropriate.

From *Belong: Group Spiritual Direction for Christian Friendship and Communal Discernment.*
Copyright © 2025 Abingdon Press. Permission granted to reproduce for personal or local church use.

Group Spiritual Direction for Communal Discernment to Consensus

Prompt and Centering Silence (up to 5 minutes)

- The facilitator or lead team offers a prompt to help people focus on the issue of discernment. This could be a scripture, quote from church tradition, or some teaching on the issue.
- The group then enters a period of silence to offer their hearts to God and to dedicate the time to God's direction on the communal issue of discernment.

Holy Listening to First Presenter/Storyteller (set time limit)

- The group listens prayerfully, without interruption, to the presenter.
- The group seeks to be attentive to God's presence in oneself and in the presenter.
- The presenter shares as honestly and authentically as possible how they sense the Holy Spirit guiding them on the issue of communal discernment through the scripture, quote, or teaching they received.

From Belong: Group Spiritual Direction for Christian Friendship and Communal Discernment.
Copyright © 2025 Abingdon Press. Permission granted to reproduce for personal or local church use.

Silence to Hear God (Intercessory Prayer) (set time limit)

- The group members listen in the silence for God's direction on the issue out of the storyteller's sharing.
- Intercessory prayer questions include:
  - God, what is your prayer for our community?
  - What do I need to let go of to hear God's direction of us through the storyteller?

*Repeat the above process for each member of the group, using the same time limit for each person. Alternatively, the group could offer life-giving responses after each person's sharing, and then do so again collectively after everyone has shared as a form of testing consensus.

Life-Giving Responses and Questions (set time limit)

- Option 1: After each presenter, the members of the group offer questions, wonderings, noticings, and appreciations for what the presenter has shared. These sharings may be in the form of images, questions, words, or music.
- Option 2: After all have shared, the members of the group offer questions, wonderings, noticings, and appreciations of their collective sharing. They also may offer what they have received as God's prayer for this discernment. They may note commonalities or differences. They may note they need to know more about the possible options for discernment.
- The circle may offer their responses to the facilitator or to the whole group.
- The group members, guided by the facilitator, might offer improvements to the option they have discerned and/or weigh the best option out of the discernment.

From *Belong: Group Spiritual Direction for Christian Friendship and Communal Discernment.*
Copyright © 2025 Abingdon Press. Permission granted to reproduce for personal or local church use.

Silent Prayer for Discernment Process

- The group prays silently for the discernment and the leading of God, seeking wisdom together.

Continue to step 9–12 in the process of communal discernment (see Guide to the 12-Step Process of Communal Discernment for Consensus handout page 271).

From *Belong: Group Spiritual Direction for Christian Friendship and Communal Discernment.* Copyright © 2025 Abingdon Press. Permission granted to reproduce for personal or local church use.

Ignatian Deliberation Adapted for Communal Discernment to Consensus

1. *Prayer:* Jesuits begin with a prayer invoking the Holy Spirit and may give space for spontaneous prayer by the community. They might read scripture, such as Isaiah 43:1-7 or John 20:19-23, or a writing of Ignatius. Time for private prayer, of about 45 minutes to an hour, may be given before the communal sessions begin.[1]
2. *Sharing Cons:* After the proposed decision/issue is described by the abbot (this issue may have been circulated before the chapter house gathering, so that community members had time to pray over it beforehand), each member of the community has space to offer any concerns against the choice, which are then recorded.
3. *Prayer:* The community takes a break, which gives space for each person to prayerfully reflect individually on what they have heard from step 2.
4. *Sharing Pros and Checking Consensus:* Out of each person's prayerful discernment, individuals report why they favor the decision before them. These "pros" are recorded. Consensus is tested to see if clarity is coming for the community on what the choice/election should be. If consensus is already clear, the community

moves to no. 7. If consensus is not clear, the gathering moves to no. 5.

5. *Prayer:* The community takes a break, which gives space for each person to prayerfully reflect on the sharing from the "pros" in the light of the "cons."

6. *Evaluation and Discovery:* The community now evaluates the weight of the recorded reasons for "pro" and "con," and then discerns the choice to which the community is called by God. If the community is in alignment with the Holy Spirit and practicing authentic discernment, the decision becomes clear. Confirmation of the decision brings a communal sense of shared peace and consensus found together in God.

7. *Prayer:* The time of communal discernment ends with a prayer of thanksgiving and offering the decision to the abbot for a reaffirmation and commitment to carry out the decision.

NOTES

1. William Barry, "Toward Communal Discernment: Some Practical Suggestions" *The Way,* Supplement 58 (Spring 1987), 108.

From *Belong: Group Spiritual Direction for Christian Friendship and Communal Discernment.*
Copyright © 2025 Abingdon Press. Permission granted to reproduce for personal or local church use.

Quaker "Sense of the Meeting" Practice in Communal Discernment to Consensus

- *Gathering:* As they meet to reflect on an issue or problem in their community, a person in the role of the "clerk" calls the meeting to order and, after a time of centering worship, offers the issue before the body for consideration.
- *Leadings:* Quakers speak out of the "leadings" they have received. They trust that the Spirit will gradually lead them to a sense of consensus without any majority/minority positions, arguments, or vote.[1]
- *Considerations:* If a Friend (another name for a Quaker) doesn't feel at ease with a proposal, that person can voice that they aren't in full support, and that Friend's reasons will be seriously considered.[2] Adaptations are made to the proposal or decision such that it aligns with everyone's input.
- *"Sense of the Meeting":* When the clerk of the meeting senses there is unity, they articulate the "sense of the meeting," and the community gives affirmation to this "sense."
- *Waiting:* If there still isn't affirmation, more time for quiet waiting is given, or the decision may be postponed until a future meeting.

From *Belong: Group Spiritual Direction for Christian Friendship and Communal Discernment.* Copyright © 2025 Abingdon Press. Permission granted to reproduce for personal or local church use.

- *Recording of the Sense of the Meeting:* If there is unity, then the "sense" is recorded as the decision of the group and read aloud at the end of the meeting.³

NOTES

1. George Selleck, *Principles of the Quaker Business Meeting* (Richmond, IN: Friends United Press, 1977), 1–2.
2. Danny E. Morris and Charles M. Olsen, *Discerning God's Will Together* (Lanham, MD: Rowman & Littlefield, 2012), 125.
3. Elizabeth Liebert, *The Way of Discernment, Spiritual Practices for Decision-Making* (Louisville: Westminster John Knox, 2008), 75.

Wesleyan Quadrilateral in Communal Discernment to Consensus[1]

(1) Movement 1: Gathering: Symbols and signs, such as a cross, candles, or an open Bible designate the space as holy. The lighting of a candle, singing of a hymn, or prayer gather people in the Holy Spirit's presence for the work of holy discernment.

(2) Movement 2: Tradition: Through sharing the stories of the Christian church throughout history, the denominational history, and the particular tradition of the congregation, participants gain new awareness and insight. Difficult stories of unfaithfulness or challenge also are shared and nudge people to the ongoing movement of God's grace.

(3) Movement 3: Scripture: The group connects their stories to the stories of God and God's people in the Bible. Participants study and discuss relevant scriptural passages for their issue of discernment. Through this reading and reflection, people gain insights and a stronger sense of God's will and direction for their communal discernment.

(4) Movement 4: Experience: The group reflects on their experience of God's presence and direction in their midst. Participants share their stories, insights, inspirations, and guidance they have received from God during the

From *Belong: Group Spiritual Direction for Christian Friendship and Communal Discernment.*
Copyright © 2025 Abingdon Press. Permission granted to reproduce for personal or local church use.

discernment process. Times of silent prayer allow for clarity as people sit with questions like "What is it that you are guiding us to do or be?"

(5) Movement 5: Reason: Through the use of a facilitator or church leadership, the group gathers the wisdom of the group. Through a process of listening, creativity, and reforming the best ideas, the group forms a consensus—which indicates complete support of the group's discernment of God's will.

(6) Movement 6: Sending Forth: After resting the discernment with God, the group offers prayers, songs, or a blessing. A leader may offer a summation of the discernment. The group may pray for particular people or practices, address any concerns, and propose the next steps. The congregation moves forward to implement their communal discernment with the Spirit of God.

NOTES

1. Adapted from Garrie Stevens, Pamela Lardear, and Sharon Duger, *Seeking & Doing God's Will: Discernment for the Community of Faith* (Nashville: Discipleship Resources, 1998), 20–27.

From *Belong: Group Spiritual Direction for Christian Friendship and Communal Discernment.*
Copyright © 2025 Abingdon Press. Permission granted to reproduce for personal or local church use.

Sample Outline of One Church's Communal Discernment Process

4:00 pm Gathering

- Welcome by facilitator
- Orientation: Name and describe the discernment issue; affirm the Holy Spirit's presence with us, short instruction on holy listening, including the mention of Elijah listening to God's voice in the cave (1 Kings 19).

4:10 pm Word

- Invitation to listen to a word or phrase that stands out to you from the speaker.
- Introduction and welcome to the speaker on the topic for the day.
- Speaker teaches for 20 minutes.
- Transition: Invite people into time of prayerful discernment. Tell story of Acts 15—people being of different mind but coming to consensus in the Spirit.
- Teaching on liberty of opinions and essential nature of love of God and love of neighbor.

From *Belong: Group Spiritual Direction for Christian Friendship and Communal Discernment*. Copyright © 2025 Abingdon Press. Permission granted to reproduce for personal or local church use.

Sample Outline of One Church's Communal Discernment Process

- Covenant/Ground rules for practice:
  1. Confidentiality in the circles
  2. Holy Listening—no interrupting, cross talk, responses, advising/correcting/fixing
  3. Openness to the Holy Spirit

4:40 pm Response (Listening Circles)

- Life-giving questions. Will engage in a practice of listening around 3 questions. After a time of silence, each person in the circle will be invited to offer their answer to the question for no longer than 2 minutes. The facilitator will keep time.
- Questions:
  1. When speaker was speaking, what one word or phrase captured your attention? *Hold a minute of silence. Hold what we have heard in prayer.*
  2. What in your past or present life made that word or phrase speak to you? What in your life caused that word to captivate you? Allow 2 minutes to share; facilitator will keep time; then receive what is said. (After 8 minutes, facilitator checks in to see that 4 people have shared.) *Hold a minute of silence. Hold what we have heard in prayer.*
  3. If Jesus were sitting beside you, what would you say to Jesus about your phrase or word? What do you think Jesus would say back? *Hold a minute of silence. Hold what we have heard in prayer.*
- Discernment into consensus: Facilitator transitions group into time of discernment with some teaching on consensus.
- Closing Prayer: Invite people into time of prayer. Offer these questions, with option of silent hand raising.
- Are you comfortable, are you not comfortable, are you unsure with our church taking this action? The circle leaders will take

From *Belong: Group Spiritual Direction for Christian Friendship and Communal Discernment.* Copyright © 2025 Abingdon Press. Permission granted to reproduce for personal or local church use.

back a "general" impression of what they saw in the consensus question (e.g., "About a third are unsure").

5:45 pm Sending Forth

- Facilitator offers a blessing and a benediction.
- Debrief: Circle leaders will report back to the facilitator what they are hearing and seeing. This will help them inform the church council about readiness and consensus.

Abbreviated Communal Discernment Practice for a One-Hour Meeting

(Abridged Version of the 12-Step Process)

1. Prayer practice: Prompt and Centering Silence
(5–10 minutes)

- Light a candle: Open your heart to the presence of God. Take a deep breath (or five).
- A prompt: Read together a pertinent scripture and reflect on it in silence or aloud.
- Prayer for indifference: Shed any ego, opinion, or desire in order to be completely open to God's will. Consider writing down what you need to shed.
- Centering silence: Listen for God's wisdom on the issue in silence. Continue letting go of any preconceived solutions or opinions. Soften your own will for God's.

2. Guiding Principle and Framing the Question
(5–7 minutes)

- Guiding principle: Set the boundaries for the process with a principle that affirms a core value or belief of your faith community in connection to the issue or question for

From *Belong: Group Spiritual Direction for Christian Friendship and Communal Discernment.*
Copyright © 2025 Abingdon Press. Permission granted to reproduce for personal or local church use.

discernment. Consider using language from your vision and/or mission statements.
- Framing the question: Develop together a clear statement of the question or issue for discernment. What is this discernment about—or what is it not?

3. Discernment: Holy Listening and Life-giving Responses (10–20 minutes)

- Holy listening: Listen for the wisdom of the Spirit as group members share their insights/reflections on the issue. Allow silence in between sharing.
- Life-giving responses: Reflect together: How might the Spirit be whispering to you in this situation or issue of discernment? Are there any improvements or alterations that could be made to the discernment we are receiving?

4. Silence to Hear God (1–5 minutes)

- Prayerfully seek God's wisdom together. Rest the discernment close to your heart.
- Pray: God, what is your prayer and will for this discernment?

5. Consensus—Stating the Minute (Proposal), Testing for Consensus (Sense of Meeting) (1–5 minutes)

- Share any insights from the silence. State the "minute," or the best option from the discernment.
- Test for consensus. What is the "sense of the meeting"? Do people have a common heart for what seems to be God's will? Members can share verbally or raise hands.

From *Belong: Group Spiritual Direction for Christian Friendship and Communal Discernment*. Copyright © 2025 Abingdon Press. Permission granted to reproduce for personal or local church use.

6. Resting Decision (1–5 minutes)

- Silence: The group prays over the decision to confirm that it is the source of God's joy and will for them.
- Testing: After the silence, the group can confirm that this option is their discernment and that they feel an inner peace. If not, they can adjourn and continue the discernment at another time; or if time remains, they cycle back to holy listening.

7. Thanksgiving (1–5 minutes)

- The group offers a prayer of thanksgiving for God's presence and guidance.
- They may distribute duties for the implementation of the discernment.

From *Belong: Group Spiritual Direction for Christian Friendship and Communal Discernment.* Copyright © 2025 Abingdon Press. Permission granted to reproduce for personal or local church use.

Listening Practices for Communal Discernment[1]

Posting

- A way for smaller circles to report their discernment on an option/proposal to the larger group.
- Practice: A delegate from the small circle/group writes on poster paper/whiteboard their discernment.
- Easy possibilities for categorization include:
  1. Yes to the proposal (indicate whether unanimous, majority agreement, or a number who disagree).
  2. No to the proposal (indicate whether unanimous, majority agreement, or a number who disagree).
  3. Revision to the proposal—revisional text is written on the poster/board (indicate whether unanimous, majority agreement, or a number who disagree with the revisions).
- Alternative process: Assign people who share the same viewpoint to small circles. This practice enables shy or timid people to feel more comfortable and at ease. Have the group's delegate identify their viewpoint or share 1–3 of the most important issues to the larger group. The larger group engages in "open forum" discussion or a delegation process (see below).

From Belong: Group Spiritual Direction for Christian Friendship and Communal Discernment. Copyright © 2025 Abingdon Press. Permission granted to reproduce for personal or local church use.

Open Forum

- With minor differences in the proposal, the large group could host a discussion to improve it until there is consensus.
- Delegates from the smaller circles might share their reasons for revision or improvements.

Delegation Process

- In a process with a large group and many small circles, a delegate from each circle meets to discern with all the other delegates.
- The delegate group may do more exploring, improving, or weighing of the options to come to a consensus.
- The delegates return to their original small circle, share the proposal ("state the minute," and gather a "sense of the meeting." If further improvements or refinements are suggested, the delegate returns to the delegate group with these suggestions.
- The movement between delegate group and small circles continues until consensus is reached.
- Delegates may meet in their group at a different time/place from the whole gathering. At a later meeting of the large group, they share their discernment. Alternatively, the delegation process could occur during the large group process, with the small circles holding the delegates in prayer as they discern.

"Fish Bowl"

- An inner circle of a few chairs (4–6) hosts people who share their perspective or opinion as they discuss the proposals or options for discernment. These "inner circle" folk could represent one perspective or be diverse in viewpoints. All communication happens in the inner circle.

From *Belong: Group Spiritual Direction for Christian Friendship and Communal Discernment.* Copyright © 2025 Abingdon Press. Permission granted to reproduce for personal or local church use.

- Most of the group sits in an outer circle of chairs. Their practice is to listen.
- After everyone in the inner circle has shared, they may voluntarily move to the outer circle.
- A person in the outer circle can then take the empty chair if they have a perspective to share. An outer circle person also can stand until one of the inner circle chairs becomes available. All are welcome to participate until everyone who desires to speak has done so.

Samoan Circle[2]

- A small group of designated speakers (3–4 people) sits in a semicircle of chairs in the front. The larger group of designated listeners sits in a larger semicircle facing the smaller group of speakers.
- The small group of speakers shares in a conversation. Each person represents a particular view or perspective on the issue or problem before them and speaks to that perspective.
- The larger group listens without offering any response.
- They then engage each other in holy listening and responses, intentionally seeking God's will for unity and consensus through their differences. Sometimes by listening and observing representative speakers work through issues together, the whole group can achieve consensus more easily.

Conflict Spectrum

- Identify one corner of the room for people who strongly identify with one proposal/option, and the opposite corner for those who strongly are convinced of the opposite of that proposal.

From *Belong: Group Spiritual Direction for Christian Friendship and Communal Discernment.*
Copyright © 2025 Abingdon Press. Permission granted to reproduce for personal or local church use.

- Invite everyone to stand in a position somewhere at or between the two corners/positions. People could be invited to share why they stood where they chose.
- Optional: The spectrum of people could be divided into three (two ends plus a middle group) or more groups. Each group then has 10–20 minutes to name the strengths and weaknesses of their position, and then offer that to the whole group for discernment.

World Café

- Small groups of four people sit at tables. They share in conversation around the same problem, question, or issue for 15–20 minutes. Identical questions or statements of the problem could be provided for each table.
- At the end of the first round of conversation, three people from the table get up and move to different tables. One participant stays at the table and shares a summation of the conversation with the group of three people who join the table.
- The new group of four may have another conversation on the same set of questions or problem. It's also possible for the focus question or problem to change.
- The group engages in as many rounds of conversation as is helpful to their process.
- A facilitator may collect key impressions and ideas at the end of the "world café."

Interviews[3]

- The facilitator selects people who represent differing perspectives/proposals/options in the discernment process for interviews.

From *Belong: Group Spiritual Direction for Christian Friendship and Communal Discernment.* Copyright © 2025 Abingdon Press. Permission granted to reproduce for personal or local church use.

- The facilitator interviews each person, inviting them first to share a little about themselves and then how they view the issue at hand. The interviewee uses "I" language to describe their position.
- Their views may be summarized on poster paper/whiteboard by the scribe and used in further discernment.

Role Reversal interview

- The facilitator/leaders selects people who pretend they are another person with opposing views.
- The interviewee tries to answer questions with the differing views. The facilitator might need to do supportive paraphrasing/guidance ("Now, tell me about your views on this issue").
- At the end, the facilitator turns to the person with opposing views and asks how well the interviewee represented them. Was the presentation of views accurate?

NOTES

1. Posting, Open Forum, Delegation, and Fish Bowl practices are adapted from Victoria Curtiss, "Guidelines for Communal Discernment," from the Presbyterian Peacemaking Program (Louisville, KY: Presbyterian Distribution Service, 2007), Appendix B: Ways to Deliberate with Large Groups, 13. Curtiss uses a source I also read in John Carroll Futrell, S.J., "Communal Discernment: Reflections on Experience," *Studies in the Spirituality of Jesuits,* vol. 4, no. 5 (November 1972), 181–84.
2. Jes Stoltzfus Buller, *Peaceful Practices: A Guide to Healthy Communication in Conflict,* (Mennonite Central Committee, 2021), 75. Samoan Circle, World Café, and Conflict Spectrum all come from this resource.
3. The Interview and Role Reversal Interview info both come from the "Structuring Dialogue" section of the workbook for conflict transformation. "Conflict Transformation Skills for Churches," (Lombard Mennonite Peace Center workbook), D-10. I received this workbook for a workshop. "Conflict Transformation Skills for Churches," Lombard Mennonite Peace Center, online workshop, May 2024.

From Belong: Group Spiritual Direction for Christian Friendship and Communal Discernment.
Copyright © 2025 Abingdon Press. Permission granted to reproduce for personal or local church use.

Spiritual Practices for Communal Discernment

Use these practices in times of holy listening, improving, or weighing during the communal discernment process.

Ignatian Examen Adapted for Communal Discernment

1. Open to the presence of God. Become aware of your inner climate. How might you need to welcome God's grace? How is God present to you right now? Reflect silently.
2. Offer gratitude for the discernment process. How have you experienced God's love or grace at work? Who has been a sign of God to you? Reflect silently.
3. Consolation: What about this proposal or option brings you joy or life? How will the community benefit from this proposal? You might write these down. These consolations could be verbalized in a small circle or large group.
4. Desolation: What about this proposal or option frightens you, angers you, or saddens you? What price will the community pay for this proposal? You might write these down. The desolations could be verbalized in a small circle or large group.
5. God's presence: How do you sense the Holy Spirit guiding you in this proposal or option? If you implemented this option

From *Belong: Group Spiritual Direction for Christian Friendship and Communal Discernment.*
Copyright © 2025 Abingdon Press. Permission granted to reproduce for personal or local church use.

tomorrow, how might God be present in it? You might pray on this silently, or these reflections could be verbalized to the larger group.

Lectio Divina for Communal Discernment

The facilitator or leadership team, or members of the group, determine a short scripture passage that applies to their situation of discernment.

1. First reading: The group members listen to the scripture, simply absorbing the text.
2. Second reading: Ask, "What word or phrase in the text speaks to you about our issue of discernment?" Reflect in silence. Afterward, the group may share just the word or phrase.
3. Third reading: Ask, "How is God working or speaking through that word or phrase into our situation?" Reflect in silence. Afterward, you may share briefly what you received.
4. Fourth reading: Ask, "What is God guiding us to do from this scripture? How is God speaking through this text into our context?" Reflect in silence. Afterward, you may share briefly.

Reflect together: What new insights or wisdom did you receive on our discernment? How do these insights influence the sense of God's leading in this situation?

From *Belong: Group Spiritual Direction for Christian Friendship and Communal Discernment*.
Copyright © 2025 Abingdon Press. Permission granted to reproduce for personal or local church use.

Creating a Communal Discernment Process in Your Church

(For Use by a Leadership Team or Church Council)

Preparing the Leadership Team

1. Naming the courage and the gifts.
2. Calling a team.
3. Calling a spiritual director/facilitator/discernamentarian.
4. Cultivating contemplative practices.
5. Naming the fears.
6. Conflict styles.
7. Challenges in a communal discernment process.

Creating a Communal Discernment Process

1. Covenant Making
   - Framing the question
   - Guiding Principles
   - Covenant
2. Kind of Discernment/Structure of the Process
3. Logistics: Time/Place/Dates/Duration
4. Recruitment and Training of Additional Leaders

From *Belong: Group Spiritual Direction for Christian Friendship and Communal Discernment.*
Copyright © 2025 Abingdon Press. Permission granted to reproduce for personal or local church use.

5. Exploring: Research of Options
6. Prayerful Preparation
    - Communication Plan and Implementation
    - Formation and Teaching
7. Gathering

From *Belong: Group Spiritual Direction for Christian Friendship and Communal Discernment.*
Copyright © 2025 Abingdon Press. Permission granted to reproduce for personal or local church use.

Acknowledgments

Many thanks to all those who believed in this project. I offer huge gratitude to Shalem Institute, and particularly Patience, who taught me group spiritual direction and through her expression of wisdom and grace, offered a practice that changed my life.

One of my mentors, Dr. Randy Maddox, assured me (when I really needed it!) that this work could represent an invigoration of the tradition of the class meeting within early Methodism. His affirmation of group spiritual direction as a traditioned practice of the class meeting and as a Wesleyan means of grace heartened me and encouraged me to write this book. Kathy Armistead, who was then publisher at the General Board of Higher Education and Ministry, expressed interest in my ideas and my direction experience, and encouraged me to write a book proposal. I appreciate the trust of people like John Clark at GBHEM who kept allowing me to submit drafts and encouraged me to continue in the project. Many thanks to GBHEM/Abingdon editors who provided invaluable insight and helped me to be a better writer.

Tania Casselle and Sean Murphy provided excellent instruction and guidance through their program, "Write to the Finish." Many thanks to the four wonderful women writers from that program's writing group—Sue, Felicity, Lisa, and Joyce's encouragement and labor with me helped so much. Later Zoom writing groups which included Sharon and Trudy also helped establish a writing habit and rhythm when I didn't think I had time.

Eventually, I wrote a second draft that was still too long and academic, and a third draft that experienced the same problems. The encouragement from beloved friends such as Carol, who told me "the church needs this book" when I really need to hear that meant so much. Many thanks to clergywomen and spiritual director friends like Kristen, Katherine, Kelly, Tiffany, Antoinette, Jenae, and Regina who participated with me in group spiritual direction and affirmed the significance of this practice. I pressed on to keep working on this book when the soil of my soul felt dry, and I just had to trust that the text would grow as it needed to be.

Many thanks to the churches who trusted me with teaching and leading them in group spiritual direction and communal discernment. I'm grateful to all the faithful people who participated in these practices and witnessed to the peace and grace of God that comes from them.

For my family, who endured my constant time in front of a screen and who encouraged me in this project, a huge "thank you." I also want to take a moment to thank myself—for my pushing through discouragement, for keeping on, for doing the work, and getting it done. Thank you to the soul within that did not give up, and profound gratitude to the Holy Spirit, who guided me in this work and directs me still with compassion and love. May I keep on listening.

www.ingramcontent.com/pod-product-compliance
Lightning Source LLC
LaVergne TN
LVHW031419031025
822579LV00007B/7